ROUNDING TAWERO POINT

ROUNDING TAWERO POINT

AN AUTOBIOGRAPHY

John Broomfield

atmosphere press

For Maggie

Rounding Tawero Point you leave sheltered waters and confront the challenges of outer Pelorus Sound. Here your boat rides swells from the open ocean and faces winds that can be extreme. The South Island lies in the Roaring Forties and gales here can lift rooves off houses. The Sound took its modern name from "HMS Pelorus," which surveyed these waters in 1838, but there is a much older name with links to primordial Polynesian explorer, Kupe. Te Hoiere is what Maori call both the Sound and Maud Island, which lies in its western reaches. Te Hoiere translates as "Kupe's Paddle," and the paddle itself can be seen on the island as a prominent peninsula with a right-angled end jutting into Tawhitinui Reach. Tawhitinui: "the great far-distant place."

Table of Contents

— Chapter One —

Meeting My Ancestors

"The past is never dead. It's not even past."
– William Faulkner

I feel great satisfaction in the fact that my first departure from New Zealand was by ship and that I returned by ship after my longest absence. Before my lifetime, the sea was the highroad travelled by all humans to reach these remote Pacific Islands. First, the greatest of all mariners, the Polynesians, and then my own European kith and kin. I delight in the story of my great-grandfather William Broomfield, crewman on the "Minerva," who jumped ship in Takapuna at the age of 25 in 1847. Despite this nautical heritage, I failed my knotting test as a Sea Cub in Invercargill at the age of ten, and it was 50 years later before I overcame the ignominy. For two decades living on remote outer Pelorus Sound after my final return to my homeland in 1994, I was in a boat virtually every day and my knots held.

"We are pure British," my mother used to say proudly, but according to ancestry.com my DNA reveals that my descent is 11 percent Norwegian. Perhaps some ancestor of mine was a Viking sailor on one of those longships that raided my Celtic and Anglo-Saxon forebears in the British Isles before settling amongst them, as many Norsemen and Norsewomen did. Perhaps, like great-grandfather William, he too jumped ship. Fancifully, I like to imagine that it was because of this Viking heritage that the longest of my ten ocean voyages was on a Norwegian freighter, the Knutsen Line's *Marie Bakke*, six weeks from California along the Pacific's northern rim and south through the islands of Indonesia to the Indian Ocean and Australia's west coast.

I am attracted by the Maori understanding of *wa* and *whakapapa*, time and genealogy. For most of us *Pakeha* (European-descended New Zealanders) it is self-evident that we stand facing the future with the past behind us, but traditionally for Maori it is the future that is behind them. They stand facing the past and their ancestors, who are a living presence in spirit. It is the vision of the ancestors that guides the present generation into the unseen future with one clear and overriding purpose: to prosper the generations yet to be born. As the *whakatauki* (proverb) instructs: "*Ka Mua Ka Muri*. Walk backwards into the Future."

Our *mokopuna* (descendants) live in us, and we live in our *tupuna* (ancestors). I use the present tense "live" because Maori often speak in the first person when recounting events in the past in which their *tupuna* participated. "In 1881 I stood with Te Whiti at Parihaka." Maori feel a continuing personal presence across generations that is an inspiration to me. Equally inspiring is the inclusion in the *whakapapa* of the more-than-human world – fellow creatures and the land itself. Despite our civilization's understanding of evolution, we do not, like Maori, acknowledge animals, birds, mountains, lakes, rivers and ocean as ancestors.

As a kid, I hoped that someday I would find I had Maori ancestry or, alternatively, that I was descended from an Australian convict. Both proved idle dreams, but I have discovered some scoundrels in my lineage. Ship deserter, William, has already been mentioned. In his teens he had served for two years in the Royal Navy to escape the wrath of his brothers whose ponies he had had impounded, leading to their involuntary sale. The family lived near the New Forest in Hampshire, where apparently Broomfields are thick on the ground, as they have been since the Middle Ages.

A few years after leaving the Royal Navy, William had signed on with ships trading in the Pacific. There are differing family stories about his 1847 desertion in Auckland, although there is general agreement that the *Minerva's* irate captain sent a search party after him. One tale has him hiding in a flour barrel (he was just 5ft 1in tall) and being discovered by a member of the party, who replaced the lid so he could go free. Another version has him hiding with a shipmate, Pritchard, in a *toitoi* bush. One of their boots was sticking out, but a member of the search party said nothing even after he tripped over it. William worked for a time in an Auckland timber yard before becoming a "waterman" ferrying people to and from ships in the stream. He also built himself a boat, the *Lady Grey*, and began trading along the coast. Unfortunately, before long his boat sank because of faulty construction.

There are other ancestors who found an illicit means of coming to New Zealand. In December 1842, less than three years after the signing of the Treaty of Waitangi, a Cornish family of five under the name Stephens embarked on the *Westminster* in Plymouth, Devon, bound for Auckland. These were my paternal great-great-grandparents, Richard and Anne Congdon, and their children aged six, three and two. Richard had assumed his mother's maiden name, Stephens, apparently to conceal two inconvenient facts. One was his conviction and imprisonment for petty larceny at the age of 21 and the other was that, at the age of 52, he was too old to qualify for an assisted passage from the New Zealand Company. A name change and some age whittling got the family free passage on the *Westminster*.

The voyage took three-and-a-half months, and the hardships suffered at sea included the death of Anne's brother. Nor was life ashore easy in the new settlement of Auckland. Richard found a labouring job, and the family lived in a *raupo whare* on Queen Street. By 1849, however, Richard was building boats on the Tamaki River, assisted by that master shipwright, William Broomfield. A year later, the Congdons had their own dairy farm on what is now Wellesley Street, but Anne died at the age of 52 in 1853, leaving three teenage children.

The eldest was Elizabeth, 16 when her mother died and already pregnant with what she claimed was William Broomfield's child. Although William denied this, he and she married in 1857 and soon after acquired a 113-acre farm in Howick. William served in the militia in the Waikato Land Wars in 1863-1864, and while he was away, a Maori raiding party appeared in the district. Elizabeth and her six children sought refuge in the stockade in Howick. She later claimed she met the raiding party on the way, and they allowed her to proceed because she spoke to them in Te Reo Maori. Elizabeth had taken a new oven with her to bury for safety, but when she returned, she could not locate the hiding place.

It is a measure of how the family prospered that the town today has a Broomfield Road, with Broomfield Cottage in Broomfield Park preserved as an historic place. Elizabeth had 12 children in 20 years, the last born in 1874, three years after William died at 52. (The date of death recorded on his gravestone at All Saints Church, Howick, was changed from 1871 to 1877 "to accommodate a daughter born after his death," as one of my cousins has observed coyly on ancestry.com). Elizabeth lived to be 89, outliving by seven years her eleventh child, my grandfather, Charles, who was struck down by the 1918 influenza pandemic.

The Congdons and Broomfields, before migrating to New Zealand, had no pretensions of being middle class, in contrast to my maternal ancestors, the Braithwaites and Hindles. The latter, originally from Lancashire, came to New Zealand from Kent, where my great-great-grandfather, Joseph Hindle, a Cambridge University graduate, was the Anglican vicar of Higham, a post he held from 1829 until his death aged 80 in 1874. He lived at The Knowle and according to a story frequently repeated by my mother, was a close friend of his next-door neighbour at Gads Hill House, Charles Dickens. Joseph and Charles had a tunnel connecting their houses – or at least, so we were told as children.

The first glimpse we catch of Joseph's son, David Burn Hindle, is in his twenties in New Zealand in the 1860s serving in the Armed Constabulary, a colonial contingent fighting alongside British Army troops in the Land Wars in the Waikato. In 1870, he went south to try his luck gold mining in Canvas Town in the Marlborough Sounds but, unsuccessful, he returned after less than 12 months to rejoin the Constabulary and receive a parcel of rich land at Whatawhata in the Waikato, land "confiscated" from Maori for having had the temerity to oppose the Crown's illegal land grab.

His increasing prosperity as a farmer allowed him to take a voyage home to England in the mid-seventies, and in 1881 in his late thirties, he went to Sydney to marry Alice Gunn. The couple had three daughters and one son before Alice died in 1887. In 1892 David married again. His second wife was Elizabeth Dillon Braithwaite and, at their wedding, Elizabeth's brother, George Bailie Braithwaite, met David's beautiful eldest daughter, Daisy, then just 11. Eight years later, George married Daisy, in the process seriously complicating the *whakapapa*. Elizabeth was now the sister-in-law of her step-daughter, Daisy.

David and Elizabeth had one son, Harold Burn Hindle, born just eight years before my mother, who had a serious crush on him in her teens (no matter that he was both her uncle and her cousin). Judging from my mother's cherished photo of him in Royal Artillery officer's uniform, Hal was dashingly handsome. He was studying at Cambridge University when he volunteered for duty in the First World War. He died aged 25 on the Somme in March 1918.

The Braithwaites were from Kendal in the Lake District of Cumbria, and my maternal great-grandfather, John Bailie Braithwaite, had married Isabella Dillon, an Ulster Protestant from County Down. The couple migrated to New Zealand when John was still in his twenties, and he became a member of the gardening team working for colonial governor Sir George Grey to create the retreat on Kawau Island in the Hauraki Gulf that Grey wanted. When John and Isabella had a son in 1866, they named him George, and Sir George gave them a gold sovereign in the youngster's honour.

After leaving Kawau Island, John became a rates collector in Mt. Albert and (according to family legend) a virulent anti-Catholic. He was said to ride out on horseback in Auckland on St. Patrick's Day wearing an orange sash and carrying a horsewhip to use on any wearers of the green he could find. This anti-Catholic bigotry was sustained in the family into my lifetime, and it was something I had to unlearn in my adulthood. I recall my father observing that if a Catholic were appointed as a school Principal, the whole teaching staff would be Catholic in no time. He also told me once (in the process revealing a second prejudice) that he "would rather Bronwen married a clean Maori than a Catholic." No doubt to my parents' gall, both my sister Bronwen and I married Catholics, more correctly lapsed Catholics.

My maternal grandfather, George Bailie Braithwaite, became a very successful and prosperous builder as Auckland expanded rapidly in the late nineteenth and early twentieth centuries with the development of tram lines and railways. He built a large house for his family in Mt. Albert, where (the story goes) he demonstrated in his later years an eccentricity to rival his father's. He is said to have erected a blackboard by his front gate and used it to chalk insults directed at neighbours and the wider citizenry of Auckland.

Even though he lived until 1952, he met me only once because my parents threw him out of our house when I was a baby and told him never to return. Grandfather George had remarried after the death in 1908 of my grandmother, Daisy, at the tragically early age of 26, and his new wife, Lilian, insisted that Daisy's older children (my mother Eileen and her sisters Winifred and Constance) be sent to boarding school. Her words were, as my mother reported them: "Either they go, or I leave with my Pekingese dogs. There's not enough room here for them and us." My mother never forgave her father for acquiescing, and almost certainly the fight in my infancy reflected this anger. I have little doubt that he had already received a rebuke with the middle name I was given: Hindle, the family name of my maternal grandmother, his first wife.

At the end of the nineteenth century, Grandmother Frances and Grandfather Charles Broomfield, like David Hindle 30 years earlier, sought fame and fortune – or, at least, an income – in the south. Charles seems to have been a jack-of-all-trades, as I suspect many settlers were in the nineteenth century. He had worked in dairy factories and had farmed. He went to Otago to work on the construction of the Waipori hydroelectric dam south of Dunedin, and it was in Dunedin that my father, Ladas John, Charles' and Frances' fourth child, was born in 1902 before the family moved back to the North Island, first to Hukerenui and then to Whangarei for Charles to become a coal merchant and cartage contractor.

In her 1996 book *The Deep Sky Waits on the Outskirts of Town*, my cousin Annette Lees writes of the stories told by her grandfather, my father's brother William Broomfield:

"That family and those they were descended from cut their farms out of the kauri forests in Northland. They had fished the estuaries. I heard about the size and numbers of the fish. I heard about their black cars that had to be pulled from the Northland mud on roads that were rutted tracks .... We heard a few stories about my grandfather's mother. All Sunday morning she and her daughters would bake – fruit pies, cakes, breads, biscuits, scones. That mother was famous for her baking. She won national prizes, beat professional chefs."

Judging by similar stories Dad told Bronwen and me, he had a happy rural childhood of which the highlights were the frequent fishing and hunting expeditions with his brothers. When he was 16 and brother William just 10, this life was brought to an abrupt end by the death of their father at the age of 48 in the influenza pandemic. On the evening of November 23, 1918, all family members went to bed in apparent good health, but by morning Charles and his second son Harry, aged 20, were dead.

Frances was left facing poverty with two teenage and two pre-teen children. My father gave us no details about how the family struggled through, but he always expressed deep gratitude for the role played by his eldest sibling, Ella. She was 24 in 1918 and already married. She arranged for Dad to become a pupil teacher and subsequently to enter the Teachers Training College in Auckland. He distinguished himself both as a teacher trainee and in sports, representing the college in cricket, rugby, hockey, and athletics, proving to be one of the province's fastest sprinters over 100 and 220 yards. His amateur athletics career, however, was stopped short when someone uncovered the fact that he had run for prize money at country sports meetings in Northland.

It was at Teachers College that Eileen Braithwaite and Jack Broomfield met and fell in love. (Away from home, Dad preferred to be known as Jack. He did not like the name Ladas, which had come from a famous British racehorse.) It was apparently no obstacle that he was a poor boy from the Northland gumfields and she a young woman from a rich family in an upper-crust city suburb who had attended St Cuthbert's College, one of Auckland's most distinguished private schools for girls. It is interesting to compare photos of the two in their late teens and early twenties. Throughout, stylishly dressed Eileen with her head of thick curls, looks confident and at ease in her circle of sisters and girlfriends. Jack evolves from a somewhat awkward and seemingly insecure boy to a poised and well-dressed young college man.

When economic necessity forced Jack to cut short his study for a B.A. at Auckland University College in 1924 and return north to teach, Eileen and he wrote each other love letters and pledged to marry the following summer. This they did just before Christmas 1925.

The primary school at which Dad was teaching was at a Public Works Department [PWD] camp at Pukehuia on the railway line being laid between Whangarei and Dargaville. It was a one-teacher school when Dad went there, but with the camp population growing, Dad was able to persuade the Department of Education to add a second teacher for 1926. Lovelorn single men in the camp were filled with eager anticipation when they learnt that a young woman was coming as the second teacher. What Dad did not reveal was that the new teacher was Eileen Braithwaite, whom he would marry before she accompanied him back to Northland. They arrived in the New Year on the only form of transport available to reach Pukehuia: a railway jigger.

Mum and Dad taught together in schools in Northland and around Auckland for six years until Bronwen was born in 1931 and mother left her career to care full-time for her baby. In 1935, when I was born, Dad was headmaster of the primary school at Onerahi, a village east of Whangarei on the harbour. He was also mayor, and in this elevated capacity, it fell to him to raise the flag on the accession to the British throne of Edward VII on January 20, 1936.

By the time Edward abdicated in December of that year, Mum was severely ill with what was diagnosed as leukaemia, considered terminal. She was hospitalised in Auckland, and when the school year resumed in February 1937, Dad had to find a way to get me looked after. Bronwen was five and already in school, so he could take care of her, but not me as well. I was therefore bundled off aged 18 months to a home in Auckland for unmarried mothers and their infants run by my Great Aunt Kitty Hindle, who was an Anglican nun. Dad and Bronwen drove down from Onerahi to visit Mum and me every weekend, and although I have no explicit memories of the period, I have a feeling I was not unhappy at the home. Undoubtedly, my mother's miraculous recovery to full health contributed to my sense of well-being.

Sometime after the family's reunification, an incident happened at a beach that gave rise to a family story repeated throughout my childhood. Apparently from the time I could walk, I was a wanderer, and on this occasion, I skedaddled into the ocean without anyone noticing. When the family did realise I was gone, all they could see was my sunhat floating on the waves. Fortunately, they quickly fished me out from underneath the hat, none the worse for wear and happy as a clam, they said. I don't remember the swim, but I do have an associated memory that involves the supernatural. I was approached at the beach that day by the black-clad figure of Death, who suggested I come with him. I laughed and said "no." This I did not tell my family.

I had a more serious tangle with death a short time later. When I was three, we were living in Auckland, and our house on Maungakiekie Avenue backed onto Cornwall Park. I would climb through the fence and play in the park among the grazing sheep. Probably as a result of drinking from one of the sheep troughs, I contracted a severe case of bacillary dysentery and was admitted seriously ill to Auckland Hospital. Of this, I have fragmentary but clear memories, though none of meeting Death personally as I had at the beach. I was desperately lonely as I waited each day for family visits, consoled only by the presence of my tatty, one-eyed teddy bear. I remember the day I dropped Teddy through the bars of my cot and wept until he was returned after what seemed an eternity. I must also have been severely dehydrated because I was left with a lifetime fear of being without drinking water. I have a vivid memory from the age of five of being inconsolable after breaking my water bottle on an Owaka school excursion.

Mum and Dad described me as little more than a skeleton when I returned home from Auckland Hospital, but I must have recovered fast because I was soon back to my wandering ways. I would frequently show up at a neighbourhood dairy, which stocked my favourite chocolate-covered marshmallow Mickey Mice. Even though the shopkeepers would say firmly, "No penny, no Mickey Mouse," I would hang around hopefully, and my mother would have to be called to come and get me.

My most infamous exploit was the humiliation I inflicted on my long-suffering seven-year-old sister when she was on a school "route march." I turned up, pushing a doll's pram and wearing only a singlet, bare from the waist down. A teacher called Bronwen out from the marching column to take me home. (I should explain that, in our childhood, New Zealand schools had the habit of sending students on regimented walks when the staff had some business to do.)

In light of this, it surprises me that one evening I was able to persuade Bronwen to go with me to a "meeting." The importance my father attached to "going out to meetings" had impressed me, and I persuaded myself that I had a "meeting" to attend and generously allowed Bronwen to accompany me. It was anti-climatic when we arrived at the meeting venue to discover it was an empty, overgrown section. We had started for home when my father turned up in the car looking for us. I don't remember the outcome, but I imagine poor Bronwen got most of the flak.

The car was our parents' pride and joy, an American Essex, bought with a small inheritance Mum had received. Dad was meticulous in maintaining it. One day when the car was sitting unattended in the driveway, a playmate and I decided to lend a hand. We turned on the garden hose, intending to give the car water, as I had seen my father do, but we could not loosen the radiator cap. We did manage to unscrew the petrol tank cap, so we put the water in there. With Dad at the wheel the next day on downtown Queen Street, the car sputtered to a halt. The diagnosis, water in the fuel, sent Dad home to interrogate me and discover my foray into car care. It took weeks for Dad to get all the water out of the carburettor.

My next vehicular adventure was more life-threatening. Whenever the baker delivered bread to our house, he gave my friend and me a ride down the street with him. When he turned up at our place, we would sit in the van awaiting his return. On this particular day, one of us released the handbrake, and the van careened down the hill, fortunately slamming into a lamppost just before busy Green Lane. I remember the two of us dashing home, squeezing past Mum and the baker chatting at the back door and diving under my bed. Mum, who said I was ashen, hurried indoors to find us while the baker raced to his van and back to the house to see if we were all right. No more rides in his van after that.

~ ~ ~

In summer 1940, the family drove the length of New Zealand, from Auckland to the Catlins, the remote southeast corner of the country, an epic journey in those days of gravel and mud roads. Dad had been appointed Headmaster of Owaka District High School. We stopped in Wellington to visit the Centennial Exhibition, where I remember Bronwen being humiliated outside one pavilion on a grill that had an updraft designed to lift women's skirts. As we travelled on in the Essex, I drove her batty (and my parents as well, I imagine) by "playing" my mouth organ incessantly.

Through the four generations since coming to New Zealand, my family on both sides had lived almost continuously in the north, but with the move to Owaka in 1940, I became a permanent southerner. In the 80 years since I have lived in places spread the length of the South Island and in several countries abroad, but I have never spent more than a few weeks at a time n the North Island. I have become a confirmed Mainlander.

The Catlins was probably one of New Zealand's poorest districts when we arrived. Its southern areas were still covered with bush that was being milled, and the farms on the cleared land had poor soil and were overrun by rabbits. In fact, the sale of rabbit skins was the best money spinner for some farmers. This meant there were many who did not throw their weight behind the national policy of total eradication of the pests, and the Rabbit Wardens had an uphill task in ensuring the rabbit laws were enforced. One of those regulations made it an offence to raise rabbits, and it is a commentary on the bizarre nature of NZ bureaucracy that the local warden welcomed our family to Owaka by giving us two baby rabbits as pets. Fred Dagg was alive in rural NZ well before the days of television!

We moved into the schoolhouse across the tennis courts from the school. The country was, of course, at war, and one of my earliest Owaka memories is watching out of my bedroom window as Dad drilled on the tennis courts at night with fellow members of the Home Guard. They carried wooden rifles and other replica weapons in preparation for repelling Japanese landings on these southern shores. Dad commented that he would feel a lot safer with the invaders than with his fellow Guardsmen if they got real firearms!

Dad had a ready wit. I remember when I was out walking with him one day, he stopped in front of an empty shop on the main street, pointing to the dead flies lying inside the window and telling me that's where they got the filling for one of my favourite slices, colloquially known as "Squashed Flies."

There was no joking about my desire to go to school, which I was very eager to do. Mum and Dad told me I could start as soon as I could read and write. I was already hard at work on these skills, and they let me enter kindergarten during the 1940 school year when I was still four. I worked equally hard on learning to swim, which I did in the frigid water of the nearest estuary at Pounawea soon after I turned five.

Some of my energy went into activities that did not earn parental applause. After school each day, I was permitted to ride with one of the school bus drivers as he took the kids home. One day I had him let me off with Neill Gorman, a friend of my age whose farm home was about two miles out of town. I told the driver dishonestly that my father had said this was OK and that he would be coming to pick me up in the car. Mrs. Gorman was surprised to see me, but at the time, the farm had no phone on which she could ring my parents and check the story. After a while, I said I would start walking home and that Dad would meet me on the way - which he did, and he was angry! I vividly remember standing with my head against the outside wall of our garage, crying my heart out after Dad told me I could no longer ride the buses.

In a more serious transgression, I became a war profiteer. I found in the house a pile of stickers designed to raise money for the Red Cross in its work on battlefields. I had seen my mother going door-to-door soliciting funds, so I took some stickers and proceeded to do likewise. People were generous with their donations, and I soon had what seemed a fortune to a five-year-old. I was working for myself, not the Red Cross, and I stowed my ill-gotten gains "securely" under a sofa cushion in the sitting room. Unfortunately, one lunch hour, my mother heard me counting my coin stash and demanded to know its source. My reply that I could not explain because I was due back in school cut no ice. When I finally confessed, she told me that when school was out that afternoon, I had to return to the houses that had contributed, confess my sin, and return the money. I felt completely humiliated.

My parents were strict but fair and consistent: far more consistent, I think than I was myself when I became a parent. They were also very loving, expressing their affection for Bronwen and me without reserve. They encouraged us to do well, and when we did, they let us know how pleased they were. I admired them hugely. Dad was an exceptional male for the period, sharing an extraordinary amount of the household work. He cleaned the bathroom and toilet daily, and on Saturdays, he and Mum jointly did the laundry and hung it on the outdoor clothesline together. Dad and I cut all the firewood, and Dad tended the fire. Mum did all the cooking, but Dad, Bronwen and I did the dishes. Dad administered the discipline, which could include a spanking or even a strapping with his belt. We kids could not "answer back" Mum or Dad without getting physical punishment.

My mother was the consummate organiser at home and in public, where she usually ended up running organisations she joined. Both Mum and Dad were completely at ease with people of all sorts, and they had a genuine interest in other people's lives. When we were out walking or driving, Dad often stopped to chat with people about what they were doing.

It was Dad's sporting prowess of which I was most proud as a youngster. During our Owaka years, he won the Married Men's Race hands down at the Kaka Point New Year's Day Community Picnic and was the star batsman in the beach cricket game. Dad played cricket throughout the summer on the Owaka team and, at the age of 39, was selected as wicketkeeper in the South Otago rep. team. He continued to play competitive cricket into his 40s after we moved to Port Chalmers.

Two events stand out in my memory of our Owaka years. One is a visit during one Christmas holiday of my cousins, Kathrine and Moragh Walker. They were the daughters of mother's sister Win, who lived in Scotland and had been evacuated for the duration of the war to the care of another of the Braithwaite sisters, Aunt Con in Dunedin. Kathrine was my age and Moragh a year or so younger. When Dad appeared dressed as Santa Claus, the poor girls burst into tears, and to reassure them, Dad had to remove the Santa beard. Rather than feeling sympathetic, I was peeved with them for spoiling the fun.

The other memory was of a summer holiday in Wanaka. We drove there in the Essex and camped at Glendhu Bay on the beach in a large canvas tent. I recall spending happy hours in the lake floating on a log. Very early one morning, I startled everyone in the tent by screaming after drinking very cold water from a billy and giving myself a sharp pain in the tummy. Before we returned home, Dad drove us to Te Anau and from there on the rough gravel road to the entrance of the Homer Tunnel, a PWD depression-years project that had been suspended because of the war. The tunnel would not be completed until 1953, and it would be 1981 before I could make the journey to Milford Sound.

As a family, we were in Owaka for only two years, but I had a much longer connection. Almost all my childhood summers were spent on the Gorman's farm. Bill and Flo Gorman and their three children, Dawn, Myrna and Neill, were our closest Owaka friends. Dawn was a few years older than Bronwen, Myrna and Bronwen were the same age, and Neill was my age. Flo Gorman was very caring and became a second mother to me. She and Mum developed a loving friendship, sustained by regular correspondence after the family left Owaka. Bill was Australian by birth and a genuine character, with an inexhaustible fund of tall stories, in most of which he played a central role. Dad enjoyed them greatly, but warned us not to take everything Bill told us as gospel truth. In one area, Bill had no need to exaggerate. As an underage teenager, he had finagled his way into the Australian Army and had fought with the Anzacs on Gallipoli. The earliest war stories I can remember were his.

Bill had an entrepreneurial streak and constantly sought ways to supplement the farm's all-too-meagre income. When car production resumed after World War II, he became the Ford agent for South Otago, which meant he always had a new car to drive. He also had a stock of soft drinks for sale in his garage. How this business worked, I never understood, but it meant there was always a large bottle of lemonade for our pic-nics. Bill tried to make an entrepreneur out of me. At the end of one summer, he sent me home on the train to Christchurch with cabbage plants, which he wanted me to sell door-to-door. Another year, I travelled home with a roll of cyclone netting, which I was to display as a sample to get orders for Bill to fill. My parents were not enthusiastic about my hawking cabbage plants and cyclone netting in our somewhat snooty Fendalton neighbourhood, and my entrepreneurial spirit was stillborn.

The summers on the farm gave me indelible memories. Out at daybreak with Neill cutting down foxgloves. The whis-tle of the train approaching Tunnel Hill. The shearing gang and the exhilarating, exhausting week in the shearing shed gath-ering fleeces to be baled. Learning to milk the cows by hand and, with more strength as I got older, to spin the manual separator to make butter. All four of us kids armed with hoes thinning turnips on the Gorman farm and up Hunt's Road at the Grays' place. The weekly bath in the tub filled with very hot water from the laundry copper; I was the first houseguest to enjoy clean water. (Bathing in hot water to this day brings back the feeling of homesickness.) Horse-drawn mower and rake cutting hay as we gathered sheaves for the haystack. Lav-ish morning teas of scones and pikelets sent out to the field by Flo. Riding back to the farmhouse at the end of the day on the draft horses. Catching rabbits in a warren with ferrets and the heart-rending shrieks of the rabbits caught in nets staked across the holes. Rabbit trapping. Learning to kill and skin rabbits, the skins stretched to dry on wireframes. Crouch-ing under the bedsheets to evade Huhu beetles flying around the bedroom at night. Listening to the number of rings on the phone to learn who was being called on the party line. The excitement of the annual Owaka District A&P show. Saturday night dances in the Owaka Hall, with the kids sliding across the polished floor before the dancing began, women on one side of the room, men on the other or outside at the back around a beer keg. The lavish suppers of home-baked goodies.

For all my 35 years overseas from 1959, it was the image of the rough hills of the Catlins that tugged at my heart, calling me home.

In the mid-1960s, when I was living in the US, by some chance I discovered one of my former fellow students from Owaka. He was Brian Stoddart from the remote timber-milling settlement of Tahakopa, deep in the southern Catlin's bush. He had become a mathematician and taught at Western Michigan University in Kalamazoo. A short man, he was married to Gillian, a tall African-American woman, and they and their three children became good friends of my wife Jenni and me. We exchanged visits back and forth between Kalamazoo and Ann Arbor, where I was teaching history at the University of Michigan.

— CHAPTER TWO —

South Island Childhood

"The thing about childhood is that you don't understand
how strange it is until you look back as an adult."
– Lisa Brennan-Jobs

The family's two years in Owaka were followed by two in Port
Chalmers, Dunedin's deep-water port. This period seems to
have been among the happiest in my life. I say "seems to have
been" because how can one make such a sweeping judgment
based simply on childhood memory? I can say that almost all
my memories of Port Chalmers are happy.

Such contentment cannot have been shared by my parents. This was the point in the war when a Japanese invasion
of New Zealand seemed imminent. As Headmaster, Dad was
responsible for the safety of the children of the primary school,
which was perched on a rocky hillside between the town's two
railways and in direct line for a bombing run from the head of
Otago Harbour to the docks in which US warships were under
repair, and the two railway stations.

The director of the World War II movie *Home by Christmas*, Gaylene Preston, writing in 2010, observed:

"The isolation of the war period may be difficult for a
modern audience to understand. There were 2.5 million
people in New Zealand, much more evenly spread than
we are now, with more people living in small towns ....

People didn't have phones. All you had was the BBC world service (on the radio) for people to hunch around to try to find out anything. News was sparse."

Working with a neighbour, wharfie "Dummy" Braithwaite (no relation), Dad dug an air-raid shelter deep into the clay in our backyard, lining it with sheets of copper "donated" from the cargo of a ship in port. This became my daily play space for war games with my boyfriend, Timmy Woods. Also, in the long grass of our large back section, there was an old car, and this gave us a tank from which to repel enemy attacks on our bunker. Inspired by cinema newsreels, I made a parachute jump off the garage roof. Fortunately, my fall was slowed by a tree that snagged my parachute, Dad's umbrella. I was offended by the fact that Dad was decidedly more concerned about damage to the umbrella than he was about my war wounds: a grazed knee and a bruised arm.

As kids, we enjoyed the practice evacuations from the school into the scrub on the hillsides across the upper railway line. We were also intrigued by the corks that were handed out, one per student. We were instructed to clench the cork between our teeth and lie belly down, holding ourselves up off the ground so bomb shock waves would not hurt us severely. The day we were given these corks, there were kids down on the ground all over town, having a whale of a time as we headed home after school. I bet we all lost our corks in no time flat.

Two other wartime memories stand out. One was the launch of the first minesweeper at a local boat yard, which previously had built fishing trawlers. Under Dad's direction, the whole school was marched in orderly ranks the mile or so to the boatyard, where we lined the road above the slip. We all cheered as the small minesweeper slid into the water – and tipped on its side. This was followed by the most entertaining consternation among the boat builders, but for us, the show ended too soon as Dad had us marched back to school. We were not taken to subsequent launches, which apparently went without mishap.

The other wartime memory is of a day when all the greater Dunedin metropolitan areas practised for a civil defence emergency. Dad had some civil defence role, so he was gone from the house early in the day while Bronwen and I stayed home with Mum. Bronwen, who was 11 or 12 at the time, had been designated as a wounded war casualty, and Mum hung the approved signal – a bedsheet – in a front window, awaiting the arrival on our street of a Civil Defence Warden. He ultimately strolled by, gave a cheery wave and was headed up the hill until Mum pointed out that he had overlooked the bedsheet. Bronwen was carried out on a stretcher and taken to the railway station to await evacuation. She lay there for several hours before getting her train and ambulance ride to Dunedin Hospital. It was dark before she returned home, a very hungry and discontented war victim, convinced she would have been left to die in a real emergency.

Although already past 40, Dad had to report for a medical examination for enlistment in the Airforce at some point in our Port Chalmers years. He failed the exam because of scarring on one lung, possibly due to the 1918 flu that killed his father and brother Harry.

Port Chalmers in the early forties was a small cohesive community in which my parents felt comfortable, allowing their seven-year-old son to wander freely with his black Labrador puppy. Even though I took full advantage of this freedom, my mother always seemed to know where I had been when I returned home at day's end. There was a very active bush telegraph.

I marvel at the contrast between the contemporary hyperconcern for children's safety with the places I went unsupervised in those Port Chalmers years. There was the blacksmith's shop at the southern end of the main street, where I would stand by the roaring coal-fired forge to watch the blacksmith hammer red-hot metal into a horseshoe on his anvil. There was the railway turntable close to the port station where I would give a hand to the driver revolving a steaming locomotive, and there were the shunting yards on the Mussel Bay side of the port tunnel, where I would play on the waggons with my friends, each of us goading the others to have the courage to walk through the tunnel. None of us was ever silly enough to do this, but we did play in the collapsing tunnel that had been dug into the hillside at Back Beach to pump through dredged harbour sand for the reclamation of Mussel Bay. This was undoubtedly unsafe.

Back Beach claimed many of my hours. This was where I swam almost every day in the warmer months. It was also where I had my first victory in a race. There were prizes on offer that drew swimmers all the way from Dunedin. I entered a handicapped event for boys, and being the youngest, I was given the biggest head start. Apparently, some of the older boys, thinking they could easily overhaul me, did not start as soon as their handicap entitled them to do. They misjudged, and I won. I could scarcely contain my excitement as I waited for my parents to arrive home from an out-of-town cricket match in which Dad had been playing. I greeted them proudly with my prizes: money and a large chocolate bar. (I am happy to report that this brief foray into professionalism did not result, as it had for my father 20 years earlier, in my being flung into outer darkness by the amateur sports fraternity.)

It was at Back Beach, perched on the half-submerged rusting hulks of old trawlers that I fished for cockabullies and sea horses with periwinkles threaded into cocksfoot stalks. My real fishing with rod and line was done off the wharves in the port, and it was there I made friends with the trawler crews as they offloaded their night's catch. They would give me throwaway fish like red cod, leatherjacket, and elephant fish, but I did not receive an enthusiastic welcome when I carried these home. Dad was fed up with having to bury them.

Port Chalmers is a town of very steep hills, not an easy place to learn to ride a bike, especially when you are a small boy learning to ride on his big sister's machine. I was too small to ride sitting on the seat, so I couldn't engage the back-pedal brake, making me reliant on the hand brake on the front wheel. If applied too sharply, this sent the rider hurtling over the handlebars. Having suffered this misfortune a couple of times, I was very grateful when my parents gave me a smaller bike of my own for my eighth birthday.

My most serious accident happened on my own two feet on one of the town's steepest streets. On my way to school one morning on Grey Street, I was walking backwards, watching my father, who was a hundred yards or so behind me. One of the shopkeepers had opened an unprotected loading shoot in the pavement, and I fell backwards down this to land on my head on a pile of coal in the cellar. I must have been knocked unconscious because the next thing I remember was being picked up by my father and carried home. I got two days off school but seemed none the worse for the adventure.

A very different threat to my childhood equilibrium was posed by a teenage boy who befriended me for a while. One day behind a downtown building, he got me to open the fly on my pants and slip my penis into his open fly. It seemed to me an absurd and boring game. I never mentioned this to my parents, but perhaps there were rumours circulating about the boy because soon after, they told me not to spend time with him anymore.

It was not he but my good friend Timmy Woods who got me into trouble. My mother found Timmy and me smoking cigarettes in the long grass in the back section. She asked if we had filled our cigarettes with dry grass, and before I could say yes, Timmy blurted out the truth that it was tobacco we were smoking. I had stolen this and the cigarette papers from my father's study, and it was because of the theft, not the smoking, that my father later punished me with a strapping.

Both my parents smoked cigarettes for years. Dad was a chain smoker, and my enduring mental picture of him is with one of his skinny self-rolled cigarettes hanging from his lower lip. At some stage, the Labour government raised the tobacco tax, and Dad developed paper filters to roll into his cigarettes. He called them his "Wally Nash beaters," Walter Nash being then Minister of Finance. It was not until he was in his seventies that Dad gave up smoking, and then only because a doctor said it was probably contributing to his glaucoma, from which he was going blind.

I attribute my success in avoiding the family nicotine addiction to the advice given by one of my teachers at Christchurch Boys' High School [CBHS] when I was 15. Ernie Hawkhead, a war hero in our eyes because he had survived five years in World War II as a prisoner of the Germans, told us that you had a crucial advantage as a POW if you could trade the cigarettes from your Red Cross parcels for items you needed. I determined then and there not to smoke.

Other Port Chalmers' memories:

- Losing my balance in an earthquake and falling to the ground under our rotary clothesline, which appeared to be about to tip over.

- Being witness to an exchange between my father and the parson from the church across the road from our house. The minister had come to complain that that morning I had flicked dried peas at the legs of the young woman who was my Sunday school teacher. Dad's reply raised him, in my eyes, to the category of super-hero. He said that I was a bright boy who must have been very bored to do that, and in future, he would find something better for me to do with my Sunday mornings. Strangely, I have no memory of Dad rebuking me afterwards, and writing about the incident now makes me feel apologetic for being such a brat.

- Running down to Timmy's house after returning from a short family vacation in a rented bach at Waikouaiti Beach to discover that not only had the Woods family gone, but that the back half of their house had been demolished. I did not have to wait for the teachings of Buddhism to gain awareness of impermanence.

Intertwined with all of my Port Chalmers memories is my black Labrador puppy, Nigger. (I am appalled now at the insensitivity of the name. At the time, it was popular, among Pakeha at least, as the name for a black dog.) Nigger went almost everywhere with me. I remember his delight in playing in a rare snowfall one winter's day in the hills above the town. Nigger was in tow the afternoon that Timmy and I decided to run away from home. We didn't get far because my plan for a supply of food – sweets from the dairy – didn't work out. Even though I was careful to say "give" rather than "sell" when I asked the shopkeeper for a bag of lollies, he insisted on our paying for them. He was unpersuaded by my explanation that we didn't have any money.

The one place Nigger was not welcome was school. My parents told me to make sure he was tied up before I left home, but one day he followed me to school and ran up enthusiastically to Dad as he was addressing the morning assembly in the playground. "Whose dog is this?" Dad asked sternly to the accompaniment of chuckles from the other teachers. I waited hopefully for Bronwen to step forward, but no such luck. I had to claim Nigger. "Take him home and report to me when you get back," said Dad. I took as long as I dared on the round trip, but when I finally showed up in the Headmaster's office, all Dad did was ruffle my hair and send me off to class with the injunction not to be a fool in future.

In 1943, Dad was appointed inaugural Principal of a new intermediate school in Invercargill, and I was told we would soon be leaving Port Chalmers. Shortly after this, I came home one day to find Nigger gone. My parents explained that when we got to Invercargill, we would have to stay in a hotel while they house hunted. It would not be possible to have Nigger with us, so they had given him "to a nice farm where he would be happy." I was devastated, and even now, writing about the loss brings me to the edge of tears. I never forgave my parents for this.

~ ~ ~

In the first weeks in Invercargill, I was very unhappy. I was sent to South School, and although I do not have any detailed memories, I have retained a bleak feeling about it. Of course, I must have been grieving the loss of Nigger, but I wonder whether a deeper root of my unhappiness was that this was the first school I attended where my father was not headmaster. I began telling Mum and Dad I was ill and couldn't go to school. When they found a house to buy, they moved me to St. George School, which was on the same street as our new house, and they asked some of the St. George teachers to give me special attention. It was not long before I was a happy camper there.

I found there were lots of schoolmates living in the neighbourhood, so I soon had a sizeable group of friends, which may explain why I didn't have one special boyfriend as I had in Port Chalmers. Our house and surrounds were perfect for play. We had a full quarter-acre section, and in the back yard were old hen houses in which I soon had an assortment of animals, including chickens, guinea pigs, and a rabbit. I had little success with a homing pigeon, bought from a boy who lived close by. I followed his instructions to keep it well fed in the hen house for a few days, so it would regard my place as its new home. When I let it out, however, it flew away, and I was sure it had "homed" to its previous owner. He denied this, and because all his pigeons looked alike, I had no way of proving him wrong. What a racket, I thought!

One section next to ours was empty, except for a macrocarpa hedge and two garages across the front. My friends and I played in the hollow centre of the hedge, and the distinctive smell of macrocarpa has lingered in my consciousness from that day to this. Behind the garages, in the empty section, we played cricket, despite objections from neighbours whose sitting-room window overlooked our pitch. Sure enough, one day, we smashed that window with an errant cover drive. The owners were in the room at the time. They refused to give us back our ball, and they told my parents angrily that their baby had been showered with glass. Dad apologised and made peace with them, promising to pay for the damage, but we lost our cricket field.

I remember Port Chalmers as a sunny place. I do not remember Invercargill that way. Possibly this is an accurate memory of Southland's bleak weather, but I suspect it also reflects the fact that I spent most of my summers during these years on the Gorman farm in Owaka. One place I remember as sunny was Awarua Bay, where I loved to go, even though it was a demanding 20 km bike ride from Invercargill. The sandhills there were teeming with skinks, which I loved to hold and feel all silky sliding between my fingers. The shallow waters of this tidal lagoon were deliciously warm, inviting a swim which the surf at Oreti Beach on Foveaux Strait certainly did not.

Throughout my childhood, I spent time alone in nature without any feeling of loneliness. I have brilliantly clear memories of "being bathed" in nature. Looking back, I realise I had a mystical connection with the natural world from the youngest age. Once I got my own bike, I would go on long solo bike rides interspersed with nature rambles. I remember a smooth track near Port Chalmers lined on each side with poplars that threw beautiful shadows on the path. When I visited in 1981 (my first return to NZ after more than 20 years), I went back to find with joy that the pathway and the poplars were still there.

Given Invercargill's general flatness, it invited cycling. In our three years in the city, I remember only two accidents. One was my own mistake in bad weather. I was biking head down into the driving rain of a Sou'westerly when I rode smack into the back of a parked car. The other was at night, close to home on ill-lit Tweed Street. Blinded by the lights of an oncoming car, a taxi driver ran into me from behind. I was not injured, which was miraculous given that the back wheel of the bike was smashed, and I landed on the ground almost under the front tyres of the taxi. The driver was appalled by what he had done. He loaded the bike into his boot before dropping me home and then driving on to take his fare to his destination. I was too traumatised to tell my parents what had happened, and they were startled when the taxi driver returned to ask after my welfare. I then burst into tears, and everyone was convinced I must be injured.

On this occasion, as after another bike accident a few years later in Christchurch, I found I could not share my feelings with my parents. Strong emotions were customarily suppressed in our family. Bronwen, in her teens was the exception. She often exploded angrily at Mum and especially Dad, but I know it took a great toll on her. There was evidence of self-harm in scar tissue along the sides of both her hands, where she bit herself repeatedly. Mum and Dad kept a tight lid on their feelings. In a rare moment of self-revelation, Dad once told me he was afraid of his own anger.

Bronwen's Invercargill school was Southland Girls' High, where she was joined by Dawn Gorman for Dawn's final year of schooling. Dawn lived with us for the year, an informal trade-off, no doubt, for my summers on the farm. Southland Girls' High was sandwiched between my Mecca and Medina – Rugby Park and Dad's Tweed Street (later called Tweedsmuir)

Intermediate. In the late 1930s, as Principal at Orakei in Auckland, Dad was one of the pioneers of the Intermediate School system in New Zealand. He read assiduously on the educational philosophy of the middle school movement in America, and he introduced some of the features of the American schools to New Zealand, most notably elective subjects. I remember his enthusiasm at Tweed Street Intermediate for technical skills such as shoemaking, book printing, and binding, which he personally mastered with the students.

My intellectual and employment ambitions at the time were modest, shaped as they were by a local figure who had what seemed to me a dream job. This was a man whose task was to keep the street gutters and stormwater drains flowing freely. With a horse, cart, and dog, he was to be seen every weekday with a broom and shovel, quietly performing his indispensable civic duties. What a perfect life, I thought.

It is with embarrassment that I have to admit that in these pre-teen years, I was a petty thief. I can give no justification for this behaviour. I was not deprived emotionally or physically and was given regular pocket money. One instance I recall was shoplifting a leather-covered calendar notebook to give to one of my parents as a Christmas present. When the present was unwrapped on Christmas morning, Bronwen asked how I could have afforded it with my meagre pocket money. I lied and said that it was on sale and I had saved up for it. I was greatly relieved that Mum and Dad disregarded Bronwen's question. A bigger theft – one without any redeeming features – was a one-pound note I took from my mother's purse for spending money at the Southland A&P Show. (According to calculations on the internet, that was the equivalent of seventy US dollars today.) It's said that crime doesn't pay, but I have to admit I had a marvellous long day at the fair, playing all the sideshow games and eating and drinking to my stomach's content. I arrived home late for dinner with an armful of tacky prizes I had won.

My thievery extended to the summers on the Gorman farm. I moved rabbit skins from the other kids' drying racks to my own and pocketed the proceeds when the buyer came to the farm. I took a liking to the cardboard model of a jeep that Neill had made and stole it. In this case, I was almost hoist by my own petard. I entered the jeep in a craft-making competition at St. George School, claiming I was the artist. When my parents announced they were coming to see the show, I realised with horror that I would have to spend the evening distracting them from seeing "my" creation. My thefts from the Gormans ended the following summer when I stole from Neill's stamp collection, which did not go unnoticed. Without telling me, the Gormans apparently searched my suitcase before I left for Invercargill, and when I got home, I found no stamps. I felt shamed, and from then on, I stole nothing during my Owaka summers, nor in Invercargill, as best I can remember.

The only money-spinning job I had in Invercargill was one winter selling programmes for the games at Rugby Park. My own competitive sport was limited to some inter-school seven-a-side rugby games and swimming as a member of the Murihiku Club's team. I attended regular coaching sessions at the Municipal Baths. I was a Sea Cub during these Invercargill years, and I remember one bleak and homesick weekend spent in Bluff with my troop. As I mentioned earlier, I failed my knotting test in my last year as a Cub and was prevented by this from automatic ascension to the Sea Scouts.

My only brush with fame at this time was having as a family GP, Dr Geoffrey Orbell, the rediscoverer in the late forties in a remote area of Fiordland of the Takahe, a large flightless bird that had been thought to be extinct since the nineteenth century. Dr Orbell was a talented artist, and he did pencil drawings of Bronwen and me. He was also at work building a large launch in his backyard, and he gained notoriety when he had to dismantle part of his house to tow out the completed boat.

It is not quite accurate to say that Dr Orbell was my only

brush with fame in Invercargill. During 1945, I also witnessed the triumphal visit of Field Marshall Bernard Montgomery, commander in North Africa and Italy of the British Eighth Army in which the New Zealand Division had fought. With the Japanese being driven back in the Pacific and the danger of an invasion of NZ gone, the war did not figure as largely in my Invercargill childhood as it had in Port Chalmers, but I do remember the press headlines and photographs of the atomic bombings of Hiroshima and Nagasaki when I was 10. I also remember the celebrations of VE and VJ Days, the latter including scary moments when my father was almost pushed off the tailgate of a moving truck full of celebrating school kids and, in the evening when a celebratory bonfire was lit on Tay Street, a drunk trying to scale the flaming firewood.

~ ~ ~

Mum and Dad were both ill during our time at Invercargill. Disturbingly, I do not recall what illness Mum had, but she was in hospital for more than a week, during which I created family folklore by arriving home one evening with sausages and asking Dad to cook them to replace his standard boiled egg breakfast. Dad had respiratory troubles and lumbago; both brought on by Southland's cold, damp climate, and his health became so bad that Mum and he decided that we would have to move from Invercargill, even though he loved his work at Tweed Street Intermediate School. With regrets, he applied for a position on the Canterbury School Inspectorate.

We moved to Christchurch early in 1946. I was just 10 at the time, and this was the sixth town in which I had lived. I stayed there until I was 24, so it's hardly surprising that I regard Christchurch as my hometown. I was technically resident in Ann Arbor, Michigan, for 20 years from 1963, but I was absent for nine of those years on research trips to India, the UK, Australia and Massachusetts. It was not until I returned to

NZ in 1994 and settled at Te Wairua on Pelorus Sound that my Christchurch residential record came under threat.

Arriving in Christchurch in 1946 was more like a homecoming than a move to a new city. On two occasions during previous school holidays, we had swapped houses for several weeks with a Christchurch family, the Nobles, old friends of my parents from Auckland Teachers' College days. Charlie Noble had been Dad's best man at my parents' wedding. The Nobles lived in Fendalton, and in 1946 my parents were determined to find a house in that suburb.

Even though we again stayed in a central city hotel for the first few weeks, Bronwen and I were sent off to school immediately, Bronwen to Christchurch Girls' High and me Elmwood Primary, where I was immediately made to feel at home. I arrived back at the hotel that afternoon to announce that I was already a member of the Elmwood Swimming Team! My Standard Five teacher, Vern Reid, was the school swimming coach, and his first question to me when I entered his classroom was, "Do you swim?" When I told him of my competitive swimming in Invercargill, he arranged togs for me and, at the morning break, took me to the school pool and had me show my stuff. He and I both came away jubilant. In addition to being a great booster of my swimming career, Vern became a dear friend. From that day forward, for the next decade-and-a-half until I exchanged Christchurch for Canberra, the Elmwood Pool occupied many of my busiest and happiest days.

The property my parents bought was on Idris Road, a busy thoroughfare in Fendalton close to Bryndwr. The house itself was nothing fancy, certainly far less distinguished than its neighbours. It had just two bedrooms, plus a sunroom that became Bronwen's bedroom. Typical of many New Zealand houses at the time, its only heating was one small open fireplace in the dining room. I think the main attraction for my parents (apart, I assume, from a price they could afford) was the quarter-acre section with lawns and gardens front and back. Both

Dad and Mum gardened, and Dad had a magnificent vegetable garden enriched by his compost, which he ran through his fingers lovingly. The garden provided all the family's vegetable needs year-round, and there was enough left over in most seasons for me to munch on raw vegetables, sitting in the garden when I arrived home from school each day.

There were tall trees along the property's southern boundary, and I spent many happy hours high in one of these, a magnificent ash. There was also a double garage, although for our first years in Christchurch, we had no car, and when we did get one in the late fifties, Dad had the garage so full of "useful stuff" that the car had to be parked on the street until space could be cleared for it. I regret to say I have followed Dad's example as a hoarder.

Since Nigger's departure, a puppy was number one on my wish list for birthday presents. My parents gave me one for my eleventh birthday in July 1946, my first birthday in Christchurch. He was a chocolate-brown cocker spaniel, the most favoured breed in New Zealand in those days. I called him Glen and adored him. Sadly, within a few months, an epidemic of distemper swept through Christchurch. Glen was infected and died. I was heartbroken again. When I went to school after his death, I felt desolate and alone as the other kids went on with life as normal. I could not believe it would ever again be normal for me.

The other animals that joined us at 40 Idris Rd. helped me get back on an even keel. There was Rufus, a Rhode Island Red rooster, who welcomed every dawn from atop our paling fence. There was our large white rabbit Flip and Tinker, the white mouse. Flip was imperious, and he was not patient. When I cleaned his cage, I would put him on the back lawn while it dried, but if I left him out too long, he would hop back into the cage and kick hard against the back wall to demand that I give him his bed of fresh straw. He had definite food preferences. Carrots were not one of them, and he would often push them out through the wires of the cage. *Puha* (milk thistle) was his top choice. Tinker, after a year or so living with us, decided to join wild relatives under the house. The result was a local tribe of piebald mice.

And then there was the indefatigable mother, Timmy, a small grey cat, whose first of several batches of ginger kittens was born on Bronwen's eiderdown (duvet) after my barely awake sister opened her window in the small wee hours to let her in, despite Mum's stern warning at bedtime not to do so. Timmy's first and largest kitten became my inseparable companion Ru (his brother was Kanga). My parents allowed us to have pets on the condition that we were responsible for their care. This resulted in one painful memory for me of transporting Ru to a vet in an apple box on the back of my bike. Ru demonstrated his disapproval of the arrangement by clawing my lower back as I pedalled – faster and faster.

In Christchurch, in the forties and fifties, bicycles ruled. Everyone seemed to ride, including my father to his central city office and almost all my teachers at Elmwood and CBHS. Even university professors rode bikes. I recall an embarrassing incident from my undergraduate days at the University of Canterbury. One frigid winter morning, a group of us was watching and applauding cyclists losing control on the icy corner of Rolleston Avenue and Worcester Street when who should land at our feet but none other than Neville Phillips, our austere and scary Professor of History. Yobs as we were, not one of us had the presence of mind to offer to help him to his feet.

I went everywhere on my bike: in the city, to the beaches and all over the Port Hills. Well remembered are some hair-raising encounters with trams on the furious descents on my return journeys to the city flat lands, with brakes scarcely coping with my reckless choice of the steepest streets. A reunion with people who were Christchurch children of my generation often leads to cycling reminiscences: friendships formed while biking to school; the exhilaration of going full tilt on a 30-degree day with a Nor'wester at one's back or plugging determinedly into the persistent cold Nor'easterly; the danger to balance on tram lines, especially wet or frosty tram lines; and the joy of crossing Hagley Park on the excellent cycle tracks.

While I was still in primary school, probably the summer of 1947-48, Dad took Bronwen and me on a weekend bike hike on the Canterbury Plains and into the foothills of the Southern Alps. We stayed the Saturday night in an Oxford hotel, where I remember enjoying a dinner of eel. On Sunday, we circled through the Waimakariri Gorge and back home to Christchurch. In 1949, when I was 14, a CBHS friend, Neil Hartley, and I biked from Christchurch to Owaka and back in the August school holidays. We were on the road for five days each way, stopping overnight at hotels en route and being accommodated by the Gormans in Owaka. We stayed on the farm for ten days. I kept a diary, which concludes:

"This was an excellent holiday, especially as we had good weather, back winds except on the fourth day and no punctures. On a holiday like this, it is the little things that make it worthwhile. We were sorry we had to take the train from Oamaru to Dunedin and vice versa, but could find no other way of doing it. The lifts from lorry drivers were very helpful and saved us much pushing."

I am amused in reading the diary at how many evenings we spent in cinemas, even going to the movies in Owaka on our first night with the Gormans. I am also impressed by the initiative we showed in Timaru, during our return journey, in hunting down the Canterbury rugby team and cadging grandstand tickets from halfback and CBHS teacher Pat Vincent for a match between Canterbury and South Canterbury.

There was more to life in Christchurch than cycling, sport, and "the flicks." In my teens, my parents introduced me to theatre and classical music. Canterbury had a well-established Repertory Theatre, and I accompanied my parents to its productions. In addition, we enjoyed Ngaio Marsh's New Zealand Players when they came to town. Nothing, however, could match the performances of the Old Vic Company, which toured Australia and NZ in 1948 led by Laurence Olivier and Vivien Leigh, who were at the height of their stage careers. The late forties also saw the establishment of the New Zealand Symphony Orchestra (the National Orchestra, as it was called in its early days), and its concerts awakened in me a lifelong passion for classical music. During my last years in high school and as a university undergraduate, I developed a keen interest in jazz. As a background to the concerts I attended and the discs I purchased, I read eagerly on jazz history and the biographies of its performers.

My parents gave me a great gift when I started high school. They told me I could choose any books I wanted at Whitcombe & Tombs, the major bookstore in town, and charge them to their account. The only condition was that I had to read them. I knew my family's income was not large, and I was immensely appreciative of this gift. I exercised the right with great responsibility.

— Chapter Three —

My Teens

"Sometimes you're the windshield, Sometimes you're the bug."

> – Mary Chapin Carpenter

After two good years at Elmwood Primary, I was due to enter CBHS in February 1948, but that year an epidemic of polio delayed the opening of schools until the beginning of March. To avoid infection, children were instructed by the Public Health authorities to stay away from other children. Cinemas and similar gathering places were closed. This included swimming pools, but several times with other Elmwood kids, I climbed the locked gate and swam happily in the green, soupy water of the uncleaned school pool. If we could survive this, surely we could survive polio!

When I did arrive at CBHS, I was unusually confident for a "new bug," as the Form Three entrants were called. I went with a sizeable contingent of Elmwood boys, and from our house on Idris Road was no more than a five-minute bike ride from the school, which felt as if it were almost in my backyard.

I entered class 3L, a choice determined by my friendship with an Elmwood schoolmate and his decision to study Latin and French. The irony is that the friendship evaporated quickly, so my future was shaped by an illusion of lasting friendship. The 3L curriculum included no maths and a minimum of general science. I proved to be a poor student of languages, and I left high school with just a smattering of French and no Latin to speak of. I did, however, get an excellent education in History, Geography, and English Language and Literature. The teacher from whom I gained the most was our History master, Fergus Murray, whose superb teaching laid the foundations for my career. He taught me how to research and write probing historical essays, on which he gave careful critical feedback. Our L stream had smaller-than-average classes with some of the best and brightest students in the school. I remedied the absence of maths in the L curriculum by arranging to study the subject in my fourth year, and I did well until I was brought up short by calculus.

I also tried to teach myself Te Reo Maori, feeling that it was absurd that NZ schools routinely taught French when our country had more than one language of its own. My parents gave me no encouragement in learning Maori as they subscribed to the official educational dictum that it was a dying language, with no value even for Maori themselves.

In my last month at Elmwood School, I competed successfully for a McKenzie-Villiers Scholarship, administered by the Canterbury Education Board and awarded on the combination of a recommendation from the candidate's primary or intermediate school and a written examination. The scholarship helped the families of recipients to cover high school costs. Mum and Dad turned over some of the money to me to manage, and I invested wisely in Cadbury Caramelo bars to which I was addicted in my teens. They no doubt kept my intellect sharp! Strangely, I felt embarrassed by the award of the scholarship, as though the fact that my father worked for the Education Board created a conflict of interest. I told as few people as I could about my success. But then I also felt perpetually embarrassed at living in Fendalton and would often say we lived in Bryndwr.

~ ~ ~

In the late 1990s, I wrote a lengthy piece for the CBHS Old Boys' Newsletter, and I think it expresses well the deep attachment I developed for the school:

"My years at Boys' High were happy years. In my book Other Ways of Knowing, I contrasted the rather dismal experience of my children in American high schools, gargantuan soulless places that they were, with my own CBHS experience: 'My high school in New Zealand had eight hundred students when I entered in the late 1940s and a thousand by the time I left six years later. This growth was already prompting concern, but the increased numbers did not erode the 'school spirit,' as our sense of community was always described. It is a measure of my feeling of belonging that to this day the school colours – royal blue and black – carry a happy emotional charge for me.'

"I have had a career in education, so in looking back at my days at CBHS my personal nostalgia is combined with professional interest. The first thing I note is the shadow that hung over my generation: the threat of polio, 'infantile paralysis' as we knew it. A vaccine was not developed until we were in our twenties, so our high school years were disrupted by polio epidemics, my 1948 entry to the Third Form being postponed several weeks by a severe one. I don't remember being concerned, apart from whining about the closure of cinemas and public swimming pools, but I'm sure my mother and father were very afraid for my sister and me.

"Our parents had had a lot to worry about in their lives, what with the Great Depression and two world wars. By contrast, we were a carefree generation. Although WWII still loomed large in the national consciousness in the late forties, our teenage view of it was unrealistically romantic because of a childhood diet of Saturday afternoon war movies in which the good guys (the Allies) always triumphed heroically over the bad (the Axis). Many of our masters at CBHS had recently returned from service, but like most NZ men they said little about their experiences. We got the chance to see some of them in uniform on the monthly Cadet Days, when they gave us rudimentary military training. We cadets envied their handsome officer garb as we suffered in our ill-fitting, regulation-issue 'sandpaper suits,' with the stiff shorts that scraped the tender skin behind our knees as we marched around the school grounds. Even so, I liked cadets, and I have to admit I looked forward to CMT (Compulsory Military Training), which awaited us when we left school.

"'Good discipline' was a phrase we heard a lot at CBHS. In those days, it was an ideal much touted in NZ society, which I suspect was one legacy of the war, despite those entertaining stories on which we grew up of irreverent behaviour by cheeky Kiwi soldiers in the face of pompous British officers! Try that at your peril with headmasters Alf Caddick and Jim Leggat!

"The authoritarian tendencies in NZ high school education had their roots further back in the Victorian English Public School tradition, which in our day was still a model for most of NZ's single-sex high schools. Christ's College, with the antiquated collars, straw boaters and all, was more given over to the charade than CBHS, but the attitudes and some of the trappings were part of our school life. The wearing of academic gowns by masters was one relic along with others that survive to this day, among them the school colours, the Latin motto, the crest, the school song and the daily assembly with the hymn singing. The school persisted with the teaching of Latin, though by then there were few takers.

"Caning was another 'gift' of the English Public School tradition, though caning by Monitors was not sanctioned as it was in some other boys' high schools of the time.

The monitorial system itself was adopted from Public School organisation, and I have always thought that this encouragement of hierarchy amongst teenagers was anomalous in a country that has always boasted of its egalitarianism. I must say, however, that I feel the stated aim of giving selected boys command responsibilities to provide training in leadership skills did work.

"Compulsory sport was another of the legacies, including the annual cross-country race, the bane of many of us. I loved sport, so apart from the cross-country this emphasis suited me very well, and even in those rather mindless teenage days I appreciated the willingness of masters to give hours of their time after school and at weekends to coaching sports. Of course the English Public School heritage was evident in the supremacy accorded rugby and cricket and the banishment from School of soccer (too plebeian) and basketball and softball (too American). Hockey was then the only other team sport allowed a toehold.

"Speaking of the masters' dedication, it certainly extended beyond sport to academics. They left us in no doubt that they truly valued learning, which is the greatest of gifts a teacher can give any student. 'Looking back on my schooldays,' I wrote in Other Ways of Knowing, 'I realise I learned most from the teachers who let me see who they really were. We teach by what we do and who we are rather than what we say.' It is my memory that our masters at CBHS in the forties and fifties were admirable models for boys growing into adulthood.

"As far as letting us see who they really were, I'm glad to say a number of them added entertainment to our classroom days by not concealing their eccentricities. Perhaps we have the quirky English Public School tradition of encouraging colourful personalities to thank for this as well. Otherwise we might not have enjoyed the likes of

Brasso, Bav, Henry Dyer, Fred Wicks, Clifton Cook, Sam Cuming, Pat Vincent and the irrepressible Dr. John Moffat, who is responsible for perhaps the most hilarious moment of all my years at CBHS. As he did occasionally, John had climbed onto his table to deliver some colourful passage from French literature at the top of his lungs. He concluded the dramatic monologue by leaping towards the door with arms and gown flailing and landed directly in the path of an entering Inspector of Schools. This poor man staggered backwards, startled out of his wits, while John, unfazed, bowed deeply – and we almost split a gut laughing."

Among the teachers I mentioned in this piece was Bav, and I went on to write more about him in 2017:

"The recent centenaries of the First World War battles of the Somme and Passchendaele raised a ghost for me, the ghost of former CBHS teacher, Harry S. Baverstock. During my CBHS years (1948-1953), Bav was at the end of a 33-year career on the teaching staff. He had begun teaching in 1920 in the old school on Worcester St. and had transferred with the school to Straven Rd., where he designed the layout of the grounds. None of this is what I, nor I imagine other members of my high school generation, remember him for. Bav seemed to me a living embodiment of the tragic history of the first half of the Twentieth Century. As a 20-year-old NZ infantryman, he had fought in the appalling Battle of the Somme, and it was either there or during the subsequent carnage at Passchendaele that he was severely wounded. In our classes, he sometimes alluded to the horrors of war, and it was clear he had suffered deeply during the Second World War as deaths of former students and teachers were reported daily in morning assembly. His war injury was as much to his soul as to his body.

"In some ways it seemed the world had stopped for Bav in his youth. It was as though he still lived in the Edwardian era, with his butterfly collar, narrow tie and old-fashioned suits in a dark green fabric. A very small man with round rimless spectacles, he looked like a sad old owl. I studied Latin with him for three years and was amongst his least talented students in that subject. Bav could never understand the contrast between my competence with homework assignments and my abject failure in class tests. He did not know that I was able to cajole my older sister, a brilliant student of languages, into 'helping' me with the homework. In School Certificate Latin, I gained the wretched mark of 23%, 13% of this undoubtedly coming from the 'antiquities' (classical history) segment of the exam.

"In his engaging memoir Singing Historian, Ned Bohan, my best mate in school, wrote of our 'L' class: 'We were the despair of diminutive Harry Baverstock. Old "Bav," gentle, polite, artistic, almost always permanently depressed, was lumbered with us as our form master for three years.' Without question, Bav was the gentlest and kindest of our teachers. During one of his classes, he asked me to explain why some of us had been giggling. My fellow gigglers hissed at me not to explain, so I said: 'I have been told to shut up.' Bav misheard me and thought I was telling him to shut up, so he sent me off to another classroom to get a cane. When I returned with it, I explained to him what I had really said. He was hugely relieved and apologised to me for his misunderstanding! Bav retired in 1952 and lived on into his late eighties."

In this piece, I referred to Ned Bohan as my best mate, but in fact, I had two "besties" in high school. The other was Dave Spicer, and he and Ned could scarcely have been more unalike.

Dave entered CBHS the same year as Ned and me, but was not in 3L with us. His passion was sport. He excelled at rugby and cricket and made it into the school's top team in both. In addition to playing on the same rugby teams, Dave and I spent a lot of our weekend leisure time together. During the winters of our last two years in school, we joined the CBHS group skiing on the Ball Glacier at Aoraki/Mt. Cook. In earlier years, we had been together in summer Cadet camps. Dave's ambition was to become an army officer, and he and I were part of the school's Special Training Unit, which prepared cadets for military leadership. (It was also in the STU that I deepened my friendship with Graham Cogswell, my close companion during Compulsory Military Training [CMT] after we finished high school.)

In his final year at CBHS, Dave became the school Regimental Sergeant Major, which helped him gain a scholarship to the Royal Military College, Duntroon, in Australia, which trains officers for both the Australian and New Zealand armies. Dave did very well at Duntroon but found he did not like the military life and dropped out. When he arrived back in Christchurch, we saw each other frequently, and I was his best man when he married Jenny Thompson in 1958. After I went overseas at the end of 1959, we stayed in touch for a while, but ultimately I lost track of him until a CBHS rugby First XV reunion in 2003.

As I said, Ned was quite different from Dave. He was intellectually articulate and assertive, also very witty, which resulted in our collaboration in our last two years at CBHS on producing humorous skits for the annual school concerts and editing the school's satirical magazine. I recall that in one of those years, whoever on the teaching staff was charged with exercising oversight of the magazine suggested to us firmly that it would be best to allow space for others to contribute. Ned and I were a bit full of ourselves!

We both had History and English as our major subjects, and we continued the study these at university. We stayed in lockstep through our Bachelor's and Master's degrees, both graduating with Honours in History, and then went together in 1959 for a year of Post Primary Teacher training at Christchurch Teachers' College. Ned's ambition, however, was to become a professional singer. He had a fine light tenor voice and devoted much of his energy in his teens and twenties to gaining instruction in singing technique and musicology. He continued this study in Australia before spending almost 25 years in the UK as a classical performer. There he also wrote fiction for children and adults and expanded his writing to nineteenth-century colonial biography after returning to New Zealand in the late 1980s. He continues to be a very productive author.

The person Ned gave most credit for launching his musical career was Clifton Cook, "a small cross-eyed man of daunting energy and an astonishingly loud tenor voice." Clifton was CBHS' music master, in Ned's words, "perhaps the most disorganised, impossible, and put-upon music master who ever stood before a class and suffered unremitting disorder .... Clifton was utterly consumed with producing music." His achievement? "There was nothing sissy about singing at Boys' High in those glorious years when our choirs entertained Christchurch and performed for a seemingly unending succession of visiting celebrities."

Ned and Neil Hartley, my 1949 cycling companion who was a bass, were both chosen by Clifton for private lessons. I sang along with them in school choirs and even attempted to become a violinist in the school orchestra, despite the fact that I could never tune my violin. Nor could I read music, but that did not prevent the minister of Fendalton's St. Barnabas Anglican parish from recruiting me for the church choir.

In my teens and early twenties, I went through a Christian period with regular church attendance. At school, I joined the Student Christian Movement [SCM], which had the bonus of joint meetings with the Christchurch Girls' High [CGHS] SCM.

We also had weekend retreats without the girls, unfortunately. I came home from these with Christian fervour, singing hymns around the house until Dad threatened me with instant execution if I didn't stop. In this period, I devoted time daily to reading scripture, and I believe my English prose was enriched by this deep exposure to the King James Bible. My Christianity, however, did not survive. I resented what I regarded as the church's constant guilt-tripping. My faith ultimately foundered in my experience in India. It seemed absurd for the Christian religion to declare that these hundreds of millions of souls were condemned to eternal damnation because they happened to be born into other religious faiths. God surely could not be that parochial.

CBHS had many extra-curricular activities, and I was a "joiner." In addition to SCM, I tried the Fencing Club, Boxing Club, and the Young Farmers Club (I quickly withdrew from all three), the Classics Club and the Library Club (both long-term), and the Debating Club (which put me into the school's debating team for competition with other high schools).

Ironically, it was during my Christian years that I absented myself from the daily school assembly because it included hymn singing. What I preferred to do was hang out in the basement for the assembly period with my classmates Ned Bohan (excused from the assembly because he was Catholic), Joe Musaphia (Muslim) and other non-conformists, amusing ourselves with what we considered hilarious imitations of the BBC radio comedy, *The Goon Show*. This was when I was in the Fourth Form, my second year in school. As was inevitable, someone on the teaching staff noticed me with the basement "dissenters" and, finding no authorisation from my parents, reported me to the Headmaster, Alf Caddick. He called me into his office and gave me a thorough dressing down and six strokes of the cane. That hurt, but I feared much more that my parents would be told of my transgression. They were not, thank heavens, and I survived with all but my dignity intact. I had to attend assembly after that but, when all was said and done, I enjoyed hymn singing!

In high school, I was a strange mix of the high-achieving good boy and a rapscallion. Interestingly, my rapscallion tendencies always made me feel that the surface good boy concealed the real me, who would be revealed one of these days. Another example of my "rascal" was a stunt in which I participated at one of the annual Sports Days. A friend and I noted that the walking race (800 or 1500 metres) had only one entrant, someone who actually knew how to walk in the competitive style. We entered ourselves and persuaded the real walker that all three of us could stroll around chatting, and then he could do his sprint to win on the home straight. We put our grand plan into action, waving to friends along the way. The Headmaster was furious at this charade in front of parents and other visitors. He had the "race" stopped to avoid embarrassment in the stands. We felt bad for the real walker and expected to be punished, but nothing was done to us. We did win points with our mates!

Sometimes I was also impertinent. Once, as our French teacher John Moffat was handing back marked homework assignments, he told the boy in the seat in front of me that his "head was just above water." To me, he commented, "You are skating on very thin ice, Broomfield." He did not appreciate my pointing out to him that at least I wasn't already in the water like the fellow in front.

~ ~ ~

As Ned Bohan observed, there was nothing sissy about singing in the years we were at CBHS. In the 1950s, an annual August holiday option for Fifth and Sixth Formers was a week's skiing at Aoraki/Mt. Cook, and on the daylong journeys there and back, we filled our bus with song. I participated in the trips in my last two years at school, 1952 and 1953, and they were great fun.

The bus journey, almost all on gravel roads, was an adventure in itself, with the final few miles a hazardous lurch along a boulder-strewn track on a glacial moraine. The standard joke from the Mt. Cook guides was, "We only lose one bus in three, and you're quite safe because we've had two buses go over the edge this week." Significantly, within a few years, the road was deemed too dangerous, and I understand access to the Ball Hut nowadays is only on foot or by helicopter.

The old Ball Hut was much larger than the present tramping hut, with possibly as many as 30 bunks divided between two rooms. Herein lay the trip's prime attraction for us lusty CBHS teenagers: the other bunkroom was occupied by high school girls! In 1952 they were from St. Hilda's in Dunedin, and in 1953, from Marsden in Wellington. We flirted a lot, but the eagle eyes of the chaperones from both schools ensured minimal physical contact.

We may have considered ourselves suave operators après ski, but we could make few claims to suave on the snow. For starters, our clothing was laughable compared to today's dapper ski wear. Like Ed Hillary, who at the time was scrambling in woollies up a much bigger hill in Nepal, we took to the slopes in woollen pants and jerseys, consequently spending our days with wet bums! Fortunately, the lower areas of the Ball Glacier on which we skied offered kind slopes, and generally, we could stay on our feet long enough to give a nonchalant wave to onlooking "girlfriends." Going up on the rope tow was a different matter. In my ill-fitting rented boots and heavy wooden skis, insecurely fastened with clunky metal bindings, I found it harder to stay on my feet in the tow ruts than out on the slopes. And falling brought the humiliation of stopping the tow and earning derisive hoots from fellow males. Teenage boys can be so kind!

Between my first and second visits to Mt. Cook, Edmund Hilary and Tensing Norgay climbed Mt. Everest. Being on one of the mountains where Hilary had learnt his skills and among

Hermitage guides who had accompanied him on some of his NZ ascents gave me a thrilling sense of personal identification with this hero.

~ ~ ~

I was very active in school sports. Dad's ambition for me was in cricket. He coached me and bought me the best bats, but to his disappointment and mine, I didn't cut the mustard. I enjoyed playing cricket, but my well-coached batting form did not produce runs. It was at swimming that I had my greatest success. I was school champion at all levels until, in my last year, Otto Snoep arrived from Curacao to become the school's freestyle star. That year, CBHS made a clean sweep of the Canterbury inter-schools competition. With Otto swimming the freestyle, I competed in backstroke and won that event.

In 1953, my last year at school, I played in the rugby First XV – occasionally, not regularly. I was in the First XV squad. The previous year, I had been Second XV fullback, but with Barry Dineen the obvious choice for 1953 First XV fullback, there was no way I would make it into the team in that position. (Three years later, Barry was fullback in the NZ Universities team that inflicted a legendary defeat on the touring Springboks.) The First XV coach, Tubby Hewland, said he could use me in the forwards, so a forward I became.

As always, the year's big match was against Christ's College, played in 1953 on the College ground. I was on the bench until the last few minutes of the game when one of our backs was injured. College was leading by three points, and Tubby sent me on as the replacement at fullback. He gave me one stern instruction, "Whatever you do, don't kick." College was defending, and they punted the ball high downfield. I gathered it cleanly in midfield and had plenty of time to run forward. The goalposts were invitingly close, and the obvious thing to do was to dropkick a goal, in those days, worth four points. If I got it over, it would put us in front. I have no doubt Barry would have drop-kicked, but Barry had far more flare as a player than I. Tubby Hewland's words rang in my ears: "Don't kick." So I ran and passed. We lost the game by three points.

The first thing my father said to me as I came off the field was, "Why didn't you try a dropkick?" How often in the years since have I seen myself kicking the goal that won the game and made me the school hero!

In our family, Bronwen was regarded rightly as the academic star. She was so brilliant that, after excelling in humanities and languages in the national university scholarship exams in her second-to-last year at CGHS, she decided she wanted to go to medical school, so she studied sciences and maths in her final year and again excelled in the scholarship exams. I could not have done this, but my academic performance at high school was strong in everything other than languages. In my second-to-last year, I was chosen as General Excellence Scholar, and the following year was awarded the school's highest distinction, the Robert Deans Medal. Increasingly, I had been chosen for leadership roles, culminating in an appointment as Monitor (Prefect) and, in my final year at school, Senior Monitor, a prestigious and powerful position in our little pond.

From its foundation in 1881, CBHS was managed by the Canterbury University College Council, but in 1949 a separate Board of Governors was created. Mum was on a committee that advised on the transition, and in 1952 she was elected Board Chairperson. I tried not to be visible to her whenever I knew she would be around the school, given that she had no hesitation in hailing me loudly down a corridor or across a room to the unfailing amusement of my schoolmates.

At this time, Dad was promoted to Senior Inspector of Schools, Canterbury, and with Mum's consuming involvement with CBHS, educational discussions were front and centre of our home life. School inspectors, principals, and teachers were frequent guests at our dinner table. My parents' deepest friendships in the educational coterie were with Elsie and Jim Burrows and Ngaire and Jim Leggat. Jim Burrows, former All Black and All Black coach, had had ten years of high school teaching before World War II, in which outstanding service saw him rise to the rank of Brigadier. In 1945 he had become Rector of Waitaki Boys' High School for five years, after which he returned to the Army and was Southern Military District Commander when he and Elsie lived opposite us on Idris Road.

Jim Leggat was another with a distinguished record as a regimental commander in World War II, after which he was Headmaster at Gisborne High School. From there, he was appointed to the CBHS Headmastership in 1951. Initially, I felt awkward with my high school Headmaster at the dinner table, but I quickly outgrew that. In addition to Jim's role as Headmaster, he and his wife Ngaire managed Adams House, the school hostel, and Ngaire and Mum collaborated in identifying and taking care of boarders who were seriously homesick. We often had two or three of these boys come to the house for lunches at the weekend.

In the 1940s and 1950s, the long summer school holidays saw most New Zealand high school and university students engaged in temporary jobs that put cash in pockets. What I valued most about my summer jobs, given the anti-intellectual attitudes of many of my fellow male New Zealanders at that time, was being able to say I had a "real job" rather than that I was a student. My "real jobs" included assisting in the delivery of Christmas mail, digging ditches and laying cable for the Christchurch Municipal Electricity Department, sorting and moth-balling Army uniforms in the Ordnance Unit at Burnham Camp, running the bottling machine for a small family soft-drink firm, working at a market garden, picking berries, writing sports reports for the *Press*, packing Bird's Eye frozen peas, repairing roads and clearing drainage ditches for the National Highways Board [NHB] and labouring in the railway goods sheds.

This last job was shortly after the 1951 waterfront workers' strike, and many of my fellow workers were ex-wharfies. I have never met such an aggressive, meanly foul-mouthed, larcenous group of men. Every shipment of goods that came into the sheds was broken into and pilfered.

The men at the NHB were quite different. They worked very little, and those amongst them who felt inclined to discuss this with me gave what they described as a Socialist explanation. The Government was their Government, and, as such, it owed them employment. They were rigorously egalitarian. On the days when we went out to work on the roads (that is, on days when there was no hint there might be rain), there was no gang boss. The decisions to go and where were decided by general agreement. When a comfortable, sheltered location was reached, the truck would be unloaded of its tools and wheelbarrows, and a camp stove lit to boil a billy. The day was organised around smokos – morning tea, lunch and afternoon tea – in between which some token work such as clearing storm- water channels might be done: nothing strenuous. I was warned on my first day to "take it easy, mate." Playing cards came out, and reading material was passed around. In my weeks as an employee of the NHB reclining in the sunshine on a tussock in the Port Hills, I gained a good introduction to Marxism through literature supplied by my fellow workers. I have to acknowledge that there were two days during that summer when we all worked hard. Because the Waimakariri River flooded, the northern highway was washed out, and we repaired it. This earned us a photograph and a laudatory article in the *Press*.

Gathering cocksfoot seed along roadsides for sale to seed merchants was a popular free-form occupation for kids in the summer holidays. I have a particularly happy memory from early in my teens of collecting seed with other boys and girls during a family vacation at Little Akaloa, one of the bays on Bank's Peninsula. I'm also reminded by photographs of a large sea lion there on the beach, the first I had ever encountered. On that holiday, we were guests at a small lodge along with one other family, the youngest of which was a frail girl of about my age whom we learnt was extremely ill with rheumatoid arthritis. My feelings of pity convinced me I was in love with her.

~ ~ ~

Two dark memories during my high school years stand out, both involving my family. The first is of my mother becoming very ill when I was only 15, at a time when my father was absent in Wellington on education department business. Mum had been in hospital to have an operation on severely congested varicose veins in her legs. I was at home with her alone when she became delirious as the result of an allergic reaction to sulfa drugs. She fell heavily, and I had to get medical help. I stayed home from school to look after her for a week.

At this time, Bronwen was in Dunedin at Otago Medical School, where she was making a considerable name for herself. She topped her class every year, an exceptional achievement in those days when discrimination against women in universities was even more extreme than it is today. Her brilliance was recognised with a research fellowship, which added a year to her programme and resulted in her graduating with a Bachelor of Medical Science [BMedSci] in addition to the standard Bachelor of Medicine and Bachelor of Surgery [MBChB]. She returned to Christchurch in 1952 to become a "House Man" (Junior Intern) at Christchurch Hospital.

One afternoon when I was at home with Mum and Bronwen, the phone rang, and Mum answered it. Suddenly there was a commotion in the hallway outside my bedroom, with Mum and Bronwen in tears. After prolonged discussion, Bronwen, still crying, came into my room to explain. She had returned from Dunedin pregnant; afraid to tell Mum and Dad she had placed an ad in the *Press* inviting couples who would like to adopt a baby to phone our number. A woman had just answered the ad, and Mum had picked up the phone. Understandably, she was completely startled by the inquiry about a baby, and she burst into tears when Bronwen explained the situation. In 1950s New Zealand, a single woman getting pregnant was regarded as an unmitigated disaster, to be concealed if at all possible to avoid shame.

As Bronwen explained all of this to me, I told her I would help her in every way I could – at the same time feeling empty and deeply sad, knowing as a 16-year-old I was incapable of helping in any way.

Mum was devastated – her hair turned grey within three weeks – but Dad and she gave Bronwen their support. They summoned from the North Island the baby's father, one of Bronwen's former Otago classmates, and he said he would marry her. She did not want that, and Dad and Mum supported her decision. They did insist on his contributing to the expenses for the baby's birth in a private hospital. Bronwen continued to work at Christchurch Hospital, wearing Mum's wedding ring once her pregnancy started to show. To conceal her condition from neighbours, Dad went for walks with her after dark so she could get exercise. When she went into labour, she entered the private hospital under an assumed name. Her baby, a red-haired boy, was immediately put up for adoption. The subject was never again discussed in the family, and Bronwen and I have not talked about it in the decades since.

It is a tragedy that thousands of women in New Zealand who became pregnant "out of wedlock" in those years were shamed and forced, like Bronwen, by the prevailing hypocritical attitudes, to have their babies taken from them and to live the rest of their days without knowing what became of them. And thousands of babies lost their mothers. I myself have often wondered sadly who and where my nephew is.

— CHAPTER FOUR —

Swimming Pool
& Parade Ground

"My work is loving the world."
                                        – Mary Oliver

I had two consuming passions in my teens and early twenties. One of them was swimming. This was an exciting time in Canterbury swimming with the opening of a new outdoor 55-yard pool to mark the provincial centennial in 1950. I was a freestyle swimmer, and I was in the top rank at the provincial level. The closest I came to national glory was fourth place in the 100-yard freestyle at the New Zealand Junior Championships in Ashburton in 1950. As I got older, I added medley swimming, becoming Canterbury medley champion and record holder and winning a New Zealand Universities Blue in 1956.

My coach in my pre- and early-teens was a man in his fifties or early sixties, whose name significantly I have blocked. He was my near miss with paedophilia, although I was unaware of it at the time. Looking back on it now, I realise it was significant that he coached only boys and did not go on coaching them after they reached puberty. He was a bachelor, who lived in a neatly kept house in Opawa, and he would invite his students round on occasional Sundays for afternoon tea and a pep talk. One Sunday, he packed four of us into his car and drove us to a secluded beach on Lyttelton Harbour – a beach with a nifty little cave – and he had us all strip naked (himself included) and do callisthenics on the beach. We had a swim afterwards, and as he helped us towel off, he said how good it was there were no girls in the group so we could be naked together. My mother wrote when I was in Australia in the early sixties to say he had been disgraced and banned from coaching by the Canterbury Swimming Association.

I was elected Club Captain of the Elmwood Swimming Club in 1950 and held this position for much of the decade. A group of us – mostly teenagers but with assistance from some older friends and family members – set to work to improve the facilities at the Elmwood pool, which, like most school pools in Canterbury, was just 25-yards long. We painted it an attractive light blue, upgraded the changing sheds, and built stands. We installed a PA system and lights so we could host evening events. The club was on the Canterbury circuit of Saturday carnivals (as swimming meets were called at the time), and we coordinated transport to ensure our club had entries in all races each week. At the time, swimmers from the Spreydon Club dominated the provincial competition, but bit by bit, we overhauled them.

We ran learn-to-swim classes for several weeks each summer and offered coaching to all our club's promising competitive swimmers. For two summers, I also offered a fortnight-long coaching programme at the Elmwood pool for aspiring competitive swimmers from other clubs city-wide, with participants paying a fee to the Elmwood Club. I was an avid reader of books and magazines with information on the latest swimming and training techniques worldwide, and in addition to incorporating the learning into my own swimming, I passed it along to my trainees. The high point of my coaching career was the success in 1956 of two of my students, Alastair McPhail, freestyle, and Derek Eaton, butterfly, in winning National Junior titles.

The Club had a long-standing tradition of annual home-and-away carnivals with the Westport Club. They came to us for a Saturday-evening carnival, and, later in the summer, we hired a bus for a return visit to the West Coast. In the 1952-1953 summer, when I was 17, I also spent a fortnight in Westport coaching swimmers at the invitation of the local club, which paid for my room and board in a hotel close to the city pool.

My love of swimming included water polo. Overall, I enjoyed team sports more than individual competition because I did not suffer the same nervous tension when competing in a team. There were inter-club games at the Centennial pool one night a week through the summer, and I often rounded out an enjoyable evening of competition by stopping at the pie cart in Victoria Square on my way home for a meal of fried Bluff oysters, eggs and chips.

Our Elmwood water polo team was never able to unseat Spreydon as provincial champions, and, as might be expected, that club provided the core of the Canterbury rep. team. I was one of the three or four outsiders who made it into the squad, and surprisingly in my early twenties, I became team captain. The Spreydon members were considerably my senior and much more experienced, but they were feuding. The Chambers brothers, Noel and Colin, former Canterbury and New Zealand freestyle champions, were scarcely on speaking terms with clubmate Hank Schout, a Dutch immigrant from Indonesia, a large and powerful man who had become one of New Zealand's outstanding players. It was a challenge to captain a team with internal enmities, but I applied skills I had learnt from my leadership positions in high school and after, combining firm decision-making with tactful persuasion. I think I surprised the "old hands" with my show of self-confidence. I rather surprised myself!

In these years, in addition to playing water polo, I refereed games and served on the national executive.

~ ~ ~

I left high school in November 1953 and, like all other New Zealand 18-year-old males, faced Compulsory Military Training. CMT, introduced in the first decade of the twentieth century, was reorganised in 1949 to comprise four weeks of basic training and ten weeks of advanced training, followed by three years of part-time service and six years in the Reserve.

As I had opted for the Army, I entered Burnham on January 12, 1954, for boot camp. As in starting high school six years earlier, I went with considerable confidence and for some of the same reasons. I had many mates entering camp in the same draft, including a close friend, Graham Cogswell, with whom I managed to get assigned to the same platoon and hut. As a cadet, I had had experience in military camps on both islands, and Burnham was especially familiar to me as I had spent an earlier summer there working in Ordnance. Having learnt a few tricks of the trade, I arrived with a second pair of boots (purchased at army surplus) already polished, so I would not have to engage in the arduous task of "spit polishing" my army-issue pair every time we had a hut inspection. I also arrived with a potato peeler in my baggage, so I would not have to peel with a knife if I were assigned kitchen duties!

There were some general principles of survival in the military that we had imbibed with our mother's milk – or more likely from the generation of men before us who had gone to war – and Graham and I observed them carefully in our first weeks in camp: Don't volunteer for anything. Stay away from the fringes of any group so no one "volunteers" you. Don't hang around with the loud mouths. Keep your own mouth shut and listen. If moving from point A to point B, walk smartly and look purposeful, preferably carrying a sheet of paper.

In the first week or two, our platoon did a lot of formal drill, but Graham and I were not among the poor sods who were given punitive drill. As the days went by, we did pull a few stunts to make life more interesting. One of these involved a Bren Gun, a light machine gun that could be carried by an infantryman or mounted on a scout car. The platoon was divided into pairs, and each pair was to disassemble, clean, oil and reassemble a Bren Gun, which was then to be taken to an NCO for inspection. Graham and I watched two of our more dutiful fellow soldiers get to work with special zest. Just as they finished reassembling the gun, we circled the hut, presented them with our untouched firearm and told them that because of their efficiency, they had been chosen to do a second gun. We would return their completed one for them. They looked rather pleased with the accolade and went to work without question. We departed quickly and happily with a well-cleaned gun.

In the third week in camp, training became more interesting with frequent sessions on the firing range. I applied myself assiduously, having been impressed by the words of a veteran sergeant: "I only wish we had had training like you are getting before we were sent to the desert. More of us would be alive today." We got to shoot with both our antiquated .303 Lee-Enfield rifles, which dated from the 1890s, and with my favourite, the Bren gun, a 1930s vintage weapon. I worked hard to improve my aim, but if I am not mistaken, Graham was always a better shot than I.

I came close to being killed twice at Burnham, but not on the range, which was scrupulously supervised. The first time was out behind the camp in a cut-over pine plantation, where I found some solitude one evening wandering amid the stumps and scrub. Suddenly, a bullet whizzed past me and ricocheted off a stone. Probably someone out rabbit shooting. I flattened myself behind a log and lay trembling as I listened for the next bullet. There was none, but I lay there a long time before I felt I could scoot back to the safety of the camp.

The other near-death experience proved that the camp was not all that safe. In our last week, we suffered a severe outbreak of dysentery. Our platoon seemed especially badly affected, and we all had to make frequent sprints to the toilets. One of my emergencies came on an evening when we were having a swimming carnival, and I was in line at the pool to swim the anchor leg for our platoon's relay team. I got back barely in time to take my turn! The problem was traced to our mess hall, and we watched with glee while our commanding officer, cursing the kitchen crew, smashed all the crockery.

It was fortunate that we were restored to health before

Queen Elizabeth and the Duke of Edinburgh arrived to inspect us. Platoons were assigned to demonstrate different aspects of training. Ours had simply to present arms as the royal couple were driven by in a Landrover, but I very nearly dropped my rifle as it snagged on my belt.

Our time in Burnham was extended by almost a week to accommodate the royal tour schedule. By then, Graham and I had decided we would join the Armoured Corps because (Graham says) we preferred to ride rather than walk. I have a suspicion we were actually attracted by the black berets worn by Armoured Corps troopers – the only berets in the NZ Army at that time, Graham has reminded me. Whatever our motivation, we were dismayed by a newspaper article on the day our posting was confirmed that the French army had just introduced an advanced armour-piercing shell that went round-and-round inside a tank, killing the crew.

After a brief home leave, we were shipped off for nine weeks at Waiouru camp at the foot of Mt. Ruapehu on the North Island. The journey began with the overnight Inter Islander ferry from Lyttelton to Wellington, where we boarded a train for what felt like the slowest journey in recorded history. The normal rail journey from Wellington to Waiouru is five to six hours. We were on our train for 12-14 hours, exploring every nook and cranny of the lower North Island rail network and shunted frequently onto side lines so scheduled trains could trundle by.

After a while, it became exceedingly tedious, and our fellow troopers devised pranks to pass the time. Graham and I came up with one that could have resulted in our suffering physical violence had we revealed our involvement. We had an over-ripe banana, and as the train was about to enter a tunnel, one of us (Graham surely?) tossed it out the window, so it splattered on the tunnel entrance and back into the faces of those looking out the carriage windows. A huge howl went up – to which Graham and I added our voices in the hope of concealing our evil. Fortunately and surprisingly, we got away with it.

We arrived at Waiouru station after dark and then, carrying our kit, had to march the two km or so to the camp before we got an evening meal.

We joined Radio Wing, where we would be trained as radio operators and tank commanders. The initial problem was that the newly arrived CO of our company, a dapper slim Englishman with a toothbrush moustache, considered "radio" an Americanism. Our unit would become Wireless Wing as soon as additional large stones had been painted white so that WIRELESS WING could be spelt out in front of the HQ building. Painting the new stones and touching up the paintwork on the old ones was our first task on our way to becoming tank commanders.

There was another problem: The NZ Army had only three of the Centurion tanks with which the Armoured Corps was supposed to be outfitted, and these impressive post-WWII fighting machines were too precious to be used for training. They were for display while we trained in 1940s relic Valentines.

With the stones painted, we started in earnest on our radio instruction. Unfortunately, the equipment was as antiquated as the Valentine tanks, and the operator was lucky if his transmission could be received even in a neighbouring room. One more in this list of complaints: Our instructors, like the tanks and the radios, were WWII remnants and not the world's best-trained teachers. The fact that they were also humourless was the last straw. Graham and I decided to break one of the survival guidelines: We volunteered to clean latrines. Our fellow troopers decided we had lost our marbles, but we had discovered that although latrine duty was for a half-day, the work could easily be completed in an hour, after which the poor benighted cleaners could disappear into the windbreak to chat and read for the rest of the morning. Any items of learning we missed could be picked up quickly when we returned to class refreshed later in the day.

Our hut mates at Waiouru were, overall, more intelligent

and engaging than those in our Burnham hut. Some we had known in Christchurch, such as Clive Tippins, a CBHS fellow student, and Peter Elworthy, former Christ's College boy and member of an eminent South Canterbury farm family. Others, like Don Crabb from New Plymouth, became good friends. We had a lot of fun in our hut and generally shared treats received in the mail. Graham and I were reluctant to share biscuits baked and sent by my mother. If our hut mates were to descend en masse, the biscuits would be gone in a flash. Inadvertently, Mum saved the day. As she had simply stacked the biscuits in the tin without any thought to the shaking they would receive in the none-too-tender hands of NZ Post, they arrived as crumbs. We had to eat them with teaspoons, which fortunately did not appeal to our fellow troopers.

My mother's shortcomings with tins continued, despite my efforts to persuade her that those sent by post needed special care. Years later, in the US, I remember watching a poor postie deposit a tin of honey on the top of our rural mailbox. Someone had wrapped it in newspaper in the vain effort to contain its sticky contents, but so much had leaked on its journey from New Zealand to America that we found the tin virtually empty when we unwrapped it.

~ ~ ~

Our Waiouru radio work was interspersed with gunnery instruction, and this finally got us into a tank, not a moving tank but into one of the Valentines parked on the gunnery range. A standard crew for the older versions of the Valentine, which is what we had at Waiouru, was a driver, a gunner and a radio operator who was the commander. The commander, sharing the turret with the gunner, also loaded the gun. Graham and I stuck together for our gunnery, which was not good for him. Although I have no memory of this, he tells me that at one stage, I fired the gun without warning him, leaving his hearing in one ear permanently impaired.

Possibly less dangerous were our excursions away from camp. Graham describes the first of these:

"At Waiouru, we had two weekend leave passes. These were adventures, so we decided to make the first break to Wellington. We arrived by train early Saturday morning to look for the cheapest accommodation possible. We found this plum of a place in upper Willis St., the dwelling of a very Irish lady and somewhat of a tyrant. The rules were worse than an army camp – in by 9:00 pm, no excess water use, etc. After the dressing-down, she gave us one rule: no boozing at all. That was like a red rag to a bull."

Off we went to a pub, underage though we were, twenty-one being the minimum drinking age at the time. As we were in uniform, I told the barman we were home on leave from Korea, and he served us beers without question. We drank too much that day, which we regretted seriously at breakfast the next morning when our landlady served us mince on toast. The mince had an ominously green tinge!

A major impediment to our enjoyment of this Wellington weekend was the presence of another trooper from our Waiouru hut, and we had no one to blame for this but ourselves. When planning the Wellington weekend, I had written to two of the former Marsden College girls I had met the previous year on my CBHS skiing trip to Aoraki/Mount Cook, inviting them to spend time with us. They said they would be delighted to do so but that a third friend would accompany them. Could we find a date for her as well? Graham and I recklessly recruited a volunteer from our platoon to go with us to make up our trio. Lo and behold, when we met up with the Wellington women, there were only the two I had known previously. The other friend had decided not to tag along. Our fellow trooper was now an impediment. We did our darnedest to shake him off, even offering to pay for him to go to the movies and explore other Wellington attractions, but he stuck like a leech, and our vision of weekend romance evaporated.

For our second weekend leave, we chose Auckland. There I parted company with Graham to visit my Aunt Olive, husband Arthur and children Graham and Joan, both considerably younger than I. Aunt Olive was Mum's youngest sister, whom I knew fairly well as she had shown up in Christchurch unannounced several times during my teens after rows with Arthur. She and Arthur Hookway, a migrant from England, ran a hardware shop in Otahuhu, and they were heavy drinkers. This resulted during my weekend visit in a very scary ride on the narrow, winding hill road to Piha with an inebriated Uncle Arthur at the wheel. The Hookways had a bach there, and fortunately, Arthur had sobered up by the time we returned to the city on Sunday after an overnight stay. I was glad to retreat to what I now saw as the relative safety of Waiouru.

After our return to Christchurch in mid-March 1954, Graham and I continued to see quite a lot of each other even though he was working for the National Bank and I was making up for lost time at university, having arrived back almost a month late to begin my undergraduate courses. Periodically, we had to attend "weekend parades" of our 19th Armoured Regiment platoon, some of them in camp at West Melton on the Canterbury Plains, where we were introduced to advanced skills. By contrast, some of our other parades were at the barracks in the city on Lincoln Road (the former Addington Gaol), which we shared with our rivals, the Canterbury squadron of the Scottish armoured-car regiment, who were not hesitant in drawing our attention to the fact that they had Korean-War-era armoured cars while we still had the old WWII Valentine tanks.

It was these tanks that got Graham and me into trouble in June 1955. On this particular weekend, the platoon sergeant (a dull-witted fellow well known to me from the Elmwood Swimming Club) had us spend hours cleaning the Valentines.

Graham and I decided enough was enough, and on Saturday afternoon, we simply got on our bicycles and left. I went to Hagley Park and lay in the long grass, feeling blissful as I watched fluffy white clouds drift across a deep blue sky. This made so much more sense to me than cleaning vehicles that would be grimy again in a week or two. There were consequences. Graham and I were summoned ten days later by the company CO to discuss our inappropriate behaviour. To our surprise, he didn't seem very perturbed and told us confidentially that we were about to be promoted!

In summer 1956, Graham and I were back together for the first of our required regimental camps, this one near Tekapo in the Mackenzie Basin. Our company drove from Christchurch in convoy, and I was pleased to be assigned to drive one of the Landrovers escorting the trucks – until I discovered we had to travel the 220 km at below 50 km per hour. It was a tedious journey.

Graham writes:

"Tekapo Camp was a rather god-forsaken place in those days in the middle of summer. The pay was lousy, about £3 a week to suffer the heat. We were supposedly in the intelligence corps, helping to plan all sorts of wars on maps."

We were still a tank regiment without tanks, so we had to load our radios into Landrovers and deploy into the neighbouring hills to practice tactical positioning. As we were never able to establish radio contact with any of our other units, the best we could do was while away the hours until we were due back in camp for a meal. Close to the camp, there was a good swimming hole in which we would spend the warm evenings.

After a week, as boredom set in, Graham and I looked for diversions. Here's Graham's description of what we found:

"While we were dodging some sort of tedious job, we came across a group of chaps in a queue who had spent all of their time learning to become drivers in the corps and had at last reached the zenith to get the prized heavy-traffic license. They were being examined by a traffic officer, Mr. Dunlop, who was observing each, in turn, driving down to the nearest gate, backing in through the gap and up the road. This was too much for John and me, so we melted into the group and passed with flying colours.

"Afterward, volunteers were called for to take two trucks to Fairlie to the local timber yard to collect saw-dust for the camp – we were all for that. So, without any road experience, we drove the trucks. I still think that was some feat; luck and the good Lord must have been watching over us driving heavy vehicles on such danger-ous terrain."

Into the bargain, my truck had a broken accelerator pedal, which made double-de-clutching difficult, but we both man-aged the journey and enjoyed the few hours away from the camp. Mostly we enjoyed having pulled off the stunt. We also prized our heavy traffic licenses. Graham tells me he still has his and has used it a number of times through the years to drive large trucks.

A few nights after this trip, there was a horrendous acci-dent in camp. In the kitchen tent late at night, someone put a Coleman lantern on a hot stove. It exploded, showering flam-ing white spirits onto the face and head of a soldier standing nearby. I was already in my bunk asleep when I was woken by the most awful screams I have ever heard. There were no air evacuations in those days, and the camp's small medical team had to rush the victim in a Landrover to Fairlie, from where an ambulance took him to Christchurch Hospital.

In 1956, the National Bank moved Graham from Christchurch to Wellington, and as a consequence, he missed the humilia-tion our platoon of the 19th Armoured suffered at the hands of the Scottish. We had a weekend camp on Birdlings Flat, Te

Waihora/Lake Ellesmere, about 50 km from Christchurch. On our first night in camp, we posted no sentries and were completely unprepared for the raid launched in the small wee hours by the Scottish. We were woken to the sound and light of exploding rockets and loud laughter. The intruders were gone by the time we stumbled out of our tents to find they had removed the distributor caps from all our vehicles. In the morning, someone had to hike the 10 km or so to the huts at the Selwyn River mouth to use a phone. Our Scottish Regiment attackers had "kindly" left a note claiming responsibility, and on Sunday, a Christchurch relative of someone in our platoon reclaimed the caps and drove out with them so we could get home.

It was a few weeks after this that I received an official letter from the Army High Command saying that the 19th Armoured Regiment was being disbanded. We were given two options: to transfer to the Scottish Regiment or take a discharge. For one insane moment, I thought of the kilt I would receive if I took option one (Graham had a kilt because he had been involuntarily transferred to the Scottish when he moved to Wellington) – but the moment passed almost instantly. I decided on option two, and my days in the military were over.

— Chapter Five —

An Australian Summer

"Australia had a wonder and a far-awayness .... Australia
is outside everything...You just walk out of the world and
into Australia."

– D.H. Lawrence

During the 1956 summer in Tekapo, our regiment was in camp
for three weeks, but I was able to leave after a fortnight to
participate in the National Swimming Championships in Wellington. I had been in Wellington a year earlier as a member of
the New Zealand Universities [NZU] swimming team competing against a touring Australian Universities team. These tours
alternated between the two countries, with the Australian visit
being followed two years later by a New Zealand team touring
Australia. On this 1955 tour, there were two tests, the first
in Wellington and the second in Christchurch. As I had just
finished my first year as a Varsity student, I felt very much a
junior on the team, for which I had qualified as a backstroke
and medley swimmer. I swam well in my events, including the
backstroke leg of the Medley Relay, which we won. Overall,
however, the Australians were too strong for us in both swimming and water polo.

There was a New Zealand universities tournament of summer sports each Easter and a tournament of winter sports in
August. The 1956 Easter Tournament was in Auckland, and I
won an NZU Swimming Blue in the 100 yards medley. (A Blue

was awarded if you swam the race under a stipulated time.) Now in my third and final year as an undergraduate, I had much greater confidence in university swimming circles, but I was still startled by the decision of the NZU Swimming Council to appoint me captain of the team to tour Australia in January 1957. I was thrilled by this fantastic opportunity. In those days, in sports other than rugby and cricket, overseas tours were almost exclusively limited to the Olympic and British Empire Games. What made the prospect of a swimming tour of Australia in January 1957 especially exciting was the fact that Melbourne was hosting the Olympics in November-December 1956, and Australia was expected to dominate the swimming events – as it did.

As team captain, I was also to manage the team selection and logistical preparations. For my first task, the Council charged me to request of its Australian counterpart that the invitation for 1957 be for a team of men and women. Up until this time, the teams had been exclusively male. The Australian Council replied that this was not possible because (unlike NZ) their men's and women's swimming had separate administrations. We considered this a lame excuse and resolved that when we issued our invitation for 1959, it would be for a team that included women. This was done, and from that point onwards, the teams comprised women as well as men.

For 1957, our touring team would be 12 strong. I sent invitations to all the NZ universities requesting that their male swimmers and water polo players who wanted to be considered for the tour send me their sporting CVs. Those who wished to be included as competitors in swimming events should include certified results for particular strokes and distances. I was assisted in the selection process by the PE instructor at Christchurch Teachers' College.

We had a selection dilemma. Among the candidates were two of the nation's top water polo goalies, Wellington's Theo Verhoeven and Waikato's Keith Boswell. I sadly assumed we would have to exclude one of them, but my fellow selector argued that they outclassed some of the swimming candidates, and for that reason, both should be included. It worked out well, as we were able to use Keith as the central pivot in the water polo team, with Theo in goal. The touring team that emerged was Jim Marks and Stanley Paris from Otago; Theo Verhoeven from Victoria; Keith Boswell, Graham Leach, Bob Leek, John Orbell and Jim Sneyd from Auckland; and Otto Snoep, Finlay Mackenzie, Ian MacDonald and me from Canterbury. Uncomfortably close to the tour departure date, Bob Leek withdrew, but fortunately, I was able to add in his place Murray Francis from Auckland, who had been part of the NZU team in 1955 and who was already in Australia for the summer.

The team's accommodation and travel expenses for the month in Australia would be paid by our hosts, but how were we to find funds to cover our travel to and from Sydney? I hit upon the idea of purchasing the maximum number of tickets permitted for the rugby test matches between the All Blacks and the Springboks scheduled to tour New Zealand in winter 1956 and selling them to the highest bidders. In Christchurch, we recruited family members and friends to queue with us in relays overnight before the tickets went on sale, and in addition to the tickets we got for ourselves, we were able to buy a large number to scalp. I put an ad in the *Press* inviting bids, and we raised a lot of money. The Auckland team members followed the same strategy, and between us, we had enough to pay all travel expenses to and from Australia.

The team assembled in Wellington on December 28, 1956, looking smart in our uniform black NZU blazers, white shirts with black ties ornamented with silver ferns and kiwis, grey slacks and white Panama hats. Our hats provoked some laughter from the Australians, who thought we looked like lawn bowlers, but they proved very serviceable in the Australian heat. I appointed Theo Verhoeven water polo captain. Approaching 30, Theo was much older than the rest of us, whose ages ranged from 19 to 21. I suggested to the team that we elect one member to join Theo and me on a management committee that, among other things, would choose the water polo team and the competitors for races in the tests. Graham Leach was elected to this position.

We boarded the *Wanganella* in the late afternoon on the 28th and sailed in the evening. My first trip away from NZ. Very exciting. Determined that the team not get rusty on the four-day voyage, Theo and I announced that we should all be on deck for exercises at 7:15 the next morning. What a ridiculous mistake! I recorded the result in my diary:

"On an empty stomach, I couldn't even face the exercises, and Theo led them. One by one, the boys disappeared, and although most reappeared at breakfast, there were a number of hurried exits, my own being typical. Latest order: there will be no pre-breakfast PT in future!"

Fortunately, we had calm weather for the whole crossing, and everyone was in good shape to party on New Year's Eve. We celebrated twice, once at 10:00 pm for New Zealand and again at midnight for Australia.

We berthed in Sydney at 7:00 am on New Year's Day 1957, and our welcoming party from the University of Sydney "staggered aboard," as I wrote in my diary. "A crowd of real deadbeats, they hadn't been to bed from their New Year's Eve parties and were dressed in clothes ranging from cabaret clobber to barbecue briefs." After clearing customs and performing a haka on the wharf, we were split up and taken to billets all over metropolitan Sydney. My host was Bill Ford, "the real hard case from the 1955 Aussie trip to NZ." Bill's father and mother were the caretakers of the headquarters building of the National Road Motorists Association in the central city. I had never experienced a major city before, and here I was, staying on the top floor of a mini-skyscraper in the heart of the Sydney CBD.

Bill gave me just time to greet his parents, drop my luggage and change into shorts before he raced me off to begin the most amazing non-stop fortnight. The first two days – the New Year's holidays – were spent with other team members enjoying Sydney's northern beaches.

> "Stretching 30 miles from the city to the Hawkesbury River, these beaches really are marvellous – great arcs of beautiful golden sand such as I have never seen in NZ. One after another, each in a bay of its own."

Swimming and sunbathing were interspersed with visits to pubs to enjoy Australian beer, which had a higher alcoholic content than NZ beer and was served cold, an improvement that had not yet reached NZ. On our second day, we were introduced to the novelty of a beer garden, where we witnessed a full-on brawl between two very drunken groups. Australia seemed to be living up to its NZ reputation!

This was intended as our rest period, and then we hit the road for successive two-day trips to Muswellbrook, a coal-mining town north of Sydney, and Port Kembla, a heavy-industrial suburb of the city of Wollongong to the south. In both, we found full-sized Olympic pools, as we were to do in almost every town, large and small, in NSW and Victoria on the rest of the tour. Here was one of the reasons for Australia's prominence in world swimming in the 1950s and 1960s. The pools were the product of the exceptional support given to the sport throughout the country. For example, in Terang, a town in western Victoria with a population of 4,000, our swimming carnival drew a crowd of 2,000!

At both Muswellbrook and Port Kembla, we swam against Olympians: Brian Wilkinson (butterfly and medley), a Muswellbrook local, and David Theile (backstroke), visiting from Queensland University who travelled with us to Port Kembla. There John Orbell and I swam against him in the 100-meter backstroke, the race in which he was Olympic champion and record holder. "I swam in the lane beside Theile and can claim to have kept up with him for the first five to ten yards. I can't quite remember if he was dressed before I finished!" In both towns, we were lavished with hospitality, which was true everywhere we went in Australia.

The next week back in Sydney was the high point of the tour: attendance at the Australian Inter-Varsity and the NSW State Championships; the meeting of the Inter-Dominion Tours Council; and our two tests against the Australian Universities team. In amongst all this, we managed to squeeze in a welcome by the Lord Mayor of Sydney and an appearance on live television, this before most of us had ever watched TV, which did not reach NZ until three years later.

The Inter-Dominion Tours Council meeting was dominated by two issues: our insistence that future tours include women and an invitation from South African universities for a joint Australian-New Zealand team to tour the republic. We decided this was not feasible given the costs of air travel. I am dismayed that my diary makes no mention of the issue of touring a racially segregated society.

Both the Inter-Varsity and NSW Championships were on separate nights at the North Sydney Pool, a very fast salt-water pool on the harbour's edge under the shadow of the northern end of the Harbour Bridge. We were, of course, extremely interested to see the standard of the Varsity swimmers. There was a handful that was definitely a cut above us, but overall we thought our team could be competitive in the tests.

The last event of the Inter-Varsity Championships was the final of the water polo, Sydney versus Melbourne. The rivalry was fierce, and into the middle of this, I was pitchforked to referee, as the scheduled referee did not show up. The first half was torrid, and I gave many penalties, with the count heavily against Sydney. Things settled down in the second half, but with Melbourne winning 5-4, there were some in the crowd who made it clear they blamed me for the hometown team's loss.

The men's and women's NSW State Championships were held on separate evenings, and unfortunately, the women's events clashed with our test matches. The men's championships produced the most wonderful swimming. There were numerous Australian records broken, but the highlight was Murray Rose's blitz of a star-studded field in the 400-meters freestyle to claim a world record.

The first Inter-Dominion Test was also held at the North Sydney pool. Our star performers were Otto Snoep, who won the 110-yard freestyle, and Ian MacDonald and Jim Marks, who outclassed their Australian opponents in the 220-yard breaststroke. Graham Leach also turned in a stellar performance in the 110-yards butterfly only to be pipped by David Theile on the post. Our water polo team had Keith Boswell, Graham Leach and Otto Snoep as forwards, Fin Mackenzie, Ian Mac-Donald and me as backs, and Theo Verhoeven in goal. It was the last event of the evening.

> "Close all the way. They won 8-6, using the brilliant breaking and shooting of Jugoslav international Nino Von Somogy, to score most of their goals. I was marking the beggar and had a torrid time. Our combination was better than theirs, and Keith and Graham were shooting very well."

Somogy had defected to Australia after the Olympics, and how he qualified to play in the test team with universities yet to open for the year, I don't know, but I'm sure we must have raised the issue. In the second test, we did a better job containing him, and the game was drawn five all. We won all our other water polo games on the tour.

We also improved on our swimming performances in this second test. In the 220-yard medley, I even managed a close third to Wilf Arnold, former Australian breaststroke and medley champion, and David Theile. Jim Marks had the flu, so Fin

Mackenzie swam in his place, taking second to Ian MacDonald in the 220-yard breaststroke. The highlight of the night was the last event, the 4 x 110-yard freestyle relay. Our team was Leach, Francis, Snoep and me. We won by a foot and set a new inter-dominion varsity record.

On the following day, January 14, we headed for "the bush," taking the train first to the NSW country town of Young and, after two days, on to Wagga Wagga. There, the water polo game preceded the swimming competition. Wagga was the NSW country champions, and I have never played in front of a crowd as passionate and knowledgeable about the game. It was a good, clean match, which we won by one goal.

By this stage, I had acquired a two-fold reputation with my travelling companions: as a humourist in the speeches I had to give at every event and as a speed drinker. This latter skill, honed as a member of the University of Canterbury drinking horn team (I was an NZU Drinking Blue), was put to the test at an evening party on the sandy banks of the Murrumbidgee River. Sweeping all before me, I earned the nickname "Terror of Wagga."

Graham Leach (no mean drinker himself) and I were billeted together, and we found it almost impossible to get out of bed the next morning to catch the 4:50 train to Melbourne. Graham and I arrived at the station at 5:10 am, but blessedly the train was running a half-hour late. Everyone in the team was dog-tired, and it was a painful journey. Fortunately, once we reached the NSW-Victorian border, we were on Australia's fastest express, and we were in Melbourne by noon.

We were met at the station by a well-organised welcoming party from the University of Melbourne, who bundled us into waiting cars to take us to our billets. Jim Marks and Graham Leach were with Olympian John Marshall, and I was with John's wife's parents, the Byrnes. I slept almost all afternoon before having my first taste of TV: the Australian Tennis Open. I decided TV was a great medium for watching sport.

In the evening, we went to the Melbourne Olympic Pool, where it had been arranged for us to have a dip before watching the Victorian State Championships. We found that the Victorian swimmers generally were not up to the standard of the NSW cohort, but there were some outstanding exceptions, the most notable being Olympic medalists Faith Leech and John Marshall, both freestylers. By contrast to Leech, who was 15, Marshall was 26. He had won his medals in the 1948 London Olympics, and, in 1950, as a student at Yale, he had set 19 world records. It was obvious from the crowd reaction at the State Championships that he was regarded as a national hero.

The following morning, we left on a day trip to Puckapunyal Army Camp, 115 km north of Melbourne, where we competed in an afternoon carnival and played two games of water polo. Our tour of the Western Districts of Victoria started the next morning, January 20th. We had carnivals on successive days in Hamilton and Terang, followed by tw -days of relaxation on the beach at Lorne, where we bunked in the surf club. I wrote in my diary:

> "Lorne is in a really lovely setting as a holiday spot. It is in a broad bay backed by 1,000-foot rolling hills that are completely bush-covered. The trees extend right down to the shops and the beach, and houses are built among them. Some of these houses are really palatial, renting for £5,000 for just a weekend. Lorne is only 80 miles from Melbourne."

We had been lucky not to lose a team member in Hamilton. When we arrived there, one woman in the local billeting contingent made no secret of the fact she was there to bag the handsomest amongst us. She went home with Murray Francis, and his later report that she shared her bed with him was thoroughly believable. During our time in Sydney, Theo had also struck up a relationship. When we returned from Melbourne, he immediately disappeared for the night and had to join us at a suburban station the next day as our train headed for an out-of-town carnival. His paramour, Margaret, became his bride, and after I went to the Australian National University [ANU] for doctoral study in 1960, I was recruited as his best man at their Randwick wedding. Otto Snoep, who was then working as a design engineer in Sydney, was his groomsman.

On January 25th, we started our journey back to Melbourne along the Great Ocean Road – "by far the best scenery we have had in Australia" – stopping in the evening for a party in Geelong. It was there we heard that John Marshall had suffered a fractured skull when a car he was driving somersaulted after a blowout in one of the front tires. He was clinging to life in a Melbourne hospital. Billeting rearrangements had to be made for Jim, Graham, and me. Tragically, John died while we were still in Melbourne, leaving a 19-year-old wife and seven-month-old baby.

Even though we were not back in the city until daybreak on January 26th, we had to meet our scheduled obligation to play a water polo match in the suburbs before noon. We confronted a much more challenging programme the following day, participation in the annual state inter-club water polo tournament, the "Lightning Premiership" in Bendigo. Graham and I slept the 160 km to Bendigo in the back of a ute and were ready to play when we arrived at 11:00 am. "The pool was a huge quarry lake. Rather dirty water but very warm." There was a record entry of 11 teams in this1957 tournament. In the first game, we played Footscray A, winning 5-4. Then it was Bendigo B, and we trounced them 9-0. This put us in the final against South Melbourne A.

"By this time, our lack of sleep and the two previous games were catching up on us. South Melbourne were quickly two goals up, but Bos scored, and then I shot a goal – a rare occurrence! At full time the score was three all. It was decided we should play another three minutes each way.

South Melbourne again took the upper hand and had us down 5-3. We gritted our teeth, and with Theo swearing at us, we got stuck in. I did the impossible to score my second goal, and Otto threw one in right on time. Five all. Another three minutes each way was ruled, and we fell back into the water to the sound of feverish hakas from our swimming teammates. They spurred us on, but the game wasn't won until Graham threw a beautiful corner to Keith, and he slammed it straight in from the air. Final score was 6-5. We crawled out of the bath after 42 minutes of polo in our third game of the day."

In presenting the team with a big cup and small replicas each, the president of Victorian water polo said it was the best game ever seen at Bendigo. After our return to NZ, the team donated the Bendigo Cup for an inter-varsity water polo competition.

All we now had left before leaving Victoria were two more carnivals in the Melbourne suburbs and a memorable evening on which two nurses with a car took Graham and me dining in St. Kilda – memorable for me, at least, because of the stroke of luck I had.

"My wallet was in the open inside pocket of my blazer, which I was carrying when I left the restaurant. As I was getting into the car, apparently, the wallet dropped out on the very edge of the footpath. We drove off, leaving it reposing on the well-lit pavement. It contained the receipt for the team's boat tickets, £5 in cash, my driver's license, a chit for my dry cleaning, and one or two less important documents. It was about a quarter of an hour before I discovered it was gone. We raced back and found it sitting where I had dropped it, with a number of people walking past the whole time. Sighs of considerable relief were the order of the night."

We left Melbourne by train at 8:00 am on February 1 and were in Sydney by 9:15 pm. For once, we got a good night's sleep, knowing that we had to leave again by train the next morning at 9:20. We were headed for Maitland, another coal town three hours north of Sydney, for our last carnival. We were accompanied by several Sydney University swimmers and Rosalyn Barton, Gary Chapman and John Devitt of the Australian Olympic team. While we were in Victoria, John had competed in the Queensland State Championships and set new world records for the 100-meters and 110-yards freestyle.

Surprisingly there was no swimming club in Maitland, and the carnival was organised by the Lions Club. It was the strangest swimming carnival imaginable, lasting from 7:30 to 11:30 pm but with only one race, a relay pitting Sydney University against NZU. We won, I'm happy to report, as also the water polo game against the same opponents. The rest of the evening was filled with swimming and diving demonstrations by the Olympians, performances by the local pipe band and a bathing beauty contest. The three judges for this were the Mayoress, a woman from Jantzen swimwear and me! It was a split decision, with the Jantzen woman siding with me against the Mayoress. Our chosen queen did not please most in the crowd.

The next morning Graham, Otto and Jim Sneyd left early to fly to Coolangatta on the Queensland Gold Coast, where they would spend a few days surfing at their own expense. The rest of us were given a guided tour of Maitland and neighbouring towns before a 2:30 pm departure by slow train to Sydney. The five-hour journey gave me a great opportunity to get to know John Devitt, whom I liked very much.

"You would never realise that he is only 18. Rather you would pick him as early 20s. He is an unassuming chap who nevertheless is quite the master of doing the right thing, e.g., when a youngster asked him for his autograph at the dinner table at the Maitland hotel, he was heard to insist quietly that the boy get those of all the other swimmers at the table as well. He made a grand impression on the boys, and they are all very much with him in his future swimming."

In addition to the time on the train, I spent the morning with John two days later at The Spit Baths, a tidal salt-water pool where he trained. We swam together and played handball in the club rooms before I headed to the city for lunch with John Orbell. Looking back, I am perplexed as to why, when I returned to Australia as a doctoral student from 1960-1963, I didn't resume the friendships with John Devitt and others I met on the tour.

~ ~ ~

Our ship for the return voyage to New Zealand was the "Monowai," and it was scheduled to depart from Sydney on February 7 at 3:00 pm. There was a big group of our Sydney friends aboard to farewell us.

"When the visitors were asked to leave, John Devitt hurried up to me and apologised for having forgotten to bring his Olympic tie down with him. He had intended to give it to me, he said, but he would post it. I gave him my NZ tie on the spot."

The ship sailed right on time, but less than halfway down the harbour, it turned back. We were tied up at the same berth in Darling Harbour by 3:45. We were told there was engine trouble but that we would sail again at 8:00 pm. This target was changed a number of times, and it was not until the 8th evening that we ultimately got away. In the meantime, we enjoyed ourselves in nearby China Town, and on the afternoon of the 8[th,] we all took the ferry to Manly for a bonus swim in the strongest surf we had experienced in our five weeks in Oz. We had just made it back to the beach after struggling out of a nasty rip when John Devitt arrived.

"He said he had heard there was a pack of rough hicks down in the water who were frightening away the girls, so he knew it must be the New Zealanders who had swum back from the ship for a quick surf. He had brought his tie for me – much to the annoyance of the others. I'll have to watch it like a hawk!"

As rescheduled, the *Monowai* left Darling Harbour at 7:00 pm, and sailing down the harbour, we had, as a send-off, brilliant purple and white sheet lightning with torrential rain. The four-day voyage was somewhat rougher than our *Wanganella* crossing, but we were all in good shape when we docked in Auckland on February 12, just in time for the National Swimming Championships.

The highlights of the championships for us tourists were Otto's victory in the 110-yard freestyle and our NZU water polo team's defeat of Auckland by 6-4 in a specially arranged match. I took great personal pleasure in the victory in the inter-provincial water polo team's relay of our Canterbury B team, of which, to my surprise, I had found on arriving in Auckland that I was captain. I swam my fastest time ever for the 55-yard lap. I was also delighted by the success of my protégé Derek Eaton in getting second place in the 220-yards butterfly and third in the 440-yards medley, an impressive achievement for a 15-year-old.

After an overnight visit with Bronwen in Hamilton, I was back in Christchurch on February 19, almost eight weeks after leaving.

— CHAPTER SIX —

Rugby Field & Lecture Hall

"Be patient toward all that is unsolved.
Live your questions now.
Perhaps you will gradually, without noticing it,
live along someday into the answers."
– Rainer Maria Rilke

Earlier I said I had two consuming passions in my teens and early twenties, one of them swimming. The other was rugby. I was not an outstanding rugby player at CBHS, but I seemed to hit my stride after I left high school. In 1954, I decided to play for Varsity rather than High School Old Boys, probably influenced by the fact that my CBHS 1st XV coach, Tubby Hewland, was now coaching the Varsity under-20 team. We won the championship, and I made it into the Canterbury under-20 rep team as a front-row forward. I came close to blowing my chance to be a rep by almost missing the trial game. I had been skiing for a week at Temple Basin and had caught a Thursday evening train from Arthur's Pass, arriving in Christchurch after midnight. My parents were away, so I fell happily into bed in an empty house and did not wake until late morning. As I got myself breakfast, I turned on the radio and was stunned when the announcer mentioned it was Saturday. I had slept 36 hours – and I had only one hour left to get myself to the trial game! I made it to the game and onto the team.

In 1955, I was chosen for the Varsity senior squad. This

was a great thrill as the team was coached by Bob Stuart, former Canterbury and All Black captain, who had led the All Blacks to Britain in 1953-54. I played my first game as a prop, but it was quickly evident I was not big enough at 82 kg for this position in senior rugby, nor did I have sufficient strength. Bob moved me to blind-side flanker, No. 6. This was Bob's old position, and he gave me special coaching. By contrast to No. 7, the open-side flanker, No. 6's job (Bob emphasised) was primarily defensive. Any opponent running the blind side had to be flattened, and Bob told me I should put no fine point on whether or not he was in the act of passing the ball. Thump him, anyway. I had the advantage of being a solid tackler, a skill honed by high-school experience at fullback. The legacy of my merciless blind-side tackling was a confrontation in Nepal, of all places, on a 1973 trek. A CBHS Old Boy who met me in Pokhara realised he was face-to-face with the scoundrel whom he remembered as having regularly tackled without the ball his hero, High School Old Boys and All Black half-back Pat Vincent, on his loping blind-side runs. He gave me a piece of his mind.

As an aside, I should observe that every year I made sure I was very fit by the start of the rugby season. As I have said, I was a relative lightweight in senior rugby, and I was not fast for a flanker. My hope was that superior fitness in the first games of the year might give me an initial edge over potential rivals for the positions on the side of the scrum.

In 1955, Bob and his old mate, team captain Jim Stewart, were working to forge a team that could win the provincial championship. The king piece was to be All Black first-five-eight, Mick Bremner, whom Bob persuaded to move from Wellington to Christchurch. He would team up with half-back Bronc Molloy, who was already challenging Pat Vincent for the Canterbury slot. From Christchurch hospital, Bob recruited three junior doctors, big men who had played for Otago University while in medical school in Dunedin and who would give our team height in lineouts and heft in scrums. One of them, Hugh Burry a No. 8, would later join Bremner, Molloy and former CBHS hooker, John Creighton, as All Blacks. John, two years behind me at school, joined our Varsity senior team in 1956.

Our team's strategy, as devised by Bob, relied heavily on strategic kicking by Mick Bremner to give our forwards the chance to grind down the opposing pack. Restricting as it did open-field running, it was not a pretty strategy, but it was effective with a strong and well-schooled pack of forwards. In 1956, we won every game but one – an early season's loss to Christchurch – and we had the championship in our pocket before even playing the last competition game. Halfway through the season, Bob was called away to take over the coaching of the All Blacks to win the test series against the touring Springboks, and Jim Stewart combined the roles of captain and coach to see us through to the championship victory.

1956 is still regarded as one of the great years in New Zealand rugby history, and right in the middle of it, sandwiched between defeats inflicted on the Springboks by both the All Blacks and Canterbury, was my 21st birthday, with Bob Stuart, Mick Bremner and other rugby greats attending the party. A month later, the All Blacks handed the Springboks a second defeat at Lancaster Park, and the icing on my cake was the subsequent historic upset victory over the South Africans by an NZU team. I went to Wellington to support my four Canterbury Varsity teammates playing in this game, including fullback Barry Dineen, who had had a meteoric rise from the Varsity Third Grade social team at the start of the season, via our senior team, to kicking the winning points against the Springboks. He has dined out on this story ever since. On the day after the game, wearing my NZU blazer, I was mistaken by a rugby fan for one of the victorious team members. He congratulated me on the victory, and I did not disabuse him, holding my arm firmly over the swimming inscription on my blazer pocket so I would not be unmasked as the imposter I was.

I played for five seasons in the Varsity Senior Team, and we won the championship in each of those years – the "Juggernaut Years," as fellow teammate Dick Hockley was to describe them in his history of the Club.

In my fifth and final year, I was vocal on an off-field issue on which almost all of my teammates remained silent. This was the decision of the NZ Rugby Union to continue to exclude Maori from All Black tours to South Africa in tacit acknowledgment of racial segregation in the republic. That year, having completed my M.A., I was a student in the post-primary division at Christchurch Teachers' College, and in May 1959, in the college magazine, I wrote an article entitled "Hypocrisy in New Zealand." The following is an extract:

> "Sport is more important to New Zealanders than the principle of racial equality. Do you think this is true?
>
> "You cannot avoid answering this question, for it has been forced upon you by the New Zealand Rugby Union. That body thinks it so important to send a Rugby Union football team to South Africa next year that it has openly approved of racial discrimination. The New Zealand Union was not requested by the South Africans to exclude Maoris from the team, but it knew that coloured men are not made welcome in South Africa, so it decided to extend the same discrimination to New Zealand sport.
>
> "Make no mistake; this question is a moral one. You must either oppose this decision or, by your silence, condone racial discrimination in New Zealand .... I am bitterly ashamed to think that some of my countrymen value Rugby football more highly than the principle of racial equality. I shall be even more ashamed if New Zealanders are so hypocritical as to permit an all-white team to leave for South Africa while bragging at home and abroad of racial harmony in New Zealand."

In the following month, disregarding the rejection of a parade permit, I was one of the leaders of a group of about 500 university and teachers' college students and faculty, which assembled at the Town Hall to present the Mayor with resolutions condemning the Rugby Union's decision. It amuses me reading press clippings to see the emphasis newspapers placed on how "well behaved and good-humoured" we were! I was a member of the nationwide protest group, the Citizens' All Black Tour Association, whose slogan was "No Maoris, No Tour." President of its Canterbury branch was the Rev. Alan Brash, father of my former CBHS fellow student Don Brash, a future leader of the National Party who was later to take a very different position on race relations.

Playing on the Varsity team in 1959, I broke my right thumb in a game early in the season, and I chose not to return to the squad after six weeks with my arm in plaster. I was focused on my impending departure for doctoral study in Australia.

In Canberra, I played for two seasons in the Australian National University team and then became coach in 1962 and 1963. In August 1963, I went to the US to teach history at the University of Michigan. Just after classes began, a New Zealand accent hailed me in my new department office. The voice belonged to Allan Levett, a sociology doctoral student, who summoned Jenni and me to a rugby party that Saturday night. We found a hearty and, as the evening progressed, loud gathering of men and women from around the British Commonwealth, with assorted Americans thrown in for good measure. I had been ambushed. Somehow, this group had learnt that I had played for Varsity in Christchurch and that I had just come from coaching the ANU team, so they had decided I should be the Michigan coach. They also wanted me to play, but I was unfit and much too busy with work and family to travel with the team for away games. I did agree to coach.

"Play Rugby, Give Blood" read a bumper sticker of that era, and the game as it was then played in the Midwest amply justified that gory slogan – and made me glad I had opted to stay on the sideline. All teams had a percentage of huge former American football players. Having played that code in helmets, face guards and other protective gear, they came to rugby with a terrifying disregard for the hazards of physical contact when you are wearing nothing more than jersey, shorts and light boots. With reckless abandon, they threw themselves face and chest first into rucks and tackles, and the injury rate was depressingly high – even at practice sessions. It was aggravated by the fact that most players were unfit. This was one area on which my coaching had no impact, but I may have had some effect on skills, tactics, and coordination.

The team won every home game for two seasons. At the time, the famed Michigan football team was in a slump, and I suggested it should move out of the 100,000-seat stadium in favour of the rugby team. I would be happy to swap salaries with the football coach! To be honest, the team's home game record probably had more to do with the presence of Whatarangi Winiata than my coaching. Whata, a superb front row forward, was a former Wellington provincial and New Zealand Universities rep until 1959 when, as a protest against the exclusion of Maori from the 1960 All Black team to tour South Africa, he declared himself unavailable for further selection. At the U-M, his MBA and doctoral studies and a young family kept him, like me, from touring with the team. He and his wife Francie became our good friends.

With the rugby connection came the supplementary benefit of a place on the "Marmite Trail." Marmite was unheard of in the US in the 1960s, and families from the Commonwealth who lived in Ann Arbor survived by establishing a Marmite trail to Toronto, the nearest large Canadian city where Marmite was on supermarket shelves. Anyone travelling to Toronto would take orders from Commonwealth friends before departure and return with jars for all of the precious breakfast staple.

~ ~ ~

When I went to the University of Canterbury in 1954 focused on making History my major subject, I knew I was choosing to swim upstream. The Professor of History, Neville Phillips, determined to raise academic standards, gave notoriously low marks to students in his classes.

Neville had returned to Canterbury in the mid-1940s after study at Oxford and service in the British Army in WWII, rising in the Royal Artillery from the rank of Private to Major. In 1949, at the age of 33, he was appointed Professor of History. Bill Oliver, who joined the department as a lecturer in 1955, described Neville as an "energetic but uncomfortable man ... who was intent upon licking into shape a department that he felt lacked rigour and discipline." He was a tall, angular aloof man, who (although NZ born) distanced himself from his fellow Kiwis by speaking what at the time was called "BBC English." As Ned Bohan writes in his memoirs, Neville was "an inhibiting, even terrifying personality in tutorials or at a one-on-one meeting in his study. He was painfully inept socially and generated such an aura that students and even his staff, with few exceptions, were invariably reduced to almost equal awkwardness."

On the other hand, he was a fine lecturer, he gave meticulous critical feedback on written work, and he recruited for his department's outstanding faculty. Ned again:

"The senior lecturer was portly and florid John Saunders, an authority on Arab history and European Liberalism, and another remarkable lecturer .... The conspicuously brilliant David Fieldhouse from Oxford was always intellectually stimulating .... In 1955 the young W.H. (Bill) Oliver arrived from his post-graduate years at Oxford and, hesitatingly and almost apologetically, started his lecturing career introducing us to Hobbes and Locke and, by example, to as elegant a prose style as any New Zealand historian has achieved .... And of course there was

Jim Gardner, who all those years ago delivered rousing lectures on the French Revolution and laboured in spite of Neville's scornful lack of encouragement to develop courses in New Zealand history."

To study history at Canterbury under Neville's regime – and survive – was to emerge a very well-trained historian. Personally, I emerged slightly scarred. The increasingly frequent need to run the gauntlet of Neville's sardonic questioning as my student career proceeded gave me a stomach ulcer by the age of 22. Neville treated with scepticism anyone like myself who harboured an ambition for post-graduate study. I did, however, persuade him to allow me to sign on for an M.A. in History, a two-year programme with tutorials in the first year and a research thesis in the second. I did not do as well as I should have in the first-year's exams because of a self-defeating tendency to distribute my exam time poorly, habitually spending far too much time on the first questions and leaving myself with room for little more than a set of notes on the final one. I was pleasantly surprised, however, when Neville told me my marks in my four papers (67, 72 and two 73s) and said they were "far and away the best."

During this year, Neville and I got to know each other much better because he appointed me secretary both to the department (a routine job keeping attendance rolls) and to the History Society, which hosted public lectures and discussions. When diffidently I proposed working for the second year on a New Zealand thesis topic, Neville swept my suggestions aside and gave me a topic in his own field: eighteenth-century English political history. Under his personal supervision, I would study the Army and Navy Members of Parliament during the American War of Independence.

Neville had returned recently from research leave in Britain armed with the inspiration of a meeting with Lewis Namier, the originator of a new historical methodology. Neville was convinced that Namier stood as one of the great names "in the history of the professionalization of history," and I was swept into his enthusiasm for the Namier school's technique of "collective biography." Neville had brought back with him voluminous notes from English manuscript collections, which, when used in conjunction with published document series, would make it possible to do original research in NZ on eighteenth-century Britain. I plunged in happily, glad to have exams behind me and to be able to research and write full time.

In his own writing, Neville liked to introduce the subject of his work with an engaging quote to give the reader a feel for the historical importance of the issues at stake. It also helped time and place to come alive. I followed his example with the opening sentences of my thesis:

> "Sitting in his Library at Strawberry Hill in the late summer of 1779, Horace Walpole commented thus on the English scene: 'All the world are politicians, or soldiers; or, rather, both.' Like many of his contemporaries, Walpole was disturbed at the divisions in the army and navy on the political issues of the day and at the activity of servicemen in politics."

I won Neville's immediate, if somewhat startled, approval. As my diary records, he "lavished" praise upon me. "Rather good on the whole," he said. Neville was not a man who gushed, but he did decide I was worthy of his attention, and from that point he gave me close support in shaping my thesis. It was a lot of fun. As I later wrote:

> "These were the early years of the American revolution, the bitter civil war of empire, but one might have thought from my cast of characters that this was opéra bouffe. They included such archetypical placemen as General Sir John Irwin, who kept himself perennially available for

superior command in lucrative and socially convenient locations by steadfastly avoiding battlefields, where even officers were occasionally exposed to risk. More celebrated because they used their political connections to gain the active commands sage fellows like Irwin eschewed, were 'Gentleman John' Burgoyne, whose dash lost an entire army and its amazing retinue of whores and cordon bleu cooks in the forests of up-state New York, and Henry Clinton, whose paranoia kept him from using his army to assist his fellow commanders, whom he suspected of imminent betrayal. Then there was 'Lee-Shore' Keppel, a portly, strutting little admiral who surely must have been Gilbert's inspiration for H.M.S. Pinafore."

My 296-page thesis, which I was able to mine later for four published articles, was awarded a First Class Honours mark of 82% by my examiners, Neville Phillips and Victoria University's Professor John Beaglehole. The lower marks on my previous year's exam papers, however, kept my M.A. to an overall Second Class. I noted in my diary that: "Neville said he considered the 2nd would make little difference in the long run." He also said that Beaglehole and he considered that I should go on for doctoral study, and both would write scholarship references for me. He told me this at a departmental gathering at his house on the night of my oral exam. My diary says: "The party went well thereafter!" But I should have added, not for everyone. As each M.A. student arrived, Neville told them how they had fared in their exams. My diary records an example of his tactlessness: "Neville met X at the door with the greeting 'Good evening Mr. X. You got a pass, but a damned poor one.'"

~ ~ ~

In 1957, I had applied for a Rhodes Scholarship, and I was chosen as one of Canterbury's two candidates, even though I doubt I had Neville's unqualified support. I think his judgment on me at that stage before my thesis won him over would have been along the lines of a comment he made in one of his tutorials. He said the paper I had presented demonstrated "a clear mind but not a very adventurous one." I was interviewed by the national Rhodes Scholarship selection committee at Government House in Wellington on December 3. I came away from the half-hour session with my optimism dented by a rhetorical question from one of the professors on the panel: "What makes you think *you* could do a doctorate?" I was not awarded a Rhodes Scholarship, but that remark motivated me in the coming years to prove its author wrong.

In diary reflections at year's end, I revealed how devastated I felt by the committee's decision:

> "The year had one immense disappointment for me: the failure to get a Rhodes Schol. Undoubtedly, there were too many people (including myself) who counted unhatched eggs, and the result was fairly painful. It took a while to get things re-oriented and to wind down the sights, but I am content now to leave my life in God's hands, where, no doubt, it has always been, despite my puny wrigglings."

In writing about the "many people who counted unhatched eggs," I undoubtedly had my mother first and foremost in mind. She was, if anything, more upset by the result than I.

My overview of the year described the swimming tour in Australia as a "great experience."

> "I am sure it made a difference to me. Apart from the fine friendships, it also meant a good deal of thinking. I realised perhaps for the first time, how materialistic our outlook can easily become. This, I think, is the great danger which threatens man as he enters 1958."

My concerns about materialism had been deepened by Soviet technological achievements. I wrote:

"Sputnik Year – which will undoubtedly be the most memorable feature of 1957. The Americans have shouted 'The race is on!' – But the Soviet success has been bought, surely, at an immense human cost. 'The free world must keep up with the Commos.' Just what they want us to do. How about stopping and thinking?"

~ ~ ~

At the 1958 departmental party, Neville gave me application papers for a scholarship for doctoral study in Commonwealth history at Duke University in North Carolina. Each year, Duke awarded one scholarship to NZ, and our national selection committee put my name forward to start in the 1959-1960 American academic year. I was also awarded a Fulbright Scholarship to cover travel and insurance costs. Things went pear shaped, however, because one of the New Zealand students already at Duke needed additional time to finish his degree, and my nomination was held over to the following year.

Meanwhile, at Neville's suggestion I had also applied for a Research Scholarship at the Australian National University in Canberra to do a doctorate. My first choice was modern Chinese history and my second, modern Indian history. ANU was not impressed that I had no Chinese language competence, but they did offer me a three-year scholarship to work in India. This would be in the History Department of the Research School of Social Sciences [RSSS], which was directed by Professor Sir Keith Hancock, whom I described in a letter to Bronwen as "*the* British Imperial historian of the day, and a degree under him would be first class." I would go to Canberra in January 1960. I was elated.

— Chapter Seven —

Into the Wider World

"Traveller, don't try to decide where to stopStay light on your feet and keep moving Speak any language, but always speak with love."
– Jalaluddin Rumi

In my mid-teens, I bought two Penguin Books that were to have an important influence on my life: *The Physiology of Sex* and the *Psychology of Sex*. (I can be fairly certain I did not charge them to my parents' account!) I read them avidly, taking to heart the message that good sex involved ensuring that one's partner had an orgasm. Soon afterwards, I found a girl who was willing to explore sex with me. Liz was one of my fellow members of the Elmwood Swimming Club, and after closing the pool, we would spend our evenings in sexual exploration. We were cautious; these were the days before the pill. I was similarly cautious with my other girlfriends in my teens, but my poor mother, who, of course, had no way to know I was acting responsibly, was deeply worried. A few weeks after Bronwen had her baby, I found a note from Mum on my pillow: "John, please be careful. After what has happened with Bronwen, I don't think I could survive it if you got a girl into trouble."

Although I may have exercised physical responsibility in my teens, I did not act with emotional responsibility. I recall with shame a meanness I inflicted on one girlfriend, Beth Hetherington. She was a student at Avonside Girls' High School when I was at CBHS, and in our last year in school, she was on the committee that organised the Avonside end-of-year dance, to which, of course, she invited me. Without warning Beth, I turned up with one of her classmates to whom I was attracted, leaving Beth feeling humiliated.

I was in my twenties before I had a steady girlfriend. She was Jennifer Skurr, a fellow student whom I started dating in our first weeks at university in 1954. I had known her slightly from her years at St. Margaret's College, a private girls' high school, when I had gone out occasionally with her cousin.

Jenni had been orphaned at the age of 10. Her father, a farmer who suffered from depression, had hanged himself, and her mother died three weeks later of a broken heart, it was said. For a short time, Jenni was shuttled between her aunts before she was taken in by her mother's parents, Maurice and Amelia Brown, and she lived with them in Riccarton until we married in 1959. Maurice was a stern old Scot who had migrated to New Zealand in his twenties in the 1890s and had been employed felling bush and working on farms in various parts of the South Island until he could afford his own farm on the Canterbury Plains. He and Millie had retired by the time Jenni went to live with them in 1946.

From our first meeting in March 1954, Jenni and I had a passionate relationship. In those days, the back seat of a car was the most common location for pre-marital sex. Occasionally Jenni had the use of her grandparents' car, but mostly we had to find some other place for our dalliances. Fortunately, I had had foresight when I was still at CBHS. On the ground floor of the school library, accessible from the outdoors, there was a tiny first-aid room with a cot. The room was always kept locked, with the key stored in the Monitors' room. During my final year in school, I had a copy made, so when Jenni and I needed a hideaway, we made use of the key. We had to listen for the occasional security rounds of the school caretaker. We lay still and scarcely breathed until his footsteps receded. He once turned the door handle to ensure the door was locked, and we almost had heart attacks. Fortunately, I always locked the door after we went in.

Jenni and I had many trips away together in our student years. She came with me to Easter Tournaments to see me swim and play water polo, and I went with her to Winter Tournaments to see her play hockey. The most notable trip, however, was to the NZU Congress in January 1958. This was an annual week-long gathering at the aptly named Curious Cove on Queen Charlotte Sound, where students from all over NZ and a few from abroad gathered to hear talks by leading thinkers from inside and outside academe. There were two talks and discussions a day, morning and evening, and the time between was spent swimming and partying. On my return home, I wrote in my diary: "Congress was really excellent. The lectures were most provocative and touched on some of the great subjects which may face our little country. There was a fine realisation of the need for a strong NZ culture." The subject of one of the lectures was "The New Zealand Intellectual," and it persuaded me that I wanted to be an intellectual. The lecturer (jokingly, no doubt) said that intellectuals were distinguished by their love of fine cheese. I decided then and there to become a cheese connoisseur!

I proposed to Jenni in April 1957, and we married on January 17, 1959, when I was 23 and she 22. Ned Bohan was my best man, and Graham Leach, my groomsman. My parents lent us the car, acquired a year or two earlier, for a 10-day honeymoon in Queenstown, where Aunt Con had rented for us a lovely house as her wedding present. The weather was scorching, which was great for daily swims in the chilly waters of Wakatipu but not at all good for the drive down and back to Christchurch. The radiator in the old family Chevrolet kept boiling on the hills of Central Otago, and as we got up speed on the Canterbury Plains on the way home, the car shed its muffler. We must have been audible from miles away, and there was Dad standing at the front gate as we roared up Idris Road. His greeting: "God, son, what have you done to the car?"

We were back in Christchurch just in time for the arrival of the Australian Universities water polo and swimming team, which this time included women. Ian MacDonald organised the tour and did a fine job. My involvement was limited to playing against the Aussies on the Canterbury provincial water polo team (we won) and serving as announcer for the swimming test at the Centennial pool.

~ ~ ~

Jim Leggat had offered me a temporary job teaching at CBHS from February to July 1958, but with regret, I had turned this down, saying I needed to write my M.A. thesis. I also declined an offer from Neville Phillips of a temporary lectureship in his department for 1959, as I was hoping to leave mid-year for Duke University. Meanwhile, I would join the post-primary division of the Teachers' College to fulfil my bursary obligations.

Before we married in January 1959, Jenni and I found a furnished flat in an old wooden house opposite North Hagley Park on the corner of Dorset Street and Park Terrace, just three blocks from the Teachers' College. Opposite us on Dorset Street was a new block of flats in one of which lived two Australians in their thirties, Gerald and Leon, who had recently opened a trendy small restaurant on New Regent Street. Leon struck up a friendship with us and decided to introduce us, the naïve young couple that we were, to "modern culture." We had a standing invitation to the flat where Leon played us the latest music and mixed exotic cocktails for us. The flat was on the social circuit of American servicemen from the US Navy's Antarctic "Operation Deep Freeze," for which Christchurch was the base, and we met a range of interesting characters.

Leon was especially determined to teach us how to eat good food, drink, and wine, so we dined at "Gerald's Beaver Bar" at least once a week. Gerald was the chef, and Leon was the mâitre d' and sole waiter. He chose our food and wine for us, ostentatiously "smuggling" the bottle to our table under his flowing apron, this, of course, being the absurd period when serving alcohol with food was prohibited in NZ. Gerald and Leon had frequent loud, theatrical disagreements, with Leon rolling his eyes and telling patrons that working with Gerald was impossible. When more than 20 years later, I lived on Beacon Hill, a centre of LGBT society in Boston, I became familiar with similar camp behaviour of many gay male couples. It shows how naïve Jenni and I were in 1959 that it never occurred to us that Gerald and Leon were gay, even though Jenni was almost invariably the only woman at their flat.

My parents were profoundly disturbed that we were wasting our money dining out, and my father warned me frequently that we would go broke if we continued our profligate ways. Jenni and I were enjoying the fact that, for the first time ever, we both had independent incomes. In this my final year of post-primary teacher training, my bursary had been increased. Having graduated with an M.A. in English Language & Literature, Jenni was teaching at Riccarton High School. She bought a Vespa scooter to get to and from work and later replaced this with a car, an old Ford Prefect, purchased with a small inheritance from her parents' estate.

Towards the end of 1959, I had a brief affair. In November, I was part of a large group of Teachers' College students from Division C, the post-primary section, who went to Auckland for a week to compete against their Division C. I golfed, swam, played water polo and debated, as well as acted in a stage play. Despite this incredibly busy schedule, I found time for a torrid three-night sexual relationship with one of the Auckland women. This was the first of many affairs I had during my 14 years of marriage to Jenni.

~ ~ ~

As Jenni and I prepared for our departure to Australia, our excitement was increased by letters received from Ian McDougall, a Canterbury University friend who had gone to Canberra to do a doctorate in Economics following a year at Duke.

"ANU is a magnificent place. Discussion with numerous overseas visitors confirms my opinion that you would do well indeed to find conditions for scholars better anywhere in the world. I am confident that you will marvel at it. The atmosphere intellectually around here is most stimulating – even more so than at Duke."

Ian explained that the ANU doctoral programme allowed for three years' work on a dissertation rather than the two years of courses and one year on a thesis at Duke. He liked this much better, and I also found it more attractive.

"To answer your question about possible work for Jenni: There are quite a number of part-time jobs available for women. P.S. You will be pleased to know that rugby is extensively played here."

I also received a letter of welcome from the head of the ANU History Department, Sir Keith Hancock, who struck a collegial note strikingly different from the hierarchical tone I was used to with Neville Phillips. Instead of saying that my doctoral supervisor would be Dr. Anthony Low, he wrote, "it would be useful, I think, if he and you could work alongside each other." Anthony's follow-up letter echoed this tone. "You will, I'm afraid, find that I am a newcomer to Indian studies, too – my work so far has been in Africa and African History. So we will have to experiment together." He suggested I plunge in right away and read widely on modern India. I was delighted by the encouragement.

On January 14, 1960, Jenni and I sailed from Wellington

on the *Monowai* bound for Sydney. My Aunt Con's farewell gift was a package of Christian tracts, and as we sailed out of the harbour, irreverent yahoo that I was, I threw them one by one into the ship's wake, chanting, "Cast thy bread upon the waters." On arrival in Canberra, I certainly did not share this story with Hancock or Low, sons of Anglican clergymen both and committed Christians.

Jenni and I spent a very hot and humid week in Sydney before taking a train to Canberra on January 25. We were met at the station by Anthony Low and Peter Reeves, a doctoral student who had arrived from Tasmania just an hour before. Anthony was driving the Low family's Morris Minor, so it was agreed that we and our eight pieces of luggage would travel in a larger car driven by Dave Buckingham, a former Canterbury student sent to meet us by Ian McDougall, who had the flu.

Dave took us to University House, where a flat was reserved for us. Providing full board for faculty and students and their partners, University House was ANU's first building, modelled after an Oxbridge college and had been opened just six years before. It was a beautiful place with residential wings, meeting rooms, library, dining hall, and bar built around ponds and grassy courtyards to which gum trees attracted flocks of colourful parrots. On our first evening, Anthony came after dinner to take us to the Lows' nearby residence to meet wife Belle and their children, six-year-old Angela and four-year-old twins Penny and Adam. We were made to feel completely at home, and in the following week, Jenni gained Auntie status by taking the children swimming.

The day after our Canberra arrival, I was installed in an office in the Old Hospital Building, one of numerous buildings on campus dating from Canberra's early history that were being used while construction of permanent buildings proceeded. I had learnt from Anthony the previous evening that we three – Anthony, Peter Reeves, and I – were to form a "unit" (as was the ANU parlance) to introduce Indian History to the university.

In the previous decade, Anthony, an Englishman from Oxford University, had held a lectureship at Makerere College in Kampala and was the London Times correspondent for Uganda. Hancock got to know him when he went to Uganda as head of a constitutional commission in 1954. He invited Anthony to switch his field of study from Africa to India and join him at the ANU, where he was about to become Director of the Research School of Social Sciences [RSSS]. Anthony accepted the invitation, conditional on his having time to finish his Oxford doctorate before he came to Canberra. After a year back in the UK, working on India at the School of Oriental & African Studies, he joined Sir Keith in 1959.

As I wrote to my parents at the end of January 1960: "Peter Reeves and I must have applied to do Indian studies here at much the same time, and apparently were just what they were looking for." Fortunately, Peter had done nine months of research in India for his University of Tasmania M.A. thesis. Generously, he took me under his wing and gave me my start. After a few weeks with other office mates, Peter and I were able to get an office together, and we were to share this amicably for three years. We could not have done that without Peter's great sense of humour and empathy.

He and I were in our mid-twenties, Anthony was just 33, three young men embarking together with great enthusiasm on the exploration of the modern history of India. More correctly, I should say there were four young men. The fourth was Bruce Graham, a New Zealand political scientist about Anthony's age, who had joined RSSS before him. He had published work on both Australian and French politics before being recruited by Sir Keith to work on contemporary India. He joined Anthony in supervising Peter's and my doctorates.

In *Other Ways of Knowing*, I describe what I found in Canberra:

"In those days, the ANU was a small research institute. Everyone – students and faculty alike – were treated as grown-ups. We were all doing research, and we were all provided with the needed resources, including offices. Everyone, from the eminent head of the school to the newest junior arrival, was expected to give a work-in-progress report each term, and everyone in the department showed up for this weekly seminar. Beyond that, we were trusted to use our good sense in going to whichever seminars were useful for our work. Or we could get together a cross-disciplinary group to organise a discussion series that met our mutual needs."

I remember vividly the excitement I felt in my first week on my daily five-minute walks from University House to the Old Hospital Building, celebrating the tremendous opportunity I had been given. In my first working sessions with Anthony, he stoked that excitement by telling me there would be funding for field research in India, and he suggested planning for two six-month trips in the Indian winters of 1960-1961 and 1961-1962. He would accompany Peter and me in the coming October on the first of these visits. I enthused to my parents: "Enough to say that the History Department is all I had hoped for and more. Certainly, I could not have hoped to work under men of such standing as Low and Hancock had I gone to Duke, nor could I have had the chance of Indian visits."

In correspondence with Anthony, before I came to the ANU from New Zealand, it was decided I would devote my dissertation research to a study of the politics of the Bengal Legislative Council in the early twentieth century, applying the same methodology of collective biography I had used in my Canterbury M.A. thesis on the eighteenth-century British Parliament. There was as yet no research on the legislatures of British India, but there was a series of studies of other British colonial legislatures edited by Margery Perham, to which Anthony referred me. Peter Reeves, for his part, would also build on his M.A. work with a study of the political activities of the large landlords in the United Provinces and the Punjab from the 1920s.

Anthony took the initiative in an attempt to find for the National Library of Australia sets of the proceedings of the provincial legislatures, which would be fundamental for our research. For me, he struck gold with a letter to the West Bengal Legislative Assembly. Back came a prompt and warm response from the Assembly Secretary (chief executive officer), Dr. Ajita Ranjan Mukherjea, assuring Anthony that the proceedings were already on their way to Canberra. Moreover, I would be most welcome to call on him for assistance when I came to Calcutta. Dr. Mukherjea was as good as his word, and in India, he became my research patron and, over the years, a dear friend.

~ ~ ~

When we arrived in 1960, the city of Canberra generally had bad press. It was a planned city developed from scratch "in the bush" between Sydney and Melbourne to end the squabble between these two rivals over which should be the nation's capital. Cynics called it "a good sheep station ruined." I gave the following picture in a letter to my parents in mid-February:

"It is hard to describe. My first impression was of a large and very well-planned army camp. Everything is orderly, newly built, or in the course of construction; things are clearly signposted; the people are equally new and extraordinarily mixed. You have no idea of the diversity of races. In town, there seem to be more non-British people than British on the streets. The place has no roots, nor do the people, and, as Jenni has just remarked, it has no atmosphere. It is very artificial, with some extraordinary contrasts. The heart of the city is to be lakes, but at present, it is rich farmland. All around this are big blocks of city flats, up to eight stories in height. Trees abound, but apart from the gums, most are half grown. Everywhere there is construction work and more construction work. Administrative buildings are met on every road, but there is nothing locally that would require their presence. Children abound (especially at the Olympic Pool) and so do ex-university men and women.

"The town is built on a series of rolling hills, in a saucer-shaped basin bounded by blue bush-covered ranges. There are lovely views, especially at this time of year in the warm still evenings. Dress here is much more informal than in NZ, mainly on account of the heat, we suppose. A car is a must as the public transport system is rotten. I may say I like the place a lot. It is ideally quiet for work, and there are an extraordinary number of interesting people for so small a city. The friendly welcome we have received undoubtedly weighs in favour of Canberra."

Proof of how easy it was to get things done in our new town is what we achieved in our first week: Jenni got a job as a Research Assistant in the Department of International Relations at a salary equal to my scholarship. Soon after, she became Department Secretary with an even higher salary. She bought a brand-new Holden station wagon in her favourite colour of sea green. I was installed in an office with a typewriter and every kind of stationery and other office supplies I could imagine. Peter and I were invited to order for both the University Library and the Australian National Library any book or run of periodicals that we judged to be valuable as the basis of a collection on South Asia. I was recruited by the ANU rugby team for the coming winter season, and I was invited to travel to Griffiths on my first weekend in town to play on the Canberra team in the NSW Country water polo championships. I had to decline this last invitation as I reckoned the return journey of more than 700 km alone would wipe me out after all the travel we had just done. A fortnight later, I did play for Canberra against a visiting Sydney University water polo team, and I became a regular member of an ANU Sunday cricket team playing other local social sides.

~ ~ ~

The most notable absence in our first whirlwind weeks in Canberra was Hancock. As I wrote to my parents on January 31:

"I have not yet met Sir Keith Hancock, although he has intended to come in to see me. His wife, Theaden, is dying from cancer, and he is nursing her. Understandably, he is terribly upset and has disappeared from the scene altogether. They say her loss will be a huge blow to him. It is a great shame. Everybody has a very high opinion of him and says he takes a great interest in his students. He has a habit of suddenly descending on one of them and taking him/her for a walk, during which he chats about anything from gardening to work. Apparently, he is the master of the searching question but, according to Low, is kind to everyone but the humbug. Aged 61, he is a little thin man, with an unruly shock of white hair."

It was the end of February before I got to meet Sir Keith. I found him as personable and friendly as I had been told. He was, however, pretty much out of circulation for the whole summer and into autumn. In May, he endeared himself to me with a remarkably thoughtful gesture. I was scheduled to deliver my first work-in-progress paper to the department, and Sir Keith took the trouble to write me a note from Theaden's bedside the previous evening apologising for being unable to be present for my presentation. Work-in-progress papers were circulated in advance, and Sir Keith had obviously read mine carefully, judging by two helpful suggestions he appended to his note.

That night I had a remarkable pre-cognitive dream that my seminar was a failure because very few members of the Department turned up. I was particularly annoyed because Sir Keith and Robin Gollan, the senior Australian historian, weren't there. In my dream, it was explained to me that Sir Keith was not present because Lady Hancock had died. All proved to be true, including Gollan's absence. He was on phone watch, intercepting calls to Sir Keith. Given the circumstances, the seminar was a lack-lustre affair, but my paper won approval from my colleagues.

Anthony kept Peter and me busy as the year went on, volunteering us to present papers in several RSSS seminars. To be fair, the papers fitted well with our ongoing preparatory work on India, and the presentations gave Peter and me positive exposure to the faculty. Lightheartedly, Anthony had nicknamed us "Sepoys," seemingly unaware as an Englishman of the irony of applying to his Australasian students this British imperial label for Indian troops under British command. As more students arrived in Canberra to work with Anthony – Ravinder Kumar, Hugh Owen, Pete van den Dungen, Bill Hale – Peter and I became the "Original Sepoys."

In mid-May, Jenni's good work with the Housing Officer got us a three-bedroom furnished house owned by the University close to the city centre, allowing us to move out of University House. During our time there, Jenni, who loved to cook, had missed having a kitchen. The new place would save us money as the rent was subsidised by the University. It enabled us to have Jenni's grandparents come to stay for a fortnight in the early winter. We were now able to host parties and entertain dinner guests. One of these was Marjorie Eyre, an English woman who had been Sir Keith's private secretary and who had accompanied him to Canberra as his research assistant. Jenni described her in a letter as "a very nice, quiet little woman, very unassuming, but quite interesting when drawn out." Marjorie became a good friend.

Jenni's work in the International Relations Department was expanding, and her leisure time was occupied with acting in the Canberra Repertory. Meanwhile, from April onwards, I was playing rugby – not infrequently two games a week. Our ANU side had an excellent forward pack, but the backs were my despair. Although we gained the lion's share of the ball, we lost as many games as we won. The grounds were rock-solid and the play was rugged. In this first season, I was rewarded with a chipped front tooth and a split lip.

Plans for Indian fieldwork were proceeding apace. Peter and Anthony would fly to India in October, but Jenni and I opted to go by sea. In September, we would drive to Melbourne, store the car, and board the Lloyd Triestino Line's *Oceania* for a voyage via Djakarta and Singapore to Cochin in southwest India. From there, we would travel by train to Calcutta, with a week's research in Madras on the way. It was all very exciting. As Anthony, Peter, and I would be in India at the same time, Anthony, with Sir Keith's support, secured approval for Jenni's appointment as a research assistant to the three of us, with her return trip paid in full.

The weeks leading up to our departure from Canberra were hectic. There was a surprising amount of formal paperwork to be done, including visas for our stopover in Indonesia and our entry to India. As the house would be occupied by others when we left, we had to put into storage all possessions we were not taking with us. We had a staggering number of farewell parties to attend, a testimony to the numerous friendships we had made in our seven Canberra months in the International Relations and History Departments, University House, the repertory company and the rugby and swimming clubs.

Ramping up the intensity another notch, two outstanding British academics arrived at ANU during our last ten days: W.H. Morris-Jones, Professor of Politics at Durham, and Asa Briggs, Professor of History at Leeds. Morris-Jones was the author of *Parliament in India*, obviously of great importance as background for my study of the Bengal legislature. I described him in a letter to my parents:

"He is a slight, balding, soft-spoken Welshman in his early 40s. In an otherwise lack-lustre Asian Constitutional Conference this week, he gave a most penetrating paper on 'Behaviour and Ideas in Political India.' Peter and I also had an hour-and-a-half with the man on Friday evening. We found him a delightful person, and he made numerous helpful suggestions on what to look for in political India, who to see, how to interview Indians and so forth. Although he knew very little of the legislatures before Independence (which shows how unworked our field is) he was able to suggest approaches which might be profitable and questions we might hunt for in our material."

Asa Briggs was visiting ANU for six months, and in a chat with him at the History Department's party, I discovered he had a high opinion of Neville Phillips and the work on eighteenth-century England at Canterbury in which Neville had involved me and others. Neville was advising Briggs on the revision of his *Age of Improvement,* originally published in 1959. A year after I met him, Briggs moved from Leeds to a chair at the new University of Sussex and, as Dean of Social Studies, recruited Anthony in 1964 as founding Director of the School of African & Asian Studies (somewhat to Hancock's annoyance). Anthony, in turn, recruited Bruce Graham and Peter Reeves.

~ ~ ~

Jenni and I left for Melbourne on September 5 and sailed from there for India on the 14th on the *Oceania,* a small passenger ship with modest facilities, at least in second class in which we were travelling. After a few rough, cold days crossing the Great Australian Bight, we were ready for our first experience of tropical heat: "like an intense Canterbury Nor'wester with gallons of water poured into the air. Most of the time, you feel you could reach out and touch the air." We were happy when the boat's small plunge pool was filled with warm seawater.

There were two ports of call on the itinerary, Djakarta and Singapore. We had a day in each, and the contrast could not have been greater. As I wrote to my parents:

"Indonesia is a police state, par excellence, with the qualification that it is the height of officious inefficiency. On the wharf to greet us were at least a dozen troops and police, all armed to the teeth with rifles, automatics and revolvers. The troops were in full battle kit. There were even two policewomen with revolvers and knives."

We had introductions to a Kiwi couple, Judith and Dick Myerscough, with whom we spent the day. We learnt a lot from them about the society and the Indonesian power structure: "Everybody wants a uniform in Indonesia." Dick was the Reuters-Australian Associated Press Correspondent, and he said he was careful with what he wrote: "the truth but not the whole truth." Although there was no censorship of foreign despatches, correspondents were not infrequently called to Army HQ to explain things they had written. "One must have a sense of humour. It is good for a laugh. Otherwise one could not remain sane."

"Dick and Judith ran us into central Djakarta, and what an eye-opener it all was. Life everywhere. It was so like a book or film, suddenly come real. Everything was so different. After a short drive around, we went to the old Hotel des Indes, once the best hotel in Asia and now no good at all. We had a long chat, drinking beer and eating sandwiches, sitting under bamboo awnings in the forecourt with fans whirring above. Then by car to the markets, the outstanding memory of our day. Hundreds of bamboo stalls under bamboo rooves, with narrow alleys between. With Judith (who speaks good Indonesian), we wandered deep into the maze, and she haggled for bananas, pineapples, oranges, and sweets for us. It was fascinating."

Our ship sailed from Djakarta in the evening on September 24 and docked in Singapore at 7:00 am on the 26th. "We thought Djakarta was a busy port, but it was Kaiapoi compared to Singapore," I wrote my parents. "We were told there is a daily turnaround of passenger vessels alone of about 20." Our guides for the day were Tony Miranda, a Singaporean Indian whom I had met at Christchurch Teachers' College the previous year, and his friend, another teacher, Singaporean Chinese Timothy Tham.

"They piled us into Tony's Morris Minor, and we did Singapore. Routine chores first at a post office and bank, at both of which the service was quiet, prompt, and polite. The contrasts with Djakarta were legion. Everything was thriving and prosperous here; the traffic was extraordinarily heavy on the roads, but it moved fast and was well controlled; roads were in excellent repair; new buildings were going up in many places; and the shops were crammed with wares. We had lunch in a Chinese section of the city, and Tim and Tony explained what was happening around us, such as a Chinese funeral. Lots of Chinese beating drums, clashing cymbals, burning incense, and looking quite happy. Tim told us that rock-and-roll music is frequently played in these ceremonies! It was nearly time for the Chinese Festival of the Moon, so vendors were selling special lanterns and moon cakes, large currant buns. There will be a big torch procession on the night of the festival.

"The smell on one Chinese street was overpowering – it was a narrow crowded street with dozens and dozens of people eating meals outside in little stalls. On long bamboo poles overhead, washing was strung, jokingly referred to as the 'state flags of Singapore.' The houses along the lane were dilapidated. We saw firewood stacked in some of the rooms and big fish hanging in the windows of others. They looked incredibly small for the number of families Tim told us would be living there."

Back on board the *Oceania* that evening, passengers were comparing prices on their day's purchases. It was clear Jenni and I had done well. We had bought a telephoto lens for our cameras and a transistor radio, and we had got exceptional bargains because Tony had played his trump card for us: a Catholic priest with clout among hi-tech retailers!

India was now just five days away. From Singapore, we sailed through the Straits of Malacca into the Indian Ocean, around Ceylon and the southern tip of India, to berth at Cochin in the state of Kerala.

— Chapter Eight —

Incredible India

"There is a moment when one is newly arrived in the East, when one is conscious of the world shrinking at one end and growing at the other till all the perspective of life is changed."

– Gertrude Bell

Letter to my parents from Sudder St., Calcutta, October 1960:

"Up until now everything was so new (and at times quite overpowering in its novelty) that I just couldn't face starting a letter about it, but at last we have settled and are finding our feet.

"We docked in Cochin around breakfast time on 1st October. We were ashore by 9.00 and enjoying our first experience of India's plentiful labour supply. Our bags were taken off for us by a string of porters. We also saw the sad side of it. In our cabin we had left a cardboard box and an orange, and these had been descended upon by the porters as soon as they realised we did not want them. Later, in the Customs shed, we saw them being displayed with great pride to all and sundry. The poverty is really very sad.

"The Customs men were polite, friendly and helpful (despite forewarnings to the contrary), as were the shipping agents who arranged for porters to take our luggage over to the Malabar Hotel, which was just across the road from the Customs shed. Again, we looked like a caravan and felt most conspicuous. We have now, however, grown quite used to having half-a-dozen porters in tow.

"The Malabar Hotel and Cochin in general turned out to be something quite out of this world. They were lovely. The hotel was spacious, built in the Indian style with very high ceilings and open connecting archways for air circulation, clean with good food. The service was marvellous. We had our own room 'boy' who waited on us hand and foot. Our bedroom and attached bathroom were immense, and our beds, with their mosquito nets and supporting frames, looked like old four-posters.

"Our first task on arrival was to arrange for rail bookings to Madras. I went to the travel agent at the hotel and asked for sleeping berths on the next day's train. His reply floored me: the first available bookings were 7th October! We found out later that we had struck the annual Puja festival holidays when there is a great deal of travelling. It was impossible for us to wait for seven days in Cochin; so we decided we must fly to Madras and damn the cost. This meant that we must send most of our luggage through by rail, and in the afternoon I took it down to the railway station. What a saga that was! Neither the taxi driver nor the porters spoke English, and I was quite certain that at any moment all my luggage would disappear from under my nose. Moreover, at every turn there were the most violent and incomprehensible arguments over how much I should pay for the various stages of the cartage. I was determined not to get 'done' and everybody else (I was sure) was determined on the reverse. In retrospect, I think I probably did rather well out of the arguments – but the physical effort was much too great.

"I finally found the luggage room and was horrified to

learn that the luggage could not be accepted unless it was wrapped in gunny (sacking). If we went by rail, however, it could accompany us as it was. I was just about reduced to tears. I headed for the booking office and at last a ray of sunshine broke through. They could give me first-class reservations for 4th October. I grabbed them, deposited the offending luggage in the left-luggage room, had another fierce argument with the porters, drove back to the hotel, had another argument with the taxi driver and collapsed into our bedroom, a broken shell of Broomfield. India had definitely won the first round!

"The experience gained was invaluable nonetheless. We have now some hard and fast rules for dealing with people like porters, taxi drivers etc.: First, decide how much they should get well in advance and have exact money ready; Second, don't look at all confused or diffident; Third, give them the money when the job is done and then take no further notice of their protests; Fourth, if possible move smartly from the impending scene of battle. It is amazing how much less one is pestered if one looks relatively confident, does not linger undecided or, alternatively, takes absolutely no notice of the constant barrage from people selling things, offering services and begging. One has to move imperiously through the streets or one would never get anywhere.

"We had now four days to fill-in in Cochin, which gave us a good chance to look around. It is rather an unusual port for a big shipping line to call at and the sort of place one would usually miss. Lying on the west coast and well to the south it has a very wet climate (over 100" a year) and a hot temperature with little seasonal variation. The port and surrounding villages are built around a series of lagoons and on islands lying within them. The houses stand half-hidden in the lush growth of coconut palms and smaller trees, which everywhere fringe the water. The effect is more like a tropical island than one's mental picture of India. One afternoon we hired a rower and his dinghy, and for two hours were rowed around the lagoon and in and out of the islands. It was beautiful. We went close to many of the villages and were a source of great wonder to the populace, the women and children being particularly fascinated with Jenni. Indians are great stare-ers. It is not as bad here in Calcutta, where Europeans are fairly common, but in Madras and further south we nearly stopped traffic every time we went out.

"Cochin was one of the first places in India visited by Europeans. The first recorded contacts go back to the 15th century. In the next century, Vasco de Gama established a trading post there, and it was in Cochin that he died 20 years later. It was there too that the first Christian church was founded in India, as early as 300 AD by the Apostle Thomas it is said, and St. Francis Xavier established a mission a few years after de Gama's death. The result is that this area has the highest proportion of Christians in India. There are 30 churches in and around Cochin, and very beautiful they look set along the water's edge among the coconut palms.

"Because of the educational work of the churches, Kerala is India's most literate state. Sad to say, it is also its most poverty-stricken. The result was the communist government, which came to power in Kerala about three years ago. The alliance between communism and Christianity was hardly a holy one, and it is not surprising that the occasion of the government's fall 18-months-ago was a clash over Church control of education. There were bloody riots and the Indian Central Government moved in to restore order. At present there is a Congress Party government in the state, with the whole place still bubbling like a hot mud pool. One afternoon while we were there, there was an R.C. festival (Our Lady of the Rosary) to which the locals flocked. At the same time the communists turned out on the harbour in a launch decked from one end to the other with red flags and hammer-and-sickles, and paraded up and down the waterfront.

"We went over to Ernakulam, a market town across the lagoon from the port, to do some shopping and were appalled by the poverty and filth. There were beggars by the dozens, and, worst of all, many were maimed, blind or diseased. Elephantiasis is notoriously common in Cochin and we saw three or four hideous cases of it. Apparently it is carried by the mosquito and has no cure as yet.

"This was the bad side of Cochin. The beautiful side was the lush growth of plants and animals – the flowers and trees were a delight, and there were hundreds of big butterflies and lizards a foot or more in length. Bird life is also very dense – throughout India, apparently. And like all other men and beasts on this overcrowded continent, they are great scavengers. There are hundreds of black crows everywhere, which will steal any small object the moment one's back is turned.

"Some of our other impressions of Cochin which we jotted down:

"1. The incessant honking of horns in the streets. This we have found everywhere we have gone. At first it nearly drives you mad, but already it has just become part of our general existence.

"2. The lack of women on the streets. This was more pronounced in Cochin than in Madras, and certainly more than in Calcutta, but the disproportion is still remarkable. Of course, in the big cities there is a very low ratio of women to men (in Calcutta it is as low as 650 to 1000) and those women apparently stay at home most of the time.

"3. The revolting Indian habit of spitting, especially when it is accompanied by betel-nut chewing. There are notices on all the railway station platforms "Spit Here," but neither on railways or anywhere else is spitting confined in any way. I remember it was one of Gandhi's great regrets that Indians did not realise what a revolting habit this was, and we thoroughly agree with him!

"4 The ubiquitous black umbrella. They are carried everywhere, for both rain and shine, and often there is a good deal more material on the umbrella than on its carrier. You see people working under them in the fields and even sitting under them in ponds. The officer in charge here told us he saw an Indian washing himself one day from a bucket, stark naked, in pouring rain, with his umbrella up! I must admit they are useful. One of my first purchases in Ernakulam was a big one, which cost me the sorry sum of 9 shillings. It is serving me well, especially as a sun shade.

"5. Indian skill at handiwork. Jewellery, wood and ivory carving, leather-work, weaving, metal work and embroidery are really wonderful – and you have no idea how cheap. We have made a policy of finding out what each area we visit is noted for, and buying some examples of that (when we can afford it). The Kerala area is famous for ivory work and we got some exquisite pieces (some for Christmas presents) very cheaply there.

"6. A strange silence in the streets, which is hard to explain at first. When you realise what it is, it seems so obvious – the absence of shoes and their consequent clatter. Most people go barefooted or wear soft sandals. It seems quite strange to hear a "shod" European or policeman disturbing the silence. Not that there is really any silence anywhere in India; all is life, movement and, above all, toil. The way most of these people live and the appalling physical exertion which much of their work involves is heartrending.

~ ~ ~

"Our train for Madras left at 1.45 pm on the 4th. We were in a six-berth first-class compartment, but for half the journey we had only one companion. He was a middle-aged Australian railwayman who had come across on the Oceania with us and was taking advantage of free railway travel (an international railway arrangement) to tour India. Quite a nice fellow. We three had the lower berths (big seats which turn into sleeping berths at night) and when two Indians got in about 9:00 pm, they took two of the upper berths. The first-class compartments are spacious, but spartan and dusty.

"The journey was very interesting while the daylight held, but it was tediously slow. We moved quite fast at times, but there were many long stops at stations and between them. It took us well over five hours to cover the first 100 miles! Fortunately, the snail was replaced by a locomotive during the night, and we did the remaining 300 miles in 12 hours.

"We got a tremendous shock soon after leaving Co-chin. We were batting along at about 45 mph when a hand appeared through the window and tapped Jenni on the shoulder! From that time on until we got into the Western Ghats, high mountains where there is little habitation, the outside of the train was festooned with beggars, fruit sellers, basket and other handiwork hawkers, and odd 'stowaways.' They moved up and down the carriages, clinging precariously to the steps and bars over the windows, many laden down with wares, but all apparently oblivious to the grave risk of death which they ran. The agility of the crippled beggars (and there could be no question of the genuineness of their maimed limbs) was astounding. One fellow with only stumps for arms swung nimbly along the outside, using stumps and toes like a monkey. We had to shut all our windows and lock the doors to escape from the barrage. It really made us feel how overcrowded India is. This sort of thing, however, does not happen on the main express trains. Fortunately!

"The countryside in the southwest was very beautiful. Like Cochin, lush and wet and closely populated. We were very interested to see our first paddy fields – how green they are – and as we climbed into the mountains, the terracing to catch the water and the tiny pocket-handkerchiefs of green where a little flat has been built up. Man and beast (the water buffalo) were everywhere, labouring knee-deep in water with the primitive one-furrow, wooden plough. At a timber yard alongside the line, we were thrilled to see an elephant stacking logs; this, we thought, was India. At every station, there were goats – dozens of them – wandering idly among the people and eating everything: straw, paper, crumbs, cloth. Equally common were the pariah dogs – many mongrels, like a large tawny fox terrier, obviously flea-ridden and often covered in sores. They all look so alike that we reckoned they were running from station to station ahead of the train (it wouldn't have been hard at the speed we were travelling), but then, being Indian dogs, they were probably riding on the carriage steps! We were later amused to note in our air-conditioned compartment on the way to Calcutta, there was a notice prohibiting animals except dogs.

"Unfortunately, the journey over the Ghats through the teak forests was done in the dark, so when we woke in the morning (after a poor night's sleep), we were well across to the east. Here was a landscape quite different. The rainfall was obviously much less (it is about 20-30 inches in Madras city, I think), and the vegetation was sparse. There were bare patches of barren red soil, and the houses, instead of being built of coconut palms as in Kerala, were mud and straw thatch. As in many of the rural areas through which we have travelled, the labourers wore nothing but a G-string or loin cloth, and the children one garment less! The housing in the country was generally better, however, than many of the hovels we were later to see in Madras and Calcutta.

~ ~ ~

We broke our journey to Calcutta for four days in Madras, reducing the time there from the week originally planned to compensate for the extra time spent in Cochin. I was in search of a copy of a doctoral dissertation about the Madras Legislative Council in the nineteenth-century to which I had seen a reference before leaving Canberra. It was nowhere to be found, and a brief survey of the city's major research libraries persuaded me there was nothing for my work that would require a return to Madras.

Two days after we arrived, Anthony flew in from Australia and recruited as a guide to the city the Advocate General of Madras, Mr. Thiruvenkatchari, whom he and I had met the previous month at the Asian Constitutional Conference in Canberra. Mr. and Mrs. Thiruvenkatchari took the three of us sightseeing that evening.

"The highlight was a visit to a very large Hindu temple, where we wandered among the throngs of worshippers and had the various idols and shrines explained to us. The Thiruvenkatcharis are orthodox Brahmins, so they were most interesting on their religion. It was a funny experience taking off one's shoes at the door and padding around barefooted in the sandy compounds. The place was full of busy, noisy people who went from shrine to shrine, gazing upon the idols, touching the holy threshold with their fingers or with their foreheads and laying flowers at the feet of the gods. In the courtyards were family groups that sat around laughing, talking or singing. The idols struck us as tawdry, but there was obvious devotion in the worship, and, besides, the whole thing was obviously a great 'evening out' for many of the families. A better pastime than lounging around a street corner in Cathedral Square! What took my fancy was a 20-foot-high round pillar covered with a sheet of pure gold. It was the only 'god' that earned my admiration."

The following morning Anthony accompanied Jenni and me on a trip to Mahabalipuram to see the superb seventh- and eighth-century CE Pallava dynasty rock carvings and temples. We were back in the city early afternoon, and Mrs. Thiruven-katchari then took us to see folk craftswomen at work.

"Our train left for Calcutta that evening at 8.15, and we really felt by that time we had had a full day. Our air-conditioned compartment was rather nice. Just two bunks, one above the other, the upper bunk folding into the wall during the day while the lower converted into a seat. The only trouble with travelling air-conditioned is that every pip-squeak of a railway porter and sidekick latches onto you and expects a tip. People in India who apparently have money are fair game. I am certain our meals cost us twice as much as they would have in 1st class even. At least they are edible and served on relatively clean plates. There was a kitchen on the train, and meals were brought to us.

"The air-conditioning worked well, and our 42 hours on board were not unpleasant. The countryside was always interesting, and it changed in character a number of times. I would never have believed India was such a beautiful country; it really is lovely. The evenings particularly have the most entrancing deep shades of purples and rich reds. The moisture-laden air must have a lot to do with it. We went through the heart of flooded Orissa lowlands and saw water stretching for miles on either side of the railway. At many of the stations, there were hundreds of refugees camped under tarpaulins and sleeping in the open on the embankments. Apparently, this recent monsoon has caused more damage by flooding to Indian railways than any monsoon in history.

"So to Calcutta. We crawled in to Howrah station two hours late. Drizzling rain rather matched our mood, but we were determined not to accept it as an omen. As soon as the train stopped, we were greeted by Provash Chakraborty, a young student cousin of our Canberra philosopher friend Nirmal Bhattacharya. Like many Bengalis, Provash found it very hard to understand our English and we his. Even so, he was a wonderful help to us, and he packed us and our luggage off to Sudder Street much quicker than we could ever have done ourselves."

I look back on this first arrival in Calcutta from a vantage point more than a half-century on, a half-century that contains the experience of ten subsequent arrivals in the city with stays ranging from a few days to more than two years at a stretch. Even though the city has become familiar to me – one of my "home places" – those initial days still loom large in my consciousness.

~ ~ ~

For starters, Jenni and I could not have chosen a more intense central location in which to live. Following a recommendation from Peter Reeves, we had booked a room at the Salvation Army's Red Shield Guest House on Sudder Street, a block east of the major shopping artery of Chowringhee. Equally close to the north was Newmarket, the city's huge covered market where, it was said, you could buy every foodstuff imaginable and anything else from a reel of thread to an elephant. In front of the market were several cinemas. Two blocks to the south on Chowringee, past the National Museum (onto which the

Red Shield House backed) and the storied Asiatic Society, was Park Street, home to many of the city's most elegant restaurants and nightclubs. By contrast, at the bottom of Sudder Street, scarcely 200 meters from our accommodation, were brothels and *bustees* (slums) occupied largely by Anglo-Indians (Eurasians).

Letter to my family, October 24, 1960:

"Where do I start in an attempt to describe Calcutta? The composite impression is so intense; there is so much that is absolutely different, or, more correctly, there is almost nothing that is familiar. What makes it equally difficult to get or draw a rounded picture is the fact that there is never any possibility of standing away from it. There is no escape from the bustle, noise and (I fear) filth of people living. On the streets, there are always people walking, talking, cooking, eating, sleeping and urinating. In our own lane alone, I should think there are a dozen or so families whose whole life is on the pavement. At any time of day, you have to pick your way among recumbent bodies of humans, dogs, goats, and cows. Inside there is no escape from the din. A novel we are reading aptly remarks that the Hindu has the capacity to live in an uproar which would drive a European mad. To make a noise seems to be a chief enjoyment."

The Red Shield Guest House was not deluxe accommodation:

"On arrival (in the rain, you will remember), we thought it a cheerless place. It seemed old, poky, and (worst of all) our bedroom and attached bathroom seemed much too small to spend six months in. There was only one wardrobe and a dressing table with two drawers. Once we had got things organised, however, it didn't seem so bad. We shall have to live out of our suitcases, certainly, but the tray of the trunk gives us another large drawer. There is a sitting room with writing tables, the laundry service is quite adequate and cheap. The officer in charge (Captain Travis) and his wife are very friendly, helpful and sensible, and (best of all) the meals are good. As I think I told you, the place is cheap (Rs.20 a day double, which is 30 shillings, food included) and is right in the centre of Calcutta. Very handy for our libraries. So we shan't do badly.

"One of the amusing features here is the tribe of 20-30 monkeys, from babies the size of kittens to two monstrous males, which inhabit the trees and rooftops outside our bedroom window. They are ugly-looking brutes, but great fun to watch and tease. Occasionally, they make forays into the street to demand tribute in bananas or nuts from passing vendors, and then they gather quite a crowd. So we think such colonies can't be too common in the city."

~ ~ ~

An initial target for my research was the holdings of the National Library of India, which included a few manuscript collections, extensive printed documentary series, and the most comprehensive body of secondary materials in the country. It was located about three miles south of our accommodation, and in the first week, we took taxis back and forth. The journey was mostly across the Maidan, the great park the British had established to provide breathing space in the central city, so Jenni and I decided to buy bicycles to reduce our transport costs. On our bikes, we were figures of considerable interest to the local cyclists, who often rode alongside of us, staring but saying nothing. When we were not on the paths across the Maidan, we learnt to be wary of buses and trams as the male passengers frequently spat out of the windows.

We also learnt to be wary during our lunch breaks. Letter to my parents, November 7, 1960:

"Each day, we eat our lunch (which we take from Sudder Street) under the trees at the National Library. There are very large birds, kites, which hover high in the air watching for prey. One day as we were munching our sandwiches, there was a sudden rush of wind and Jenni's sandwich disappeared from her hand. A kite had swooped down and snatched it with its talons. Since then, this has happened three more times, and the last time I lost a lump of skin from one of my fingers as well. We keep watch as best we can, but the wretched birds wait until our backs are turned and dive in like bombers. They are really quite frightening. The only solution is for us to eat our lunches under unfurled umbrellas!

~ ~ ~

In the first month, our intention was to work at the library six days a week and go sightseeing on Sundays. For our first excursion, we recruited Provash Chakraborty, our welcoming angel at Howrah Station, and a friend to take us to a Jain temple complex in the oldest part of the city, North Calcutta, and from there to Belur along the Hooghly River further north in the suburbs. It was at Belur that the nineteenth-century Hindu reformer Ramakrishna developed his syncretic religion that subsequently sent monks across the world to found missions.

Arriving back at the Red Shield House in the afternoon, we were quizzed by Captain Travis as to where we had been. The hissy fit he had when we told him we had been visiting Jain and Hindu shrines forced me to revise my earlier judgment that he was a sensible person. He said he was appalled that we would visit such dens of iniquity, especially on a Sunday. He then launched into a lament that he and Mrs Travis had been exiled by the Salvation Army to such a degraded place as Calcutta. It was their martyrdom, he said, and he trusted this would be recognised when their superiors ultimately called them back to London.

A few weeks later, we were to meet a Salvation Army officer who could not have been more unlike Captain Travis. This was Major Dudley Gardiner, a former British Indian Army officer who had returned to Calcutta in the 1950s to manage a food distribution programme in the *bustees*. He exuded a calm self-confidence despite the fact that one side of his face was horribly scarred, the result of acid thrown on him by slum dwellers who took exception to food handouts to some of their neighbours. Dudley worked seven days a week, feeding the abjectly poor and attending to the sick and dying. One Sunday, he invited Jenni and me to accompany him on his rounds. We visited some of Calcutta's most desperately needy living in horrific conditions. Fifteen years later, when my mother told me that Major Gardiner had been awarded an MBE in the UK, I wrote her to say that the day spent with him "was the most horrifying and one of the most instructive experiences of my life." That day I realised that I was rich, and that awareness has stayed with me ever since.

The day also brought into sharp focus the overwhelming question that India posed for me: What could I do to help? There was no doubt in my mind that I had a moral duty to do something, but what should that be when the problem was so huge? In the years that followed, I observed the whole range of reactions by foreigners to Indian poverty, from the total commitment to service exemplified by Dudley Gardiner to an angry rejection of India by those who blamed the society for causing them emotional discomfort. Some excused themselves from engagement by saying it was the duty of rich Indians to help their own poor.

There was no easy out for me, given that I was committing my academic career to Indian studies. Initially, I felt overwhelmed by the enormity of the suffering, but my long-term resolution of the issue of what to do has been to support individual Indians with whom I have become involved. From these early student days onwards, I have tithed, giving 10% of my annual income to individuals in need and to charitable organisations, and where possible, I have recruited others to join in group aid efforts in India.

I might observe that Calcutta in 1960 had untold numbers of refugees living on its streets. Unlike the west, where the main "exchange of populations" – Muslims emigrating from India, Hindus and Sikhs from Pakistan – took place close to Partition, in the east, the main exodus of Hindus was delayed by the hope that communal relations in East Pakistan would be relatively amicable, a hope encouraged by some East Pakistani leaders. It proved a delusion, and in the mid- to late-fifties, millions of Hindu refugees poured into West Bengal.

— CHAPTER NINE —

Further Afield

"Keep walking, though there's no place to get to. Don't try to see through the distances."
– Jalaluddin Rumi

At the end of a very busy first month in Calcutta both Jenni and I fell ill. Jenni's illness preceded mine and was much worse. Running a temperature of 103 degrees, she had a splitting headache for a week, sharp pains in her back and limbs whenever she walked and vomiting. The diagnosis was dengue fever, probably from a mosquito bite in Madras, where there were no mosquito nets on our beds. The good news was that once you have had dengue, you never get it again. I had similar but milder symptoms in the week following Jenni's recovery.

I was on my feet again just in time for Anthony Low's arrival on Saturday morning, November 5. He had come to see how we had settled in and to survey the library and record holdings in Calcutta. I wrote to my parents:

"We have had a hectic and marvellously profitable week. On Saturday afternoon, we went to Firma K.L. Mukhopadhyya, a bookseller from whom I had purchased books while in Australia. It was a funny little show in a backstreet, but Mukhopadhyya himself could not have been more friendly or more helpful. We spent a delightful afternoon drinking his tea and rummaging through his books.

"Following up on the letters of enquiry I wrote from Canberra some months ago, Anthony and I devoted the rest of the week to searching the city for every likely source of historical material which might be of value for me in the first instance or for later members of the ANU India unit. Our search has unearthed nearly everything I could have hoped for my work. I am elated with our finds. I must say, Anthony is a tiger for getting people to do things for him. He goes into action with a great deal of charm but, at the same time, with the air of one who owns the place. The results he gets are quite wonderful, and the week has really provided me with an excellent training in public relations.

"What a week! All I can say now is – let's hope there's no 'Great Fire of Calcutta' in the next 18 months! The rest is just hard work and much inspiration."

In a week of warm welcomes, the warmest of all was that of Dr. Ajita Mukherjea at the Legislative Assembly. He gave up most of an afternoon to introduce Anthony and me to the Assembly, and after setting aside an office for me beside his own, he insisted on our taking our places in the VIP gallery to observe an Assembly session. A few days later, he called me back to the Assembly to show me a letter he had written to Dr. B.C. Roy, West Bengal Chief Minister, requesting that the CM instruct the Government Archivist to make available to me official records for my research. He lent me his car with driver so I could deliver the letter personally to the CM's Private Secretary.

Among the many fascinating people we met during this week of exploration were Gouri and Abu Sayeed Ayyub. They were that rare commodity in India, an inter-religious couple. Gouri was Hindu and Ayyub Muslim. He was 48 and she was 23, and they had a son who was two-and-a-half. Ayyub was a philosopher, and he had just been appointed to direct a new

Indian Studies Department at the University of Melbourne. Jenni and I became good friends with them before their departure for Australia in February 1961. Regrettably, Ayyub found neither the Melbourne climate nor culture to his taste, and after a year, he resigned from the position to return to his beloved Calcutta.

After Anthony's departure for New Delhi on November 13, Jenni continued to work at the National Library, where she now had tasks assigned by Anthony, and I followed up on new leads in other parts of the city. We had trips away planned for December and January, so I was eager to become familiar with as many documentary sources as I could before then.

On December 8, Jenni and I flew to Dacca in East Pakistan to continue the search for documents and people useful for my research. We unearthed some manuscript sources that would make a longer visit valuable, but where we struck gold was in gaining access to old Muslim politicians and journalists who had been prominent before Partition in undivided Bengal.

Letter to my parents, December 18, 1960

"I was very interested in getting the Muslim side of the story to counterbalance the aggressive Hinduism of Calcutta. Among those I interviewed were Abu Hossain Sarkar, a representative of a rapidly disappearing race: Muslim supporters of the pre-Independence Congress Party; Maulana Akram Khan, 86 years old, who edited Muslim League newspapers in Calcutta before Partition; and Fazlul Huq, who entered the Bengal Legislative Council as early as 1913 and was subsequently Chief Minister of both undivided Bengal and East Pakistan. Unfortunately, the old fellow, now in his 80s, was not very coherent, but his 48-year-old nephew, Azizul Huq, was a real find. He revealed that he was his uncle's lieutenant through the 1930s and has the old man's political career at his fingertips. Moreover, he is very keen to help me as he hopes I may show what a great man Fazlul Huq was."

Quite apart from the research, we discovered ourselves in the middle of an unexpected drama in Dacca. In preparing for our visit, our main contact had been the head of Dacca University's Political Science Department, K.J. Newman, who had been very helpful but unexpectedly had fallen silent in the month preceding our arrival. It transpired that in November, he had been attacked and injured on campus by a mob organised by a post-graduate student who alleged that Professor Newman was discriminating against him. Newman, who had been in Dacca for ten years, suspected a political motivation for the attack. He believed the government was trying to force him out of the country.

~ ~ ~

Jenni and I spent Christmas Day, 1960, on a train travelling across the dusty Gangetic Plain.

> "We had a 'dinner box' each from Firpos, one of Calcutta's posh British-Indian restaurants: chicken, ham, tongue, tomatoes, lettuce, bread rolls. We also had some of our Christmas cake and a small bottle of wine to wash it down. Not a bad Christmas after all!"

Our destination was Aligarh, where we were to join Anthony and Peter at the Indian History Congress, an annual gathering of hundreds of historians drawn from the length and breadth of the country. The host institution in 1960 was Aligarh University, an impressive place both in architecture and the quality of its faculty. Founded with British backing in the 1870s as Aligarh Muslim University, its original and successful aim had been to promote higher education among Muslims as a counter-balance to the Hindu passion for univerity study.

We quickly discovered that "quality" was not a word that could be applied equally to the 1960 History Congress. The papers and ensuing discussions on the first day were so bad that

Peter and I (with Anthony's support) considered withdrawing the papers we had contributed. We did not do so, but I decided not to stay on to present mine. Peter, a guest in Aligarh of a Nawab who was one of the great landholders whose political activities under the British were the subject of his research, did stay. Jenni and I, with relief, took a two-hour bus ride to Agra, where for a few days, we explored the Taj Mahal and Red Fort and nearby Fatehpur Sikri.

"The Taj is the most beautiful building we have ever seen (how inappropriately prosaic is the word 'building'), and we were impressed by its preservation. The white marble is still white. The exquisite marble carvings and diamond cut work found in each of the outside bays is in excellent condition. The tombs are the centre of the building, divided from surrounding chambers by a trellis-work screen of white marble, delicately carved. The screen and the tombs themselves are inlaid with semi-precious stones (such as onyx, jasper, bloodstone, lapis lazuli and turquoise) in intricate floral designs."

We visited the Taj first on an afternoon and stayed through a lovely sunset until darkness fell. We were back at 6:00 the next morning to see it at sunrise before spending the day at Fatehpur Sikri.

"This, to my mind, was the best day of our trip to the northwest. Fatehpur Sikri, built from 1560 by the Emperor Akbar 23 miles from Agra, was the capital of the Mughal Empire. It was abandoned early in the seventeenth century, not long after being completed, because the water supply was not healthy. Today it stands in a magnificent state of preservation, surrounded on three sides by a colossal wall seven miles in circumference. On the fourth side there was, in Mughal times, an artificial lake some miles in length which protected the city from attackers in the north. All is built in the bright red sandstone of which the area has an abundance, and things are so well preserved that the rich and splendid life of the court can be visualised with ease."

I was so entranced by Fatehpur Sikri that I returned perhaps a dozen times in later years.

After Agra, we had a week in New Delhi, dividing our time between work in the National Archives (me), shopping (mostly Jenni), sightseeing, meeting people to whom we had been given introductions, getting acquainted with the staff at the NZ High Commission, and welcoming in the New Year with Anthony, Peter and friends. We departed on the evening of January 4, 1961, on a "slow express," which took 33 hours to reach Calcutta. We had an air-conditioned two-berth compartment, which made the journey very pleasant and virtually dust free. Jenni calculated we had spent a total of 120 hours on Indian trains by the time we rolled into Howrah Station at 7:15 am on January 6.

~ ~ ~

As we were leaving again on a Himalayan excursion in just over a fortnight, we plunged into research, work at the National Library being combined with a sampling of the holdings of other political organisations with which Anthony and I had established contact during his visit in November. I had not yet, however, been given access to the West Bengal government archives, which I considered crucial to my research. A visit to the Keeper of Records produced what by now had become a time-worn reply that "permission would come through in a day or two."

Letter to my parents, 15 January 1961:

"As it was now two months since I had applied, I was most annoyed and said so forcefully. From there, I went to see our good friend Mukherjea at the Legislative Assembly, and when he heard of my trouble, he got on the phone. He discovered that, in fact, the police Intelligence Branch [IB] had vetoed my application on security grounds, and at this he hit the roof. He rang everybody from the Home Secretary down to the Keeper of Records, demanding that those 'bloody fool policemen' be told where to get off. The Chief Minister himself insisted that I be given full access, he said, and the Chief Minister was not a man to be trifled with. What we should do without Mukherjea, I really don't know!"

Dr. Mukherjea had become my *dada*, elder brother. In regard to my research, he was my patron, teaching me by practical example how invaluable it is in a hierarchical society like India to have the backing of a person of influence. Using his clout and unbelievably wide circle of contacts, he opened many doors that I doubt I could have entered by myself. He also secured interviews for me with old administrators and politicians.

It wasn't until late February that I was granted access to the government files, the permission possibly coming as much from my own doggedness as from the backing of Ajita Mukherjea and Chief Minister Roy. As I told my parents:

"I had some hard words with the Deputy Secretary, Home Department, earlier in the week. I was thoroughly sick of his smooth excuses for not doing anything, so I really flew off the handle. In India, that really seems to be the thing to do because it was startling the difference it made. I now have my foot in the record room door, and with Dr. Roy's assistance I should think it may soon be wide open. Let's hope it's worth all the trouble."

It most definitely was. The government archives proved to be a gold mine.

Increasingly, Ajita Mukherjea was occupying our leisure time. Like all Bengalis, he was immensely proud of the regional culture, and he embarked on an enthusiastic crusade to expose Jenni and me to as many aspects of it as he could manage. He started with food, inviting us frequently to dine at his house, where he and his wife Nihar assisted their old cook in preparing delectable regional dishes. I have never eaten better than at Mukherjea Bhavan. Along with other friends, the Mukherjeas also ensured we sampled every kind of Bengali sweet, another object of regional pride. My love of these delicacies earned me the nickname *Mishti Mukh*, sweet mouth.

My lifelong sweet addiction had its consequences for my teeth, which began to ache to welcome in the New Year. Fortunately, our Canberra Bengali friend, Nirmal Bhattacharya, had given us an introduction to a Calcutta mate of his who was a recently graduated dentist. He was delighted to have me as a patient, and when I went for the appointment, I found he had invited a number of his dental school junior colleagues to witness his labours in my mouth. Disconcerting as this was, it was far less upsetting than the effect on his drill of fluctuations in the electric power supply. His surgery was in that part of the central city, which was still on direct (rather than alternating) current. It was also located beside a tram line, and each time a tram approached, the drill ground to a halt in my mouth! I was grateful for his treatment, but I have to admit that when I returned to Calcutta on my second visit, I found another dentist whose surgery was in the AC part of town.

~ ~ ~

Our Himalayan excursion was a week on a Darjeeling tea estate. Our hosts were the estate managers, Bill and Susan Whisker, a couple about our age. He was a Scot, and she an Australian, and our introduction to them was a present we were carrying for Susan from a Canberra friend of hers.

Letter to my parents, February 5, 1961

"Our week in Darjeeling was wonderful. The estate at Poobong was a little paradise compared to Calcutta. We flew early morning on January 23 and after a two-hour flight, we were surprised to find when we landed at Ambari, which is just 35 miles from Darjeeling, that we were still on the plains. Darjeeling is at 7,000 feet, so you can tell how sharply the Himalaya rise. An idea of the steepness of the country can be gained from the spur to which Poobong Tea Estate clings. The main road, which is close to the top of the slope, is at 7,500 feet, and the bottom of the garden is at 3,400 feet. The Whiskers bungalow is about halfway down, and on a fine day, one can see right out over the plains, ten miles down the valley.

"The house is beautiful, and we had a lovely room with an attached bathroom. The best thing of all after the incessant din of Calcutta was the quietness at night, even though one thousand workers and their families live on the estate. Susan and Bill are a lovely couple, and they were marvellous hosts. Bill is very busy with his management tasks, but Susan has little to fill her time, given that the house is run by servants. She is rather lonely, hence her delight in having our company. She urged us to stay for a second week, and I wish we could have done so had research not called us so insistently back to Calcutta.

"On our second-to-last morning, we got up at 3:30 and drove ten miles to Tiger Hill (9,000ft), which overlooks Darjeeling and the Testa Valley, to see the sunrise on Kanchenjunga and Everest. Standing no more than five miles from the northern border of India, we could see the hills of Bhutan away to the east, and running behind them and to the north, the mountains of the Tibetan

Plateau, high and jagged. Between these and where we stood were the hills of Sikkim, at present full of Indian Army troops for the Chinese are camped just beyond the passes into Tibet.

"Immediately in front of us was the Kanchenjunga massif – a colossal group of mountains, all between 20,000 and 28,000 thousand feet. Kanchenjunga itself the third highest in the world at 28,146 feet. The basin below the mountain falls as low as 4,000 feet, so you can imagine the impression this mountain makes. Kanchenjunga is only 45 miles from Darjeeling, and Everest is 120. We could see the latter only as a small peak jutting above a range of lofty foothills. Both Kanchenjunga and Everest are in Nepal, so that morning, we looked out upon five countries.

"Engrossed as I was in the spectacle of the mountain sunrise, I disregarded a tugging at my back. When I finally looked around, I found that a billy goat had swallowed the tail of my shirt. To free myself, I had to pull the shirt out of its stomach! It was a garment quickly assigned to the rubbish."

A memory equally as vivid as the sunrise on Kanchenjunga was an encounter a few days earlier on the streets of Darjeeling with a contingent of Khampas, strikingly tall men in traditional brown robes and black knee-length boots. Armed to the teeth, these were fearsome guerrilla fighters who, with the support of the CIA, were resisting the Chinese occupation of their eastern region of Tibet.

~ ~ ~

Back in Calcutta, with just two months left before our departure for Canberra, I felt a great urgency to push ahead with the research. Jenni resumed work at the National Library on tasks requested by Anthony while I continued with material held by political organisations in North Calcutta. Finally, in February, I was given access to the State archives. What excitement I felt as I entered the Writers Building, the huge West Bengal Government Secretariat in the central city, where the records were kept.

Early in March, I wrote Anthony enthusing about the archival gems I was mining. His reply was a shock. From New Delhi, March 14, 1961:

"I think I should let you know I am a wee bit disturbed. It seems to me of very great importance that you should now begin to look for the shape of the wood amidst all your trees. I don't think you can wait for this quite as long as I sense you are doing. You can very usefully spend the stray moments between now and your return to Canberra mulling over what your whole study is all about anyway. You must begin to have some penetrating insights. You will no doubt amend them, elaborate them, even reject them, but the process of eliciting insights must begin .... What I want to see you produce is a perceptive and critical study. I have no doubt whatsoever that it will be meticulous and accurate, but it must be thought-provoking too."

I was very miffed, as my reply indicated. From Sudder Street, Calcutta, March 21, 1961:

"Your letter came as a great surprise to me as I had no inkling you were worried about my work in that way. I am already quite clear in my own mind as to the theme I am developing in this study, and I believe I have quite a number of significant insights. In other words, I am sure I know what my work is all about and that I can offer provoking thoughts as well as facts.

"I think that your worry on this score may be the result of our different methods of working on historical problems. Whereas you delight in discussing ideas as they occur to you from your work, toying with them and subsequently discarding them if they don't hold true, I immerse myself in the material, slowly building a picture, piece by piece like a jigsaw puzzle, withholding my judgments, from discussion at least, until I have a large number of pieces in place. This does not mean, however, that I don't have a firm idea of what I am trying to build or that I am not seeking explanations of why some pieces fit here and some there."

The backdrop for this exchange was a work-in-progress report I would give in Canberra in May, and feeling thoroughly put out by Anthony's criticisms, I determined to write a paper that would prove him wrong. As I was to comment in print years later: "I thereby learnt a lesson from which my own students continue to suffer: a well-timed kick in the backside stimulates the brain." The 30-page paper I produced – "The Vote and the Transfer of Power: A Study of the Bengal General Election, 1912-1913" – not only earned applause from Anthony and others in the ANU department but was subsequently published in the *Journal of Asian Studies*. It brought a deeply appreciated letter from W.H. Morris-Jones: "Most sincere congratulations on your article in the J. of Asian S. This is a beautiful piece of work. I look forward to much more historical illumination of this kind of modern Indian history from your pen."

I was similarly delighted by a letter from Neville Phillips, May 13, 1962: "To have got into the *Journal of Asian Studies* so early in your career is worth congratulations from anyone." To my surprise, Neville proceeded to offer me a lectureship in History at Canterbury from the following academic year. He wrote: "I have plans for building up a team of Asian historians strong enough in two or three years to justify our applying to the Grants Committee for recognition as a School of Asian Studies." Immensely flattered as I was, I declined the appointment. At that stage, my aim was ultimately to return to teach in New Zealand, but aware that, in the post-colonial mentality still prevailing amongst New Zealand academics, an Australian doctorate was rated below the UK and the US, I decided my next move should be to one of those countries.

Although the analytical structure of my dissertation was well developed in this paper, it gave only glimpses of my core argument. It would be almost a year before I had that fully worked out. As the British scholar Nigel Barley says in his entertaining *Adventures in a Mud Hut: An Innocent Anthropologist Abroad*: "Most research starts off with a vague apprehension of interest in a certain area of study and rare indeed is the man who knows what his thesis is about before he has written it."

— Chapter Ten —

Scholarship & Tragedy

"Life is not a walk across an open field."
– Russian proverb

My March 21, 1961, reply to Anthony was posted on the day Jenni and I flew from Calcutta on the first leg of our journey back to Canberra. We stopped for a few days in Bangkok, where we were guests of Kiwis Marie and John Cranko, friends of Bronwen. John worked for Shell Oil, and my most treasured memory of our time with the Crankos was a luxurious breakfast excursion aboard the company launch on the *khlongs*, the city's colourful, crowded waterways.

We now had Thai urban images to lay alongside those of Indonesia, Singapore and India. Between Bangkok and Sydney, a stopover in Hong Kong gave us another great Asian city for comparison. On March 28, we flew into Sydney and simply changed planes to travel on to Christchurch, arriving for my father's 59th birthday. I had asked my mother not to publicise our visit – "I haven't been away very long, really, you know, and I should much rather sneak quietly home, have a good rest, see a few people and then head for the bush again." Despite this, she had a busy fortnight organised for us, and we were glad to get away on April 12 to pick up our car in Melbourne and drive back to Canberra.

On arrival, I immediately began writing my paper for the work-in-progress seminar scheduled for early May, and Jenni found a position waiting for her in the International Relations Department. Rather than resuming the Department Secretary job, she now became the personal research assistant to the department head, Arthur Burns. Soon after we arrived back, Anthony proposed that Peter and I should have our Scholarships extended for six months beyond the basic three-year period to take account of the travelling and other time-consuming consequences of Indian fieldwork. We duly applied, and the extension was approved by the Faculty Board. This meant we would have financial support through April 1963, giving us a clear 13 months to write our dissertations after returning from our second period in India.

The University had provided Jenni and me with another furnished house, this one in the suburb of Ainslie. Jenni had decided not to return with me on my second research stint in India so that she would keep this house during my absence.

I have a poignant memory from our time in Ainslie. Next door to us lived a sweet couple, an Australian-born woman, Alice, and her older Ukrainian-born husband, Mike, who daily expressed an almost child-like joy in living. It was clear Mike had mental health problems, and we understood why when he told us his life story. As a child, he had faced starvation as millions of fellow Ukrainians died in the Stalin-engineered famine of the 1930s. As a teenager, he had been conscripted into the Soviet Army and saw battle against the invading Germans. He was captured and deported to a slave labour camp in Germany and was barely alive when the camp was liberated by American troops in 1945. Australia was a shining light for Mike at the end of a long and horribly dark tunnel.

~ ~ ~

Before leaving on my second research stint in India, I stored all my dissertation notes in a bank safe deposit. I did not want to suffer the same fate as that of a small group of ANU doctoral students in 1960 who lost all their research materials when a building burned to the ground.

I began my return trip to India on September 21, 1961, with stopovers in Singapore, from where Tony Miranda took me on a two-day excursion to Johore State in Malaya to attend an Indian Christian wedding, and in Rangoon for a week as a guest of the British Embassy. I had been invited by a staff member, Esther Evans, whom I had met a few months earlier when she was on holiday in Canberra. I was given my own flat in the embassy compound and ate breakfast and some other meals in the staff dining room. For most lunches and all dinners, however, I was taken out to city restaurants by one or more of the Embassy personnel, and every night there was a party, the last in my honour on the Saturday evening, the day before my departure. Everyone at the party seemed to be planning to come to Calcutta during the winter while I was there to show them around. In fact, only three of the women turned up en route to Darjeeling.

During the week, I was able to spend a few hours on the campus of Rangoon University with two visiting English faculty members, who had horror stories to tell of political interference in the university's affairs that had destroyed academic standards. The highlight of the week was a half-day visit with Esther to the Shwedagon (Golden Pagoda), one of the greatest stupas in the world. I described it to my parents:

"It is set on a hill and rises gracefully 300 feet to a point. The top 20 feet or so are encased in solid gold, and the remainder is covered in gold leaf, rubbed on by Buddhist devotees. From anywhere in the city, you can see this magnificent pinnacle sparkling in the sunlight. There are gateways from each of the four points of the compass, and leading up to each gateway are magnificent stone steps guarded by twining serpents and dragons. The main pagoda, which is more than 3,000 years old, is surrounded by a courtyard of white marble, and in this are numerous smaller pagodas and shrines donated by rich families."

When I visited Rangoon, it was still monsoon time, and I was delighted to experience the torrential downpours. "Every now and then, the heavens would open, and the streets ran ankle deep in places. The humidity was intense just before the downpour and then the air was delightfully refreshed." Perhaps I would not have been so enthusiastic had I known the monsoon had lingered in Eastern India, causing flooding on my first few days back.

I arrived in Calcutta on October 1, 1961, a year precisely after my first entry to India. I returned to Sudder Street in the central city but moved across the road from the Salvation Army Guest House to a small private hotel, the Lytton, run by an Armenian family. At first, I occupied a small single room, but after a few weeks found a Chicago University doctoral student, Warren Gunderson, with whom to share a large twin room.

I was champing at the bit to get back to work on the government records at the Writers Building, which had eluded me on my last Calcutta visit except in the final month. I spent a great deal of this second research trip mining this rich seam. How fortunate I was to have access to these materials was underlined by the news in November that Peter Reeves had been denied permission to use the Uttar Pradesh records. The source of my good fortune, of course, was Legislative Assembly Secretary Dr. A.R. Mukherjea, who in my absence, I discovered, had sustained the pressure on the Keeper of Records and recruited the Home Secretary to do likewise.

My workload was lightened by the fact that the Bengal Secretariat, unlike many other British Indian provincial secretariats, had maintained complete indices of the records. In addition to brief summaries of content, these indicated which files had a security classification that put them off-limits to a lowly researcher like me. I found a way around this. Once

I had won the friendship of the clerks who hunted out the files for me, I was able to persuade them to save themselves work by simply bringing me a shelf full of one government department's records in a given time period, e.g., "everything from the Political Department in May 1923." I told them they could leave it to me to sort out what I needed. Every now and then, in a batch of files, there would be some marked "Confidential," and I did get useful information I might not have seen otherwise. None of this, I should add, had any relevance to post-Independence West Bengal. These were ossified classifications from British days.

There were no photocopying facilities at that time, so I had to take all my notes longhand. As time pressure mounted towards the end of my stay, I sometimes took my camera surreptitiously to the archives to photograph especially long documents. The resulting prints were readable, but only just.

There were some amusing entries in the indices:

"**Red Tape**, To reduce consumption of.

"**Umbrellas**, Principles to be observed in the supply of
for the use of menials.

"**Traffic**, In naked pictures.

"**Elephant**, Purchase of for Mr. Smyth.

"**Chandeliers**, Cost of lighting the King of Oudh.

"**Corpses**, Unclaimed.

"**Muddle, Mr. M.A.**, Suggestion for his transfer to the
United Provinces."

On this last item, I commented to my parents: "Imagine the bizarre career that Mr. Muddle must have had in his Indian service! Who would want a man of that name in their Secretariat? Trust Bengal to push him off onto the U.P."

I was being called on more frequently than on my previous

stint in Calcutta as a tourist guide to the city's highlights for travelling New Zealand and Australian friends and friends of friends. Word had also gone out to US doctoral students that there was this New Zealander who knew the lay of the research land in Calcutta, so I was engaged in introducing them to libraries and booksellers.

November 1961 brought unexpected news from Canberra: The University Housing office had told Jenni that the Ainslie house would be needed in February for a family with children. Rather than return to University House, she decided to take advantage of an ACT government loan scheme to buy a new two-bedroom house in Deakin. Her letters for the next six weeks were full of decorating and furnishing plans and the laborious business of moving our possessions across town on her own. She had my unqualified sympathy.

My own days were very full. I put in long hours at the Writers Building, skipping lunch to maximise the time available with the records, and I usually worked in the evenings at one or other of the political associations. In this period, I also discovered the D'Souza & Doucett Charities in what I had come to regard as my own neighbourhood. On Free Street at the bottom of Sudder Street was this charitable organisation giving support to indigent Anglo-Indians. When I inquired after their records, they said they had 50 years of case files and would be happy if I took off their hands as many of the inactive ones as I liked. With a couple of days of hard work, I sorted out perhaps 200 to ship back to Canberra. In later years, I drew on this source for one article before donating the collection to the Chicago University Library.

I was always looking for interviews with old politicians, but not all worked out. Letter to my parents, November 26, 1961:

"Saturday's paper brought me a big disappointment. On Friday, I had received a letter from Sir Bijoy Singh Roy's secretary, acknowledging a request I had made for an interview and saying that Sir Bijoy was indisposed and would contact me as soon as he was well again. What do you think he did? That afternoon he up and died! I must admit that the disappointment was no doubt greater for himself but for a man of 67 who had been in the Bengal legislature from 1921-1946, who had three times been a Minister and had kept all his political correspondence, to die when I was on his doorstep was a cruel blow. I had one interview with him last year, but at that time I didn't know enough to ask him the really vital questions. Now I shall have to try to worm the papers out of his family – after a decent interval."

I'm happy to say there were better things in the offing. Letter to my parents, December 10, 1961:

"In this past week, I have had three interesting discussions with Professor Nirmal Kumar Bose, Director, Anthropological Survey of India. A first-rate mind, I would say, and a powerful personality. After our first meeting, he insisted I come back for more. He has written excellent articles on caste and politics and is highly thought of overseas. He proved to be everything and more than I had hoped. He is a man of about 60 but looks much younger and has fine, sharp eyes which hold your attention while he talks. He has intimate personal knowledge of Bengal politics as he was a close follower of Gandhi from 1922; his secretary during Gandhi's efforts to put an end to communal violence in East Bengal in 1946. He had some wonderful stories to tell me of the Congress Party and of Bengal politics in particular. We talked of caste, of Hindu-Muslim relations and of communal electorates."
In a letter to Anthony, I added: "I'm glad to say that my conversations with Nirmal Babu have reassured me that I have grasped the essence of provincial politics here."

These conversations helped crystalise the theme that had been emerging from the hundreds of biographies of Bengal politicians I had now compiled. Enlightenment – my *satori* moment – came on a daylong train journey from Delhi to Jaipur on January 15, 1962. I finally had my thesis: In the twentieth century, Bengali rural and urban society differed in many fundamental respects, yet they shared at least one feature: a common dominant elite. In city, town, and village, there was one group of Bengalis who claimed and were accorded recognition as socially superior to the mass of their fellows. These were the *bhadralok*, literally the "respectable people," the "gentlefolk." The bhadralok were economically dependent on landed rents and professional and clerical employment. The group kept its distance from the masses through its acceptance of high-caste proscriptions and its command of education. It shared a pride in its language, its literate culture and its history.

This elite, I saw, was pivotal to Bengal politics. At the time, the in-vogue category for the shakers and movers in Bengal's twentieth-century politics was the "educated middle class," but this categorisation (I believed) was a misleading term because the bhadralok were not a homogeneous economic class, and their status was high, not middling. At the suggestion of doctoral co-supervisor Bruce Graham on my return to Canberra in April 1962, I dipped into the writings of Max Weber for the concept of "status group" to describe the bhadralok.

If I may look ahead a few years, I would note that my characterisation of the bhadralok as a status group in my 1968 book *Elite Conflict in a Plural Society: Twentieth Century Bengal* was contested in Bengal, most severely by Marxist historians who reacted against my rejection of class analysis. Despite this disagreement – possibly because of it – the bhadralok as an analytical category, has become widely accepted in West Bengal and Bangladesh. Concluding his introduction to the 50th-anniversary edition of *Elite Conflict*, the Bengali historian Sekhar Bandyopadhyay says:

"The social and political history of Bengal cannot be written without referring to this social group.... Although historically constructed, the image of bhadralok has now entered the Bengali common sense. One of the earliest historical works in which this image was first theoretically defined was Elite Conflict. Therein lies the historiographical significance of this book."

~ ~ ~

To restore chronological order to this memoir, I backtrack to my departure from Calcutta headed for Delhi on January 5, 1962.

Letter from Defence Colony, New Delhi, to my parents, January 7, 1962:

"I left for Howrah station at 10:30 am on Friday with my taxi piled with baggage and stood in the long and disorderly queue to check my bedding roll into the luggage van. With two porters staggering along under the remaining half-dozen items, I reached the platform just before the air-conditioned third-class vestibule train (Howrah/Delhi 81 Up) puffed its incongruous bulk backwards into the station. I climbed into coach No. 1, in which my ticket said I held a reserved seat and was promptly told that I was, in fact, in No. 2 coach. I climbed into the coach marked No. 2 and installed my luggage in the racks (plural as there was so much luggage) and was politely informed that I must have misread my ticket as it was, in fact, in coach No. 1 in which I held a reserved seat! I left. I returned to the No. 1 coach. I found my seat. I deposited my luggage for the third time. I paid the long-suffering porters a premium. I bought a bag of oranges. I spat orange pips onto the rails, and my equanimity returned. Well, that's travelling in India, I said with a shrug. And I spat out some more orange pips.

"The train left on time, 11:40 am. Pretty good, eh? Yes, but it was done at great personal inconvenience – to the passengers, as half the baggage had to be left behind. Well, you can't expect to have everything! We got away on time; next trip, perhaps, we'll leave late and take the luggage with us!! Halfway along the journey, an old bearded luggage man came through with the list of the baggage numbers that had been loaded, and we all crowded around him with our baggage checks to see if we had been lucky in the lottery. 'Is my number there, Baba?' 'Patience, son. Patience.' Yes, mine was loaded. Delight and a feeling of superiority over one's less fortunate travelling companions. From this point onwards, I repeated with great relish and at not infrequent intervals the sad story of the week's delay that attended the arrival of our trunk at Howrah after it had been left behind, in similar circumstances, at Madras in October 1960. It's the little word of compassion that cheers others in their misfortune!"

I did not suffer any such difficulties ten days later on my rail journey from Delhi to Jaipur. From there, I took an early morning flight to Udaipur. I went to the Jaipur airport by cycle rickshaw, and as I was pedalled through suburban lanes, the sunrise painted the sky a vibrant rose and pink. From the tops of walls on each side of the lanes, peahens and peacocks, of which there was an abundance in Jaipur, looked quizzically down at me. To make everything exotically perfect, we had to pause close to the airport amid fields yellow with mustard flower while a camel train crossed our path.

I was attracted to Udaipur by the renowned beauty of its location and architecture. The Mewar Rajas had chosen it as a new capital for their state in the sixteenth century and over the next two hundred years, had built splendid fortresses and palaces on the shores and islands of interlocking lakes. As in all places I travelled in those days, Ajita Mukherjea had arranged for me inexpensive government accommodation. I was staying at the Udaipur Circuit House. I described it to my parents:

"It was a lovely place on the top of a little hill overlooking the old town on the one side and two of the lakes on the other. What was more, it stood beside the house where Prime Minister Nehru was coming for lunch before addressing an electioneering gathering. Immediately on arrival, I joined the crowd waiting to see him drive up the hill. He was in an open car, and as he passed, he looked directly at me and smiled."

While I was unpacking my suitcase at the Circuit House, I was handed a cable. It was from Jenni. "Happy Anniversary, darling, arriving Delhi 1:00 am Friday 19th to celebrate. Please meet." What a surprise! Initially I couldn't believe it wasn't some sort of practical joke, but once I accepted it was not, I was thrilled that in two days' time, we would be back together. On arrival, Jenni explained she was unbearably lonely in Canberra and had decided to come – and damn the cost.

~ ~ ~

We stayed in New Delhi until January 31 and had just a week in Calcutta before flying to Dacca for 12 days of archival research and interviews. The political situation had deteriorated since our last visit in December 1960, with the Pakistan military intervening directly in the politics of the East Wing and enforcing gag orders on many formerly eminent politicians. We arrived to find university students rioting against a visit by the President, General Ayub Khan. As might be expected, the willingness of old politicians to talk with me was decidedly mixed.

The most striking memory from this visit is of cats. Patron Ajita Mukherjea had demonstrated that his reach extended across international borders by getting us a room at the Dacca Circuit House, and among the residents, there was a retired British civil servant from the days before Partition. Daily he fed all stray cats who chose to come to his room – and about 50 responded to his invitation (there were so many it was impossible to make an accurate count). It was a lovely gesture, but the result was a stench of feline urine that pervaded the entire building!

Back to Calcutta on February 19, 1962, and almost immediately to Santiniketan, a village 165 km northwest of Calcutta where the Nobel Laureate Rabindranath Tagore had built the university of Visva-Bharati. The University had the papers of Tagore's fellow teacher and close friend, English radical Charles Freer Andrews, and had granted me access to them, only the second scholar to be given such permission. Andrews was also a friend and political collaborator of Gandhi. Disgusted by the racism of his fellow British in India, Andrews was active in the nationalist movement, and the papers are rich with accounts of his energetic involvement in political action. He gave his untarnished views of the political leaders with whom he worked. Though in admiration of the cultural achievements of Bengali bhadralok, he was critical of bhadralok exclusiveness.

~ ~ ~

I had three final weeks of intensive archival research in Calcutta before Jenni and I left on March 20, 1962, for a fortnight's visit to Poona and Bombay. From there, we flew directly to Bangkok for another brief stay with the Crankos and then treated ourselves to 12 days divided between Macau, still a Portuguese colony, and Hong Kong. I visited the University of Hong Kong, perched high on the island with magnificent views across the harbour to Kowloon and China proper. I spent a little time with members of the History faculty and was invited by the head of the department to consider joining his colleagues and him in a lectureship when my doctorate was completed.

We were back in Canberra on April 14, and I plunged into writing immediately. While Peter and I were still in India, Anthony had floated plans for a Commonwealth seminar series, and Peter and I had agreed we would insist that our dissertation writing must take precedence to seminar papers of any kind. We did not want to be Anthony's "show ponies." We were relieved to discover that, with the presence of four new "Sepoys," we were no longer in the spotlight.

Beside matters academic, I had domestic affairs to attend to. Jenni was pregnant, with the baby scheduled to arrive in early November. In this circumstance, it felt good that we had our own house. There was a lot of work for me to do: levelling the section; laying a lawn; digging and establishing a garden; and planting shrubs and trees, which were supplied free by the ACT development authority. It was a good antidote to long hours of writing and typing.

Those hours became longer in June for Peter as well as me. Sir Keith was leaving for Europe at the end of the month, and Anthony suggested we both do our required work-in-progress seminars before he left. I already had a draft of my first dissertation chapter completed, so this became the basis for my paper. It passed muster.

With just nine months of scholarship support left, I started looking at job possibilities and post-doctoral fellowships. Of the latter, I was attracted by Duke University in the US and the University of Leicester in the UK In the second half of 1962, I followed up on job possibilities in the UK at Durham and Leeds, in the US at Cornell and Michigan, and at the University of Malaya in Kuala Lumpur. The Durham job was in Morris-Jones' Political Science Department, and to a personal inquiry, he responded that I should stick to my last as a historian. Peter had already secured a lectureship at the University of Western Australia in Perth, and he would take up this position at the start of the 1963 academic year.

As Jenni's pregnancy approached full term and a ship carrying my parents left the Panama Canal for Fort Lauderdale, Florida, en route to England, Fidel Castro, Nikita Krushchev and John Kennedy teamed up to distract our attention with the Cuban Missile Crisis. Blessedly Mum and Dad and the Western Hemisphere survived, and Jenni gave birth on November 9, 1962, to a ten-pound boy, Stephen John.

Letter from Chermside Street, Deakin, ACT, to my parents, midnight, November 17-18, 1962:

"The baby is home and has woken everyone (dog included) by his insistent demands for a feed. Jenni is complying, and I have risen, bleary-eyed, from a disturbed bed to occupy the broken minute on a typewriter. Stephen's first week in the hospital was unremarkable. It was indeed difficult to distinguish the future genius infant Broomfield from the other 20-odd little replicas of Genghis Khan! (This is written for later quotation in the great man's biography.)"

Shortly after Stephen's birth, I began growing a beard, and it has remained with me for the rest of my life.

~ ~ ~

With life intense at home and also at work, as I tried to complete my dissertation by the April 1963 scholarship deadline, I plunged recklessly into a passionate affair. What followed in the next six months was the most painful period in my life, which left me with deep remorse. It is exceedingly difficult to write about, in part because I was so traumatised by what happened that I distanced myself from my feelings.

My lover, Kaye Norris, was a 22-year-old undergraduate

student. I met her at an ANU dance early in 1963 while Jenni was in New Zealand, introducing Stephen to his relatives. After Jenni returned, Kaye and I met mostly in my university office at night when I was purportedly writing. Before long, I told Jenni about the affair and said I was in love with Kaye. She reacted by taking an overdose of sleeping pills and being rushed to Canberra Hospital. When I told Kaye I could not leave Jenni and Stephen, she took an overdose and ended up in the same ward as Jenni. One of my most uncomfortable situations ever was sitting in the hospital waiting room as the visiting hour approached, being glared at by female friends of both women.

My doctoral supervisors agreed that they and their spouses would provide pastoral care. Anthony and Belle Low took Jenni under their wing, and Bruce and Naomi Graham took me. Bruce startled me by saying that I should have sympathy for Jenni for the affair she had had while I was on my second India trip; she had done it only because of loneliness. He seemed to assume that my involvement with Kaye was in retaliation, but Jenni's affair was news to me. I discovered that the man with whom she had been involved was an older student in the History Department. Apparently, she had rushed to join me in Delhi in January 1962 to put an end to the affair.

When it became clear that I would not have my dissertation writing completed by the April deadline, I applied for and was granted a scholarship extension till the end of July. Meanwhile, Kaye found she was pregnant, and a lawyer contacted me, saying Kaye would bring a paternity suit against me unless I committed to paying child support. I did not think the child was mine, as the dates of our relationship did not fit, and I knew she had other lovers. Feeling guilty and very sorry for her, however, I agreed to pay child support.

With my dissertation finished by late June, Jenni and I went with Stephen for a quick vacation to the Queensland Gold Coast. When we arrived back at our Canberra house, there was a newspaper wedged in the door with an item circled. It was a death notice for Kaye Norris. She had taken a fatal overdose of sleeping pills. The horror was compounded by the appearance the following morning of a police car in our driveway. Two ACT Police officers had come to question me, suspicious as they were that I had assisted Kaye in her suicide. Despite my statement that Jenni, Stephen, and I were on a trip to Queensland when Kaye died, the police insisted I attend the coroner's inquest and formally repeat my statement. I was deeply hurt that a farewell letter Kaye had addressed to me was read aloud in court without my ever having been told of its existence.

I was left shell-shocked and profoundly saddened by Kaye's suicide, as well as deeply ashamed at my part in what had happened. When all this was over, Jenni insisted that we never talk about it again, and we never did.

~ ~ ~

In the meantime, my job enquiries of the previous year had been rewarded with the award of a year's Leverhulme Visiting Fellowship at the University of Leicester and offers of lectureships at the University of Malaya, Kuala Lumpur, and the University of Michigan, Ann Arbor. I chose the latter as it was for two years, with the possibility of renewal. To cover travel costs, I secured an Australian Fulbright Scholarship, but aware that the scholarship terms would require me to return to Australia within 24 months, Michigan came up with a travel grant of US$1,500. It was very exciting to look forward to going to the US.

It had been decided that my dissertation examiners would be C.H. Philips, Director of the School of Oriental and African Studies, London, and Robert Crane, Professor of History, Duke University, Durham, North Carolina, whom, I discovered, had held the South Asian history position at the University of Michigan to which I had now been appointed. Philips sent Crane a list of questions for me to address in my doctoral oral exam, which I took with Crane at Duke in late November 1963. By Christmas, my Ph.D. had been formally approved by the ANU.

Impending departure to the US had us selecting and packing belongings and preparing the house for rental and the car for sale. There were innumerable documents to be submitted for entry to America, along with medical examinations and vaccinations. Chan, our Pekingese, had to have a veterinary examination. He would be cared for by friends until we had housing in Ann Arbor, at which time he would take wing to join us. Blessedly, no quarantine was required for his entry to the US.

We had intended to travel to the US by ship, sailing for San Francisco from Sydney on August 5, but the required US immigrant visas did not come through in time. Ultimately the University of Michigan had to recruit a US Senator to put pressure on the Immigration Department, but it was not until August 22, the day we flew to America, that our visas were stamped into our passports at the US Consulate-General in Sydney. The most amusing part of the process was the attempt to thumbprint 10-month-old Stephen, whose tiny paw produced an indecipherable black smear. The Vice-Consul in Sydney seemed resentful of the fact the visas had been hurried along by the Michigan Senator, and he warned us ominously that we might be turned back at our point of entry because of the absence of our parents' full names on the copies of the birth certificates we had submitted.

Our flight landed in Honolulu soon after daybreak on August 22, 1963 (hours earlier than we had left Sydney because we had crossed the International Dateline), and a laid-back immigration officer gave us a warm "Welcome to the United States."

— Chapter Eleven —

Taking the Long Way Home

"In the twentieth century all inhabitants of the western world, and eventually all city dwellers anywhere on the globe, lived mentally in two countries, their own and the USA .... America did not have to be discovered: it was part of our existence."

– Eric Hobsbawm

I lived in America for 31 years, with India, Britain, and Australia woven through like threads in a tapestry. India was a thick multi-coloured thread, Britain and Australia thinner and more muted. Everything was framed by New Zealand, my home to which I always intended to return. I did not take US citizenship as I always identified as a New Zealander. I went to America with a New Zealand wife; I returned to New Zealand with an American wife; in between, I had a German wife. I arrived in the US with one Australian-born son, and while in America, I fathered another son, adopted a Native American daughter and became step-father to another daughter and two more sons. My Australian-born son returned in 2013 to live in the country of his birth. My two other children and the two step-children who are still alive all live in the US.

For my first 20 years, I lived in Ann Arbor, Michigan, and taught at the University of Michigan. The great winds blowing in the sixties and seventies – the civil rights, anti-war, environmental and women's movements – swept me into political activism, and this involvement transformed my teaching. In the classroom, I was unwilling to continue with business as usual. To my teaching on South Asia, I now added courses designed to jolt students into the realisation that contemporary organisational and technological developments could have disastrous results, including ecosystem collapse.

I left Michigan for California in 1983 and for the next 11 years lived in the San Francisco Bay Area, first as a teacher and administrator at the California Institute of Integral Studies [CIIS] and then as a networker between organisations committed to spiritually based transformative work in education, health, and environmental protection. Of all of this, I have written in *Carried on Great Winds: America and India, A Memoir 1963-1994.*

~ ~ ~

My first return to New Zealand was in 1981 as an interlude in a year spent as a Visiting Fellow at ANU in Canberra. I arranged to give lectures at Otago, Canterbury, Victoria and Auckland universities. After 20 years away, I was excited and determined to see as much of my homeland as possible in the four weeks I would be there.

I flew from Sydney to Christchurch on Sunday, July 12, arriving mid-afternoon. I took a rental car at the airport to drive straight to Dunedin, where I gave lectures at the University of Otago over the next two days. My first on Monday evening was a public lecture. The subject, "Technology and Gandhi," could not have been better timed. As part of the Muldoon Government's "Think Big" strategy, an aluminium smelter was planned for salt marshes at the entrance to Dunedin Harbour, and there was a major environmental campaign underway to prevent this. On Monday afternoon, I dropped by the "Aluminium Action Centre" to hear the pitch for the smelter and to pick up literature from which to draw material to incorporate into my lecture. I faced a packed auditorium, and the lecture was very well received. The following afternoon, I gave a paper to a History Department seminar. Not a lively response.

The next morning I set out on a five-day sprint around the South Island. My immediate destination was the Catlins, to visit the Gormans on whose farm outside Owaka I had spent those memorable childhood summers. I left Dunedin in falling snow, the heaviest I had seen in New Zealand outside the high Alps, and I arrived at the Gorman farm early afternoon in bitterly cold, grey weather. With the old farmhouse and a companion patch of bush gone, I had trouble deciding upon the right house. When I knocked on the door, it was opened by a woman. "Is this the Gorman's?" I asked. A voice from inside said: "Come in, John. We've been expecting you." The speaker was my childhood friend Neill Gorman, and it was his wife Betty who had opened the door to me. They had seen a newspaper advertisement for my Monday lecture in Dunedin.

As I recorded in my diary, reminiscences flowed thick and fast.

"Neill remembered how I had eaten 18 potatoes one lunchtime when we were thinning turnips at the Greys' place. Mrs. Gorman Senior recalled my picking up two handfuls of baby mice from chaff bags and being bitten on every finger. I have never forgotten that! Neill and I had gone into Owaka town for afternoon tea with her. Neill agreed with me that the area is looking far more prosperous than it did in the forties. Few rabbits now; the plagues are geese and possums. Mrs. Gorman and he are proud of the progress in the community.

"I hit the road for Invercargill about 4:15 pm, running into heavy snow at the head of the Owaka Valley – also fog. Even so, it only took me two hours to reach Invercargill, and once I was out of the Catlins, the sun shone through to give a marvellous sunset, with fog patches drifting and pink wash across the snow-covered tussock hills."

In Invercargill, I spent only one night and long enough next morning to drive by my old home and primary school before heading for Milford Sound, where I had not been before.

"In the Eglinton Valley with tall, thick bush around me, the clear blue river over stones beside me and the mountains towering directly above – with bright blue sky – nothing left but excitement. Through the Hollyford and up to the Homer Tunnel, a road between towering rock walls and vast peaks above, reminding me of the Modi Gorge in Nepal. On the massive cliffs were frozen waterfalls. Just outside the eastern entrance to the tunnel, to my delight, a kea, but I couldn't stop as it was in an avalanche zone. Later I learnt kea wait there to be fed by tourists. The tunnel was a great surprise: cut from solid granite, unlined, unlit and sloping steeply down from east to west. On the Milford side, it ends in a vast semi-circle of cliffs – and more avalanche warnings. The road continues down very steeply, winding through forest to the fjord."

I made it onto the last Sound cruise of the day, and when I returned to shore, there was time to explore some bush tracks before dark. The mid-winter overnight clientele at the large hotel was two couples and me – and, as I noted in my diary, "a mouse who ran through my bedroom to the bathroom early in the morning."

It was raining heavily when I awoke, and I was concerned as to whether I would make it out.

"No one at hotel reception knew anything about the road, but the advice I was given was to wait until after ten when the graders would be out if needed. Off I went right at ten, exhilarated at the challenge ahead. Ice was detected on the road early on when I tried my brakes; then freezing rain; increasing amounts of frozen slush on the surface as I neared the tunnel, and sleet falling. Into the steep, fantastic tunnel, holding my breath as to what I would find on the other side: four to six inches of fresh snow on the ground and very heavy snow falling. Blessed my Michigan winter driving experience. Even so, a narrow, steep gorge road with sheer drop-offs is no picnic under such conditions.

"A few miles down, I met the incoming bus drivers putting chains on their vehicles and cars without chains being turned back by the highway crews. Despite the difficulty of the drive, it was so beautiful: heavy snow on the thick bush, ferns white; bare mountains of yesterday now snowclad. About 30 miles down, the road was clear and dry."

My destination for the night was Queenstown. After dinner, I went for a drink and struck up conversation with a woman, perhaps in her early thirties, sitting on her own at the bar. She told me the saddest story. A few weeks earlier, her partner had accidentally shot and killed himself with his hunting rifle. Naturally, she was devastated, and her Invercargill family (bizarrely, in my opinion) had bundled her off on her own for an all-expenses-paid vacation in Queenstown. In mourning, the last thing she needed was to be on her own in a resort town. The family's action suggested to me that, like so many pakeha New Zealanders, they were incapable of dealing with strong emotions. I stayed with the woman as long as she wanted to talk and then gave her a ride to her hotel.

~ ~ ~

The next morning was Saturday, and with a lecture scheduled in Christchurch for Monday evening and mid-winter weather closing mountain routes, the sensible thing would have been to return up the eastern coastal road. But I wanted to see the Haast Pass, through which a road had been built only since my 1960 departure from the country, and South Westland, where I had never been. This reckless venture would necessitate a return crossing through Arthur's Pass, the most rugged of the South Island's three alpine passes. I set forth boldly, and having successfully negotiated both the Haast and Arthur's Passes by Sunday midday, I decided on an additional mad venture south along the eastern side of the Alps into the high McKenzie Basin to see Aorangi/Mt. Cook. The Basin was a white frozen expanse, above which Aorangi and his companion peaks towered in icy splendour. I felt thoroughly rewarded for my foolhardiness as I dashed for Christchurch on Monday.

My lecture in the evening was to the Canterbury Historical Association on a subject suggested by the Association: "Passages in the Life of an Indian Historian." In the audience were several of my lecturers from University of Canterbury undergraduate days and my high school History master, Ferg Murray, whose superb teaching had laid the foundations for my career. I had great affection for him, and I was very touched by his parting words after we had spent the next morning together: "I had been *so* looking forward to your coming."

My arrival in New Zealand coincided with that of the Springboks, South Africa's national rugby team, to start a tour over which New Zealand opinion was bitterly divided. Many said the country should not be hosting a sports team from a racially segregated nation. Others were eager for the tour to proceed. This issue had history for me, given my outspoken opposition in 1959 to the exclusion of Maori from the All Black team to tour South Africa the following year. In 1981 my sympathies, of course, were with the anti-tour group, and I was pleased that Ferg Murray agreed. He told me he took pleasure in young people's resistance to the Muldoon Government's support for the tour. If he were teaching now, he said, he would emphasise the dangers of the growth of the power of the executive.

"Wednesday July 22, 1981, 11:45 am The marchers assembled in Victoria Square for an anti-Springbok-Tour rally coordinated with others around the country on the day of the first match in Gisborne. I joined people of all ages. Some schools had let the kids come if they wished. A very large procession, we wound our way through the city centre and down Ferry Rd. to Lancaster Park. I worry for the safety of these people when the rough stuff starts. They have no apparent experience or training in civil disobedience. As we march, I made friends and was invited home for dinner by one couple."

From Christchurch, I drove north to Nelson, my first time in this attractive small city built on hills along the southeastern coast of Tasman Bay. I was here to visit my mother's sister, Constance Braithwaite. Aunt Con was a nurse who had capped her career as Matron of Stafford, a private hospital in Dunedin, which she and a group of doctors had established. She had retired to a small house in the Nelson suburb of Stoke, expecting her longtime companion, Joan Vale, to join her. Joan chose to stay in Dunedin, and Con told me she was heartbroken by Joan's decision. Of course, as a devout Christian, Con never acknowledged that Joan and she were lovers.

From Nelson, it was back to the North Island and back to the hubbub provoked by the resistance to the rugby tour.

Tuesday July 28, 1981, Taupo: "Somebody will be killed before the Springbok tour is over. The anti-tour protesters did a superb job at Hamilton in forcing the abandonment of the Waikato game, but the brutalities of the 'rugger buggers' were extreme and, in some cases, calculatingly directed to 'sort out' the leaders. If another game is blocked, I think the brutes will kick someone to death or fracture someone's skull with a full bottle or can or a four-by-two. And the police cannot be relied upon to prevent attacks. Tour protesters have already been injured by police batons. The Government is too weaselly to take the responsibility to call off the tour. To be among the suburbanites, with their pro-tour attitudes and implicit racism, is horrible."

This last comment reflected uncomfortable days I had just spent as a house guest. In Wellington, where I lectured at Victoria University, I stayed with my 1957 Australian tour NZU water polo teammate, Theo Verhoeven. He was extremely conservative and considered the anti-tour people social scum. I followed this with a few days in Taupo with an old high school and army friend, Graham Cogswell, and his family. He was less outspoken about the tour, but when he took me for a drink at the local RSA (Returned Services' Association) we were surrounded by men loudly expressing hostility towards the tour protesters.

From Taupo I went north, with a full week available before my scheduled seminar with the University of Auckland History Department on August 4. I first visited relatives from both sides of my family. Almost all those on my mother's side I had met in my youth, but I had met none of my father's relatives. My cousin, Edna Mason, took me to see houses where my mother and father had grown up and where later they lived with Bronwen and me in our earliest years. I saw the maternity wing in Whangarei Hospital where I was born (disappointed there was no plaque recording the momentous event), and I visited ancestors' graves. (*They* had plaques!) I then went on my own for a drive around Northland.

"This time spent in Auckland and North Auckland has been a fascinating pilgrimage into family history. Driving north into towns with names familiar from my father's life was tantalizing because I know little about their significance to him."

~ ~ ~

I returned to Canberra on August 6, 1981, and it was another six years before I visited NZ again. In 1985 I had married California-born Jo Imlay, and I was eager to show her New Zealand in the hope she would agree it was a country to which we might move. We went in November 1987, rented a car in Auckland and set out to camp our way down and back through both islands. Unfortunately, having been out of the country for more than a quarter century, I had forgotten that summer rarely arrives in New Zealand until the second half of December. Although we were blessed with a few fine days in the Coromandel at the beginning of our journey, we had rain on almost every day for the rest of our five weeks. On a few mornings we crawled out of our tent to find the ground white with frost, and the white on the hillsides around the Fiordland lakes was freshly fallen snow!

Apart from brief glimpses of Aoraki/Mt. Cook and Mt. Tasman, Jo did not see the peak of any of the country's magnificent mountains, and I was so convinced that the weather had doomed our plan to move to New Zealand when our time at CIIS was over that I burst into tears as we hunted in vain for a decent campsite in Wanaka, the southernmost point of our trip. After we had settled for a motel for that night, Jo assured me that the weather was not a game-changer for her. She was finding many things to love in New Zealand.

On our return journey north, it was a rainy day and a consequent retreat for two nights to an old lodging house in the Marlborough Sounds that precipitated a momentous decision. When we woke on our first morning in the lodge, the tide was creeping up the beach below our bedroom window, with the gentle sound of small waves. Jo said suddenly: "This is where I want us to live when we move to New Zealand – in the Marlborough Sounds." I agreed that would be marvellous.

Extracts from a 13-page letter I wrote to my parents describing the entire New Zealand journey can serve to capture some of the things that delighted and impressed us.

"Our first camp was in the Kauaeranga Valley, east of Thames, amid forested mountains alongside a river with delicious swimming holes – one right by our camp, which we enjoyed greatly despite a rather chilly wind. The native birds were also numerous and in good voice; there were pigs snorting and crashing in the bush just after dusk; I met one of the numerous possums one night; and, delight of delights, there were glow worms all along the streams ....

"We found a lovely spot to camp deep in the Buller Gorge between Murchison and Lyell. There was even a small beach here, and we had a good swim in the late afternoon in tolerable water temperature. The greatest pleasure was the bird song – Tui, Cuckoos, Parakeets, Fantails, Shellducks and Bellbirds. Our tent was pitched under low trees – mainly willows – and at dawn the sound of the Bellbirds was unbelievable. It seemed as though we had the Royal Philharmonic perched in the branches overhead!

"In the meantime, we had made the acquaintance of two other phenomena of the Buller: 'gentle overnight rain' and sandflies. The rain was heralded just before sunset by a double rainbow, and by the time we were in our sleeping bags, the skies had opened. It seemed as though it would never stop, and it was certainly as heavy as any monsoon rain I have experienced in India. Frankly, I worried that the river would rise the eight to twelve feet needed to engulf our tent. Obviously it didn't, but judging by the accumulation overnight in our pots and pans, there must have been a fall of at least two inches, and the deep clear river of the previous day was muddy and much more rapid. I had forgotten the delayed effect of sandfly bites. We spent the following two weeks trying not to scratch. Jo reacted more severely than did I and was saved from insanity by a Wanaka chemist who prescribed an effective salve ....

"You will be pleased to know that gardening is alive and well in NZ and that the display of flower beds and flowering shrubs in both public and private gardens remains superb. It is hard to choose the best, but I think the highlights were the public rose garden in Te Awamutu and the Pukeiti Rhododendron Trust in Egmont National Park. The hydrangeas from Taupo through the Waikato to Auckland also were a sight to see. What I hadn't remembered was the beauty of the wildflowers in NZ. On our way here, I thought to myself: 'Well, we won't have wildflowers like the ones we saw in the Colorado mountains two years ago,' but happily I was wrong. In the bush and everywhere else there were beautiful wildflowers, and the variety is greater than in the Rockies. My vote for the most spectacular goes to the lupins along the roadsides and river banks all through Central Otago and the McKenzie Country: mauve, purple, buff, yellow, pink, maroon ....

"One thing is quite certain: New Zealand is having to work out a new relationship between Pakeha and Maori. There is a strong Maori cultural revival underway, with successful demands for the development of a bicultural education system. Already there are primary schools in some Maori majority areas, such as the East Cape, where Maori is the sole language of instruction for the first two years. As you drive around the North Island and some places in the South, you now see frequent road signs for marae. The most explosive political issues concern land and fishing rights. There is a Waitangi Tribunal re-examining all contested land transfers from Maori to the Crown, and as a result of its findings, both Parliament and the courts are restoring large amounts of land to tribal control or compensating tribes for previous illegitimate land alienation.

"It is a remarkable phenomenon. I think personally the whole effect to come to terms with the racial hypocrisy that existed in the country is very healthy, but as you can imagine, it has produced an angry, and, in some cases crude, racist backlash from a fringe of the Pakeha community. Robert Muldoon is one of the most prominent spokespersons for this viewpoint. NZ will not have a comfortable time of it for the coming 10-20 years, I would guess, and I would also guess that the goodwill and idealism are present in both races to make real NZ's claim to be a decent multi-racial society."

~ ~ ~

In November 1989, Jo and I led a six-week CIIS programme in the Kangra Valley of the Indian Himalaya, and after we left CIIS the following year, we decided to build on that experience by leading tour groups in India and New Zealand. The first tour we had planned was a return in Spring 1991 to Kangra and its neighbouring valley, Kullu. This fell through because of the US invasion of Iraq in January 1991, so we decided in the time set aside for that programme to treat ourselves to another trip to New Zealand.

We departed for Auckland on March 11, 1991, on free business class tickets with United Airlines "earned" with airpoints we had accumulated with the travel involved in our organizational networking. A friend from our 1989 Himalayan trip, Carol Dommet who lived in Palmerston North, also offered us the use of her family's camper van for our travels around the country.

Our first objective on arrival were visits to two retreat centres, Aio Wera in the Waitakere Ranges west of Auckland and Mana on the Coromandel Peninsula to the east. Physically, Mana was the more impressive. Founded in the previous decade by Rainer and Shanti Heubner and Sol Petersen, it was in a spectacular location high on the hills looking northwest across the waters of Hauraki Gulf. Rainer, a physician from Germany with no previous building experience, had designed and constructed an exquisite meeting hall and an accommodation block, and the team was at work on the addition of a meditation chapel. In later years, I would bring tour groups to Mana and lead workshops there.

This was also true of Tauhara Centre in Taupo, the next stop on our journey. Tauhara had a much longer history than Aio Wera (founded in 1970) and Mana (founded in the early 1980s). Although its origins were also spiritually inspired, Tauhara had been more successful than the other two centres in attracting secular conferences and seminars. Jo was befriended at Tauhara by Igor, the centre's Rainbow Lorikeet, who waited each morning on her shoes outside her bedroom, imitating the yowl of the resident cat, whom it teased mercilessly. When Jo appeared, it would fly to her shoulder and endanger her hearing by shrieking with delight in her ear. We were very sad to learn a few years later that Igor had disappeared during a severe storm.

In Taupo I had hoped for a reunion with my friend Graham Cogswell, with whom I had been out of touch since my brief visit in 1981. When I phoned, his wife, Jill, told me Graham had recently left her and gone to Australia with a Dutch girlfriend. Even though extremely upset and angry, Jill spent an afternoon with us, and we all had a good time at a café in a bird sanctuary on the Waikato River.

Palmerston North was our next stop, and sadly we found

domestic bliss absent from Carol and Keith Dommet's place as well. Carol was her warm welcoming self, but Keith was downright churlish, apparently resentful of the fact that Carol had promised us "Sophie," the camper van. We left a tense household and headed for the South Island in Sophie, an old but comfortable vehicle.

When we arrived in Picton in the Marlborough Sounds, the South Island terminus of the inter-island ferry, we dropped in to a real estate office to inquire casually about available properties. We mentioned that we wanted to find a house at some height above the shoreline because of the predictions of global warming and consequent rising sea levels. The real estate agent was momentarily disconcerted, but then she said brightly: "You shouldn't bother with that. Global warming's not going to happen here."

Reassured that New Zealand was excluded from negative global trends, we drove west across the top of the island to Golden Bay, where we set up camp at secluded Totaranui in Abel Tasman National Park. What a wonderful place! It was nestled in thickly forested hills. Along its western edge was a lagoon and, to the north, it fronted onto a golden-sand beach with warm, clear water and gentle surf. Cinnamon-brown weka and blue-black-and-red pukeko, NZ's most prolific flightless birds the size of domestic hens, were busy in the campground mugging campers and trampers for food handouts. Our most persistent weka, who quickly learnt to knock on Sophie's door, developed a preference for noodles dipped in peanut butter.

We had intended to visit Tui Intentional Community in Wainui Bay, which bordered Abel Tasman National Park, but when I phoned I was told it was not a good time to come as the community was involved in a process of internal assessment. Jo and I were delighted to have our Totaranui stay extended as a consequence.

After a visit to Takaka, a small town that amazed us with its hippy vibe, we headed from Golden Bay east to Nelson.

There, 86-year-old Aunt Con, now living in a retirement home, took us walking to a nearby park and impressed us with her assertiveness and vigour. We would be crossing Main Road, Stoke – NZ's fifth busiest road, she informed us – so she would understand if we preferred to cross at the traffic lights, but she customarily j-walked, dodging the traffic – which is what she proceeded to do!

It was now April 8 and, with our scheduled return flight to California just 10 days away, we headed for the Picton ferry to return Sophie to Carol and Keith on the North Island. We were less than half-way from Nelson to Picton, when Sophie's transmission started to grind alarmingly. We limped on gingerly to Havelock, where a garage mechanic told us Sophie's differential had given up the ghost. He located a used differential in Auckland, which could be flown in, but the shipping and repair would take three days. Nothing for it but to hole up in the pleasant Havelock Garden Motel. The unexpected delay gave me a chance to take a daylong cruise on the Pelorus Sound Mailboat to see what our future property options might be.

Before Sophie was restored to full health, the crews on the inter-island ferries went on strike. How were we to get Sophie to the Dommets and make it to Auckland in time for our April 18 flight home? We worked out a strategy on the phone with Carol. We would park Sophie at Nelson Airport for one of them to retrieve. Meanwhile, we would fly direct to Auckland, sad though we were that we would not be able to thank Carol in person.

Celebrating what she had found in New Zealand, Jo wrote to a friend:

"I went there sorely aware that I needed a respite from the barrage of events that convince me that America is a very sick society. I have come back a Kiwi in my heart if not on my passport. I found myself exulting in a small, sane, exceedingly humane society."

~ ~ ~

We were back in NZ in less than a year with our first tour group. Fifteen in number we assembled in Auckland on February 10, 1992. Our time would be divided almost evenly between the North and South Islands, with about ten days in each. In addition to the country's natural beauty, the tour would focus on Maori culture, and we spent our first afternoon in the superb Maori galleries at the Auckland Museum, preceded by the standard rousing welcome by the resident *kapa haka* group.

The next day we drove to Mana Retreat Centre on the Coromandel, where we were met by Michael King, who spoke with the group about Maori-Pakeha relations. Michael, as a Pakeha journalist working on the *Waikato Times* from the late 1960s had followed the unusual career path of learning Maori and immersing himself in *Maoritanga*. I had discovered him through his 1977 book *Te Puea*, a superb biography of a *kuia* (female elder) who revitalised her Waikato people, Tainui. Surviving a period of severe criticism by Maori intellectuals for his "intrusion" into Maori history, Michael was to become the country's leading interpreter of New Zealand's multi-cultural society, greatly admired by both Maori and Pakeha.

Michael's introduction for our group to Maori and Pakeha cultures was given further depth by two richly informative evenings at Tauhara Centre in Taupo with Maria Kapa, a Te Arawa elder, and a week later, a full day in Christchurch with TV personality from Tuhoe *Iwi*, Te Hata Ohlson.

Our stay in Taupo included a day's excursion to Waiotapu Thermal Reserve near Rotorua. At Waiotapu, roped paths guide visitors past geysers, boiling mud pools and steaming lakes in brilliant hues of green, yellow and pink. Numerous signs warn of the dangers of leaving the paths to walk on the brittle surfaces closer to the thermal areas. Halfway through the park, Jo and I realised suddenly that one of our group members had disappeared. We had lost Amy, an American woman in her twenties, whose parents had contacted us before the tour to ask that we give her special attention as she had no travel experience. We had already observed in the few days she had been with us that she seemed disoriented.

I alerted a security guard to Amy's disappearance, and together we raced back along the path in search of her. To our horror, we spied her sitting off the track on the far side of a steaming lake. The only way to get to her was across the fragile crust. Thankfully, we were able to reach her without mishap and to lead her to safety. She seemed utterly confused, and when we got back to Tauhara, I rang her parents in California to tell them that Amy must leave the tour. They revealed that she had mental health problems and said one of them would fly immediately to Auckland to take her home. Jo went with Amy to Auckland airport and, once her mother arrived, flew to rejoin us in Wellington, our next stop on the tour.

In the South Island, we spent a few days in Christchurch before flying to Queenstown and from there visiting Te Anau and Milford Sound. On the return flight to Christchurch, our group had a small Air New Zealand plane all to ourselves. The day was brilliantly clear, and the pilot followed the Southern Alps north, flying below the summits of the main peaks. We came so close to Aoraki/Mt. Cook that we felt we could almost reach out and touch it.

The tour ended in Christchurch. From there, Jo and I flew to Indonesia to spend a fortnight mapping out a future tour of Bali and Lombok. Then it was on to New Delhi, where we enjoyed almost a week on our own before a tour group of nine assembled for a three-week journey in Himachal Pradesh.

An issue surfaced during these first tours that would become such a problem for Jo that she ultimately decided not to accompany me on most tours. She found the tour members' chatter on the bus rides an intrusion on her desire for silent reflection. My insistence that we had no right to tell our paying customers to be quiet made her angry with me as well.

— CHAPTER TWELVE —

Return to The Happy Isles

"Last, loveliest, exquisite, apart –\
On us, on us the unswerving season smiles.
Who wonder 'mid our fern why men depart
To seek the Happy Isles!"
                                    – Rudyard Kipling

With our income dependent on our entrepreneurial skills, Jo and I worked very hard in 1992 and 1993. We were still based in the San Francisco Bay area but were travelling almost incessantly to network, offer workshops across North America, and lead tours in South and Southeast Asia. We entered 1994 feeling more comfortable financially. We had decided to start taking my retirement pension, and the first monthly payment was deposited in our bank account in October 1993. The assurance this gave us of a steady, if small, income made us more confident that we could relocate to New Zealand in the near future.

Our focus in 1994 was on New Zealand. I left for Auckland on February 14 to lead a three-week tour, and Jo joined me a month later to search for "our land" in the Marlborough Sounds. We had arranged to exchange our Bay Area house with a Marlborough couple, and we moved into their comfortable Blenheim home on March 18. The following morning, a Saturday, I strolled around the downtown and in the window of the first real estate office found a listing for a 50-acre property on Pelorus Sound that seemed a good fit. The office was closed for the weekend, and to my dismay when I went back first thing Monday, the listing in the window was gone. My inquiry in the office, however, revealed that the place was still on the market, but being handled by another company. It took a week before the agent could arrange a boat to take us from Havelock to the Outer Sound, a two-hour journey.

In January 1991, I had taken a two-week workshop at Esalen Institute in California with the great shamanic teachers Michael Harner and Sandra Ingerman, during which I was given significant spirit guidance for the move we hoped to make to New Zealand. The first information came from a shamanic journey I did myself. An Eagle took me flying over the Marlborough Sounds and showed me a remote property in such detail that I was able to draw a sketch map: the position of the house in relation to two garden plots; the boat shed; the jetty; the shape of the bay.

The other information came from a journey in which we paired up with another workshop member to find each other's Spirit. My partner was a Canadian woman, Gladys, who knew nothing about me other than my name. In her journey she saw me on a boat approaching a shore and being greeted by a Maori *haka* party. That, at least, was my interpretation of what she was shown. She described them as men with spiral markings on their faces dancing in "grass skirts" – maybe Africans, she thought. Their leader held a stick, shaped at one end into a bird's head, and, as I stepped from the boat, he drove the stick into the beach and a dove flew up. This symbolised my work, Gladys said.

The stick was particularly significant, as Jo and I had found just such a stick with a bird's-head shape on one end in a riverbed in North Canterbury on our 1987 New Zealand trip. Jo had oiled and polished it to serve as a "talking stick" for the Spirit in Nature workshops we taught.

In March 1994, when we went with the real estate agent to the property in Outer Pelorus Sound, we took with us the sketch map I had drawn after my shamanic journey at Esalen. To our delight, everything fitted exactly. This was the place to which my Eagle had flown me. We knew within ten minutes that there was no need to look at other properties. As we walked back to the boat, Jo kissed me and said: "Welcome to your new home."

Then we got cold feet. What were we getting ourselves into? Could we live in such an isolated place? Did we have the necessary skills? More immediately, did we even have the money to make the purchase? We decided we needed more time on the property before making a final decision, so we arranged with the owner, Stuart Graham, to spend Easter, the first weekend in April, as his houseguests. This time we drove to the property, a three-hour journey from Blenheim, with Stuart and his partner Robin Wright guiding us for the last 10km across neighbouring farm tracks.

The more we saw of the land, the more we loved it. Apart from half-an-acre around the house, all was regenerating bush. The property was on the lower slopes of a 750m mountain, with a pine forest directly above and protected native bush stretching for miles beyond that to the north and northeast. The land sloped down to a beautiful bay, with five streams (one with a ravine and a 10m waterfall) and three shingle beaches. Across an 800m channel to the east was a large island, Te Hoiere/ Maud Island, where Department of Conservation [DOC] rangers cared for endangered species. No houses in sight, other than our own.

The two-storey house had four bedrooms and a large "rumpus room," which we saw as perfect for Jo's studio. We did not like the mish-mash seventies décor, but that could be changed. There were three outbuildings: a sleep-out, a shed and a two-storey workshop-garage. There was also an excellent jetty. Stuart was offering to sell the property "with chattels:" furniture, workshop tools and a boat, a six-meter aluminium runabout with a 90hp outboard and trailer.

Our major concern was that road access was across the neighbouring farm. Stuart eased our concerns about this by saying that, although there was no formal right-of-way, the farm family had no objection to neighbours driving in and out by this route. This proved to be the most serious of numerous lies he told us, and it was something we should have checked, especially as his realtor hedged on the subject.

When we returned to Blenheim, we decided to proceed with the purchase, and feeling that the guidance I had had from Eagle was a message that the property was to be ours, we made an offer $50,000 below the asking price of $320,000 for property and chattels combined. Initially, Stuart would not budge, but our insistence that he was asking too much resulted, by week's end, in his accepting $290,444, chattels included. We retained a lawyer, an accountant and a mortgage broker, and on Friday, April 8, 1994, we signed a contract. We decided to give our new land a Maori name, Te Wairua, "Place of Spirit."

We were back home in California a few days later, and I immediately put together the paperwork on our finances needed for the Blenheim broker to get us a mortgage. We had a huge advantage in the fact that the exchange rate was very favourable. The equivalent of NZ$290,444 at the time was just US$163,500. The mortgage took a month to finalise, and the NZ bank was willing to lend only 75% of the purchase price because of the remoteness of the property. We were able to take a personal loan from our US bank to bridge the gap.

The next task was to prepare our Fairfax house for sale. We wanted to get it on the market in June, and if it sold quickly, we would ask the buyer to rent it back to us for several months. We had networking and teaching commitments in the US until November 1994, and we were excited to have found a freighter with passenger accommodation sailing from Los Angeles to Auckland late that month. We felt that a two-week voyage would give us space for the immense transition of exchanging one country for another.

Our booking was on the British freighter *California Star*. As so often with freighters, its departure date was pushed back from late November to the second week in December. On the afternoon of the 9th, we drove to the port of Long Beach to board the ship accompanied by Cynthia Stringer, a young woman who had been working with us on our networking project since August. She and her boyfriend Vincent were taking my Toyota pickup to sell for us. We would spend our first night on a silent ship moored at the wharf, and after dark, as we strolled the deck, Christmas lights twinkled from yachts in the marina. At daybreak on Saturday, December 10, 1994, the *California Star* sailed for New Zealand.

~ ~ ~

With just nine passengers, the voyage was a quiet one socially. There were few of the celebrations that typically punctuate a journey on a passenger ship. As we approached the equator on our seventh day at sea, the Captain simply invited the passengers to join him on the bridge so he could tell us when we entered the Southern Hemisphere. To our delight, just as we crossed the line, a very large pod of dolphins surfaced ahead of the ship, and after keeping us company for about 15 minutes, they swam away south at great speed. Jo and I felt warmly welcomed by Tangaroa, the Polynesian god of the ocean.

Our voyage to Auckland was supposed to be direct, but we were given the bonus of a day in Suva courtesy of two Fijian men who had stowed away when the ship was loading there on its way to the US. They were duly returned to the Fijian police while the rest of us enjoyed tropical sunshine and warmth as we explored Suva's colourful markets. The *California Star* headed back to sea in the late afternoon, and three days later on Christmas Eve, as we sailed down the east coast of New Zealand's North Island, the Filipino cooks served a roast pork feast traditional to their homeland. Half the officers and all of the crew were from the Philippines.

On Christmas Day 1994, we sailed into Hauraki Gulf to anchor in the roadstead to wait for the port to get back to work on Boxing Day. A traditional British Christmas dinner was served that evening. It was much more to the liking of the Captain and other British officers, whose table we shared, than the previous evening's feast of pork. They had made Jo and me uncomfortable throughout the voyage with their snide remarks about the Filipino cooks. They seemed totally unconcerned that their racist cracks were heard by the Filipino officers who dined at a separate table.

The following afternoon the ship docked in Auckland, and new passengers came aboard. An affable Auckland couple, Margaret and Nelson Tollerton were the new occupants of our cabin, and when I remarked that Jo was hoping someone would welcome her to her adopted homeland, Nelson hugged her, welcomed her to NZ and wished us both well. It was late afternoon before Customs officers cleared us for disembarkation, and Jo and I and our 18 pieces of luggage were set down on the wharf from where we had been told a van would ferry us to our city motel. It seemed, however, that the shipping agent was still on holiday, and no van appeared. After an hour and a number of near misses by massive container transporters, the wharfies found a van to take us to the entrance gate and from there, we were able to call a taxi. It was a small sedan, but the driver cheerily squeezed us in with all our possessions. We must have been a comical sight at the motel, struggling out from under the pile of luggage.

Our major task in Auckland was to buy a four-wheel-drive vehicle that would be tough enough for the tracks at our Marlborough Sounds property. I had always had in mind a Landrover, but the advice we had from NZ friends was to get a Toyota Hilux. In America, this would be described as a small pickup truck, but in NZ, it went by the name of a utility vehicle, colloquially shortened to "ute." I asked Nelson Tollerton for his opinion, and he not only gave his vote for a Hilux but also recommended a Toyota dealer in the Auckland suburb of Otahuhu. As it turned out, this dealer had a used Hilux with low mileage in good condition, and the salesman, who volunteered that he had had a disappointing Christmas sales season was open to some bargaining on price.

On New Year's Day 1995, we drove out of Auckland to begin our journey south in our double-cab Hilux, which we nicknamed "Pelorus Jack." It proved to be a great vehicle, giving us 20 years' service on the rugged terrain in the Sounds, interspersed with innumerable trips on the challenging French Pass Road to and from Nelson and places well beyond. From Auckland, we had expected to be heading for the Coromandel to spend a couple of nights with Michael King and Maria Jungowska, but they had apologetically cancelled their invitation when a houseful of relatives arrived for the holidays. We drove instead straight to Wellington and the Picton ferry.

~ ~ ~

While Jo and I were crossing the Pacific on the *California Star*, daughter Nikki was making a significant crossing of her own. My first wife Jenni and I adopted Nikki in 1968 when she was nine-months-old. She was the daughter of an unmarried 16-year-old Ojibwa girl in Michigan's Upper Peninsula. During the 12 months preceding our departure for New Zealand, Nikki had sought my help in an effort to find her birth mother. Under Michigan law at the time, anyone who had been adopted could make an application to the Department of Social Welfare to be put in touch with a birth parent. If the Department had the relevant information, it would inform the parent that the child wanted to be in touch, but it was left up to that parent to decide whether or not to make contact. Nikki heard nothing until one day, there was a knock on the door of her Mt. Clemens home, and there stood a middle-aged woman accompanied by three younger people. The older woman was Nikki's mother, Rose. The others were Nikki's half-siblings, Nicole, Stephen, and Phillip.

Rose urged Nikki to bring her six-year-old son Phillip to join them in Watersmeet in the Michigan Upper Peninsula, a reservation for the Lac Vieux Desert Band of Lake Superior Ojibwe. She told Nikki she would be given a house and a job at the Lac Vieux Desert Resort and Casino, which was owned by the band. Nikki was happy to have found family, and she made the move without hesitation. Soon after arriving in Watersmeet, she began a relationship with Henry (Hank) Hazen, and they married in June 1997, by which time they had a son, Tyler. Hank, a Vietnam veteran, was the band's lawyer and leading figure in a move to pool resources to guarantee housing, health insurance, and subsidised education for all members of the band.

Jenni and I had two other children: Stephen, born in 1962, ten months before our move from Australia to the US, and Alastair, born in Michigan in 1964. Stephen had a very troubled childhood and adolescence, including alcohol addiction, and he had spent some of his teen years in juvenile detention. He was in touch with me only off and on in his twenties and thirties until he cut off all contact because I refused to continue giving him financial handouts to cover the periodic emergencies he claimed he was facing. I did not want to support his addictions, whatever they were. We had been out of touch with one another for three years before I left the US for NZ in 1994.

Alastair, by contrast, had a relatively smooth passage through childhood and adolescence. He excelled at sports, especially baseball, in which he was selected for state junior teams for both his pitching and batting. Unfortunately, his pitching arm did not hold up, so he did not play ball for his college, MSU. He graduated in 1988 and moved from Michigan to the East Coast, where two years later, he married his college sweetheart, Debbie Pesano. With a friend from MSU days, he was then building a labour recruiting company in Maryland, which they called GloboMax and taking an advanced course for certification as a Microsoft Network Systems Engineer.

~ ~ ~

By Friday, January 6, 1995, Jo and I were in Havelock, ready to drive to Te Wairua, and Stuart Graham and partner Robin insisted on accompanying us in their vehicle. We thought this unnecessary, but in fact, the twists and turns of the public roads and the farm tracks would have had us bamboozled had they not been there to guide us. We were on the land by 10:00 am, and Stuart spent the whole day hiking me around, showing me where things were and how they worked. I was weak at the knees by the time he revealed that we had been invited to afternoon tea by neighbours. These were Anneke and Rob Schuckard and their two pre-teen children, Ewen and Esther. I pleaded exhaustion, so Jo and I did not stay long. At last, we could be on our own at Te Wairua.

We had two other sets of close neighbours, and we met them both two days later. Over a small ridge to the east of our land was a bach owned by a couple from Christchurch, the Bridgemans, who visited the Sounds only occasionally. They dropped by on Sunday morning to invite us for afternoon tea, and when we arrived at their place we found our neighbours on the west also there. They were Mary and Derek Searle, who had the property between the Schuckards and us. They had owned the place for about 20 years but had moved permanently from Christchurch just six years before our arrival.

We discovered that the question uppermost in the minds of all our neighbours was what we planned to do about possums on our land. When I was growing up, the "pest" that gave rural New Zealanders sleepless nights was the rabbit. By the end of the century, it had been supplanted as a worry by the Australian Brush Tailed Possum. With no natural predators, 90 million possums were destroying the native bush, and their numbers were increasing despite poisoning, trapping and shooting. Jo and I had no ready answer, and we kept silent about our aversion to the slaughter as the neighbours regaled us with hair-raising tales of aggressive possum behaviour.

It was not the possums that troubled us on our first weekend at Te Wairua but a fairly large earthquake and gale-force winds, neither out-of-the-ordinary in Outer Pelorus Sound, our neighbours assured us.

Possums, earthquakes, and gales were safe subjects for discussion. We discovered that our explanation of the renaming of our property was not so safe. Jo noted in her journal: "Dead silence when we explained what Te Wairua means. One man looked as though I had said something distasteful, as so often is the case when Maori are mentioned in front of older Pakeha."

On Monday, January 9, our household goods shipment arrived: two very large crates. I had cleared these through Customs in Wellington on our drive south from Auckland, and now they were on the last leg of their journey from Havelock on Johnson's Barge. We were making our acquaintance with a service critical to the settlers scattered along the shores of Pelorus Sound. We got to admire Peter Johnson's skills as he grounded the barge at low tide on the closest of our beaches and brought each crate off on a fork-lift, which he then backed up the gravel roadway 150 meters or so to deposit the crate close to the house. We set to right away opening the containers and moving items into the house, but we made little progress until the following day when Rob Schuckard came to lend a hand.

The Schuckards, we discovered, had migrated from the Netherlands to New Zealand only a couple of years earlier and had settled in the Sounds, so Rob, an ornithologist, could study the sea birds that were prolific in the area. Rob had already become an expert on Kawau/King Shag, an endangered species of large cormorant found only in the Sounds.

Unlike our other neighbours who, as good Kiwis avoiding potentially contentious topics, had not touched on the question of what had brought us to Te Wairua, Rob asked outright what motivated us to settle in a remote part of New Zealand. Jo said she was looking for solitude, a place to be away from people for long stretches of time to deepen her contemplation. I said I wanted to be in a place where I could learn to listen to the voices of critters, trees, plants and the Earth itself.

We also told Rob we were hoping, with an assistant in the US, to maintain our networking organisation, the Eagle Connection, which facilitated the dissemination of information, skills and personnel between organisations committed to transformative work in education, health and environmental protection. In the weeks that followed, however, it became clear that this hope was unrealistic. Cynthia Stringer, our American assistant, found the networking overwhelming without us there to give direction. She threw up her hands and left with her boyfriend Vincent for a two-week European vacation. In her absence, we decided to fold the network, and we arranged to transfer the subscriptions of Eagle Connection members to the Institute of Noetic Sciences and New Dimensions Radio. Twainhart Hill generously stepped in to facilitate the transfer. We retained the Eagle Connection business name for the continuation of our workshops and tours.

An issue we faced on arrival in 1995 was the underdevelopment of the internet in New Zealand. It was in its start-up phase, and the remoteness of Te Wairua added problems. Our phone connection, through which our computers accessed the internet, was by radio relay, and this often blocked transmission. Had we arrived two or three years later, we would have had a satellite connection to the web.

~ ~ ~

Our first weeks at Te Wairua were exceedingly difficult. January and February 1995 were extraordinarily wet months, so we were working for much of the time in falling rain with mud underfoot. Making matters worse, Jo's energy was still severely depleted by CFS. We were surprised to find that (in contrast to the US) CFS was widely recognised in New Zealand as a disease under the names Tapanui Flu and ME (Myalgic Encephalomyelitis).

We had so much to learn about the property. We also had to deal with the fact that Stuart Graham had left almost everything in poor condition. Some of this, we decided, was a result of his inability to keep up with maintenance tasks, such as managing the water system, clearing the roadway and other tracks, and weeding the gardens. Some of it was because of his incompetence (among other things, the chains on the chainsaws were incorrectly fitted, and the saws were in serious need of servicing), and some of it was because of his penny-pinching. For example, he had drained petrol from the boat, the lawn mower, and other equipment and then included a can of petrol among the items for which we should pay him!

Visitors were the other problem. In all of our nine years in Fairfax, the number of self-invited visitors did not add up to as many as we had in just this first month at Te Wairua. People eager to make our acquaintance showed up at our door on an astounding total of 16 of our first 27 days. Most brought small gifts for which we were grateful – freshly caught fish, dredged scallops, homebaked goods – but time out for yarns over cups of tea ate deeply into our work time, and the repeated cautionary tales of the disasters of settler life were not uplifting. It was pleasing to discover that almost everyone was glad that Stuart had left, and initially, we enjoyed stories of his skulduggery, but even these began to wear thin, and we just wished him gone completely from our life. The one exception to the dislike of Stuart was the Schuckards. Mysteriously, they had found him good company.

We were sitting at our dining table with Mary and Derek Searle on one of these afternoons when a pod of Orcas swam into our bay. The Searles said it was only the third time they had seen Orcas in all the years they had been coming to the Sounds. We were thrilled and felt the Orcas had come to welcome us. Over the decades ahead, we were visited frequently by dolphins, but Orca visits were rare events.

Meanwhile, there was plenty to keep us busy on our new property. For starters, Stuart had left us with a dysfunctional water system. This took us back six years to our stay in the Himalayan village of Naggar in the Kullu Valley, where, for our first month, we had to carry water to our house in buckets. It did not come to this at Te Wairua. On a supply run to Blenheim, I purchased new pipes to replace damaged ones in the creek to get water flowing to the house. The absence of settling tanks and adequate filtering, however, resulted in muddy water after each major rainfall. I worked steadily on improvements and ultimately, we had a constant supply of clean filtered water.

Stuart had left us with other problems that convinced us he was a charlatan. In the main bedroom, we found that the queen-sized bed we had purchased among the chattels had gone, and in its place was a narrower double bed from the spare room. Stuart swore we were mistaken, but the marks left on the carpet by the queen said otherwise. Fortunately, we had yet to pay for some of the chattels, so we deducted part of the value of the queen bed. This brought a letter from Stuart's partner Robin Wright, written on the letterhead of the Blenheim law firm where she was a secretary, threatening us with a defamation suit if we did not make a formal apology and pay all monies owing. We now nicknamed the couple Ratman and Robin.

A bigger shock was to come. A week after our arrival at Te Wairua, I set off on the drive to Blenheim. As I was crossing Te Towaka, the neighbouring farm, I saw the farmer, Harry Leov, and stopped to introduce myself. As we were shaking hands, Harry said to me: "You are aware, aren't you, that you don't have road access?" He said he had told Stuart that the informal road access he had enjoyed was not being extended to the new owner. Stuart, in selling the property, should make it clear it was boat access only. I was horrified by this news, and I told Harry we were in a tough place because we did not have a boat large enough to come and go to Havelock in all weathers. It was clear to me that Harry was not surprised to learn that Stuart had lied, and he told me he understood the difficulty of our position. With obvious reluctance, he said that maybe something could be worked out, and in the meantime, we could continue to come and go across the farm.

We were encouraged by a phone call from Harry a few days later inviting us to Te Towaka Sports Day. This was an annual event on the Leov farm on the third Saturday in January, and the 1995 Sports Day was special, marking as it did the 50th anniversary of the founding meeting at the end of World War II in honour of troops manning a gun battery on Maud Island. The army sent a contingent to compete in the running races in 1995, and there was a larger-than-usual public attendance.

The invitation to Sports Day suggested we had been accepted as agreeable neighbours, and we stopped worrying about road access until, in June 1995, we received a rather curt letter from Harry saying we could not continue to drive in and out. I rang him immediately and suggested that Jo and I come over for a discussion with his wife Liz and him, but it was not until September that they agreed. They met us outside their garden gate and did not invite us in for a cuppa, even though Jo arrived in the prescribed Kiwi manner bearing a plate of freshly baked biscuits. They insisted on having the matter out while we all stood by our ute, and they gave not an inch on the road issue. No matter that we had been misled by Stuart, we would have to make other arrangements. We were both very shaken, and we left with Jo in tears.

Subsequently, we learnt that farmers and other property owners were under siege because of urban New Zealanders' lack of respect for the privacy of rural land. If there was a drive-able track, many Kiwis saw it as an opportunity to go exploring. The law of the land, meanwhile, imposed on the landowner responsibility for the safety of anyone travelling their tracks, no matter whether or not they were uninvited intruders.

Jo and I spent the day following the uncomfortable meeting at the Te Towaka garden gate sunk in gloom as we tried to figure out what we could do. Should we buy a second vehicle to park in Havelock or closer at Elaine Bay? But our boat (as I had explained to Harry) was not big enough to be relied on in all weathers for either voyage. Besides, this arrangement would require that every item brought from town be off-loaded and re-loaded twice. We were still wrestling with the dilemma late in the afternoon when the phone rang. It was Harry. Liz and he had been thinking a lot about our situation and didn't want us "to be put us in that difficulty," he said. So they had decided we should have the limited road access for which we were asking. However, we would have to bring in visitors, including tradespeople, by boat. We were immensely grateful, and we kept our end of the bargain for all of the 20 years we lived at Te Wairua. Harry, Liz and their children became close friends.

The day after this astounding phone call, we received an-other equally astounding from Te Hata Ohlson, Maori shaman in Christchurch, whom (I might note) knew nothing of our road access problem. He said that his wife Jan and he had been holding us in golden light and the day before had done a special ceremony for us. I told him of the miracle that had happened on the very afternoon they had done the ceremony, and he simply chuckled.

— Chapter Thirteen —

Te Wairua

"Of all that God has shown me,
I can speak just the smallest word,
Not more than a honey bee
Takes on her foot
From an over-spilling jar."
                    – Mechtild of Magdeburg

Our friendships at Te Wairua were not limited to humans. Our most numerous companions were *weka*: flightless birds the size of domestic hens when fully grown, with glossy cinnamon and brown feathers, orange beaks and legs, and bright red button eyes. In Maori tradition, weka are our older and wiser relatives, procreated by the goddess Haera-awaawa and the forest god Tane before he fathered humans. They were once found all over New Zealand, but in the twentieth century the spread of human settlement with the accompanying dogs had decimated weka populations in all areas other than the Chatham Islands, Stewart Island and the northern and western coastal fringe of the South Island. Happily, they were still plentiful in the Marlborough Sounds.

Weka are feisty, companionable and very intelligent. As we learnt about them, they learnt about us – and it went beyond knowing how to cadge food. Most remarkably, they showed a desire to be helpful. One of my early tasks at Te Wairua was clearing out junk such as plastic cartons and milk containers thrown into the bush by former property owners. The weka caught on to what I was doing, and they assisted my search by pecking loudly on concealed items to lead me to them. Most touching of all was the gift of a plastic bottle stopper dropped at my feet by a weka as I was chopping wood one day.

Jo began gathering antlers and bones from the land for her artwork, and as she organised her studio in the largest of the downstairs rooms, she adorned windowsills with these. When weka saw what she was doing, they started dropping gifts of bones at the downstairs door.

As we got to know weka better, they revealed to us a rich language. We learnt to distinguish from their vocabulary which were adults and which were young, which were single and which were couples, which were fighting and which were copulating, which were feeding babies in the nest and which were feeding older offspring on the move, and which birds were on their own territory and which were on another's. The most dramatic of their communications, sounded with voice and stomping foot, was their alarm signal, which would send every weka within hearing diving for cover when a predatory hawk flew overhead. Most endearing was the "roundup," a full-throated high-pitched call sounded by a single weka or a duo most commonly in the evening before dark and relayed by weka for miles across the hillsides.

Several years after our arrival at Te Wairua, I spoke on the behalf of weka in a letter to the *Listener*, August 28, 1999:

"Mark Revington concludes his timely though disturbing article on threats facing the kiwi ('Gone bush,' August 7) with the observation: 'If they die out, you can take it for granted that a lot of our other native birds are in trouble.'

"The plight of the weka proves his point. Gone already from almost all of the North Island and from the South Island east of the Alps, the weka appears to be losing further ground. For example, in the past decade, its numbers have dropped dramatically in Golden Bay, where previously it thrived. Unlike the kiwi, the weka gets little media attention, with the consequent danger that it, too, could be pushed towards extinction before serious notice is taken.

"Where we live in the Marlborough Sounds, these inquisitive, companionable birds are still numerous, but sadly many people here regard them as pests and casually allow their dogs to kill them. Let's not wait until yet another flightless bird is added to the endangered list before we recognise the weka as the treasure it is."

~ ~ ~

At Te Wairua, the evening weka calls were followed once it was dark by the less strident but equally distinctive calls of little blue penguins connecting with their partners as they came ashore to nest on the land. On a calm night, we could hear them from all along the shoreline and from Maud Island across Apuau Channel. In the lights from the house, we would often see them singly or in pairs making their way up our road to nests in the bush. Over the years, we had nesting boxes built to attract more to Te Wairua. What a gift to share our land with these 10-inch-tall miniatures of larger species to be found all around NZ's South Island, on the sub-Antarctic Islands and on Antarctica itself.

We shared our beaches with Oyster Catchers, jet-black wading birds whose pink legs, long orange bills, red eyes and excitable disposition led to our calling them Clown Birds. When we first arrived, there was a small flock on our beaches, but as Pelorous Sound's stocks of fish and shellfish were depleted over the years, our resident Oyster Catchers were reduced to one pair, who treated us with affection. They would call loudly and run towards us whenever we went down to the shore. They would also show off their babies to us in the years they managed to produce a brood.

Another precious resident was the *kiore*, a rat brought by Maori from tropical Polynesia. I described my first meeting with one in a letter to an American friend in December 1995:

"I stepped out of our truck a few days ago about a quarter-of-a-mile above the house and there at my feet was a kiore, small and chubby like a hamster. It just sat 18 inches away, checking me out. I reached out to it, and it retreated slowly into the grass on the edge of the track."

Kiore had been almost totally eradicated except on Stewart Island and a few other islands around the NZ coast, so I considered it a rare gift to have them at Te Wairua.

Another gift on the land, less rare, was glow worms. They are small, no larger than a grain of rice, and they suspend themselves in wet banks beneath ferns and along streams. To catch insects, they drape down long luminous silver threads, somewhat thicker than spider webs, with a gentle pulsing light. In her journal, Jo wrote: "It is a most remarkable sight which reminds me of being across the Bay from San Francisco and seeing the lights of the city through dense shifting fog."

To complete this inventory of the wild "animals" on our land, we go from the smallest to the largest: from glow worms to boar and deer – leaving possums aside for now.

~ ~ ~

My objective when we moved to New Zealand was to continue to lead both workshops and tours. I envisioned two tours a year and several workshops. In initiating the tours while still in the US, I arranged everything myself, except international travel for group members. I recruited participants through magazine advertisements and sent out flyers to mailing lists built up from membership rosters of transformative organisations. I arranged transport in the target country and reserved accommodations. This was a huge job before the internet, as it had to be done by mail. I continued in this way once we got to Te Wairua, but over the years, the work got easier as almost everything could be done by email, and my Eagle Connection website brought participant enquiries.

I was eager to have workshop and tour groups come onto our land, and we were able to do this by utilising the two holiday houses the Leovs rented out at Te Towaka. Group members travelled daily between Te Towaka and Te Wairua on a hired launch. Jo did not enjoy having groups visit Te Wairua, and each year she resisted the arrangement, urging me to meet with the groups instead at Te Towaka. I argued successfully that we couldn't take tax deductions for Te Wairua unless we worked with groups on our land.

My original vision had gone even further. I saw Te Wairua as a place for transformative teachers and writers from around the world to come for sabbatical retreats. I would have treasured the interactions, and I regret we did not implement this.

~ ~ ~

After our move to Te Wairua, my first tour was with a group in New Zealand from late February 1995. Initially, there were four women signed on, but one withdrew in mid-January, forfeiting her deposit. I was due to depart from Te Wairua by float plane on February 23, but I had to cancel the flight because of bad weather. Fortunately, the Searles were driving out that day, and they gave me a ride. It was a wild journey in torrential rain, and we barely made it to Havelock through Pelorus River floodwaters, which closed the highway behind us. With no buses running, I teamed up with 10 other people stranded in Havelock to rent a van to get to the Inter-Island Ferry in Picton. I was in Auckland to meet my tour members (two Americans and one Canadian) and start exploring from February 25.

The aspect of the tour that was strengthened this time was Maori contacts.

Letter to Nicky Mendenhall, May 17, 1995

"It is a time of great upheaval in Maori-Pakeha relations, as Maori language, cultural self-expression, and spirituality revives. This is accompanied by forthright challenges to Pakeha to make good on the nation's claim that we consist of two equal peoples – some of the challenges are very confrontative and deeply disturbing to many Pakeha given that they are couched in traditional forms and most often demand restoration of tribal lands. I find it a very exciting and creative time, and it was wonderful to have the opportunity on the tour to discuss the issues with Maori women and men who are active in these movements.

'Maori time' is rather like Indian time: You can never be sure that scheduled events will happen until they actually do. Concerns of family, community and tribe – particularly where rituals are involved – take precedence over anything involving outsiders. I felt it was a healthy learning experience for our group to be thrown off-balance on two or three occasions when things didn't happen at all as expected. Of course, there's always some other rich experience that emerges, as we have found so often in India."

Jo was delighted that my month's absence gave her a chance to be alone at Te Wairua. In her journal, she wrote:

"I love the silence, the lack of interruption, the seamless flow from one activity to another. Imagine no other houses or humans in sight, except for an occasional boat; no lights at night, only stars and the moon in all its phases; no sound other than a distant boat, the water cascading down the little valley on one side of our house, the native songbirds, the wind through the forest, the cicadas, the gentle lapping of the ocean as the tide changes. How utterly wonderful it is to be this alone. I truly love it! I feel so blessed with this new way of life, to finally be free from having to explain so much about how I love solitude."

~ ~ ~

It was March 23 before I was back at Te Wairua, and the following week Jo and I took the big step we had been planning ever since the death of our old cat Sam in Fairfax three years before, i.e. to find his reincarnated spirit. She was a fluffy grey tabby kitten waiting for us at the SPCA in Nelson, and we named her Rai after the beautiful valley through which we drove to and from Te Wairua. I persuaded Jo to get a second smooth-haired black kitten as a companion for Rai. We called him Kia, which in Maori means "good wish" or "intention."

All our neighbours warned us when we told them we were getting a cat that cats are killers of native birds, and some of them urged us not to proceed with our plan. We were not as naïve as they seemed to assume. Quite the contrary, Jo had an extraordinary ability to train her cats not to attack birds, and this she did with Rai and Kia. What was more, in driving off feral cats, they almost certainly helped to protect the birds.

The relationship Rai and Kia developed with weka was fun to watch. The first thing the kittens had to learn was not to fall asleep outdoors in a place where the weka could get to them. If they did, a weka would invariably sneak up from behind and peck them. For their part, the cats would chase a weka for fun every now and then – but always an adult or adolescent weka, never any of the fluffy black babies.

A fortnight after we got the kittens, I took the boat to Havelock to pick up Carol Dommet, who was visiting for five days. She had joined my group in February and early March for the North Island section of the tour, so by now, she felt like an old friend. She and Jo had a great time discussing ideas for the redecoration of the house, and Carol volunteered to return to help with painting, which she said she enjoyed.

I had arrived home exhausted from the NZ tour, and Jo and I decided we should cancel plans to travel to the US to teach in the 1995 Naropa Summer Program. We were scheduled to lead a Himalayan tour in September-October, and we saw that the turnaround time between the two programmes was insufficient given the amount of work it took to maintain the property. To our great pleasure, we had also received an invitation to lead a five-day workshop at Esalen over the 1995 Thanksgiving weekend, and this we were successful in having moved to late June 1996.

~ ~ ~

Letter to Bronwen and John, May 21, 1995:

"Just after Easter, we went to Nelson and lugged back in our truck a BRAND-NEW WASHING MACHINE! Can you imagine what sort of excitement that is for us settlers? The machine washes real loads of laundry. Jo is in seventh heaven. And the old one (circa 1965), which came with the house and which washed one sheet per load if it was having a good day, sits dismembered outside the back door. Weka regularly steal coloured plastic items, jandals, scrubbing brushes, etc., but they seem impervious to our pleas to drag the washing machine into the bush! Perhaps they are slightly discouraged by the fact that it has a one-foot-square lump of concrete as a counterweight in its base. I think it was constructed in a local blacksmithy. Jo commented that our driveway looks like 'Ma and Pa Kettle Move In.' If the weka fail us, perhaps elves will miraculously hoist it into the back of the truck so it can go to the dump on our next trip to civilisation.

"More wild excitement: Modular furniture for our two

studies, ordered from Nelson six weeks before, arrived at our wharf at 11:00 am on a recent Sunday on Johnson's Barge. What fun the kittens and we had breaking open the cartons, finding all the pieces, scratching our heads over the incomprehensible instructions, searching out all the really difficult tiny fastening things and putting them together. Oh, I forgot the circus trying to clear enough space to erect the new beauties in offices already full of makeshift furniture."

Letter to Edie Farwell, December 23, 1995

"Our hard work on the land keeps us fit, if often very sore. This is our excuse for our big indulgence: A hot tub, more correctly, a spa pool. As you know, we're hot-tub freaks and don't mind admitting it! This one is close to the house on the edge of the bush, with a lovely view down to the beach and bay. The 'neighbourhood builder,' Michael Brennan, and I poured a concrete platform back in August; our next-door neighbour, Derek Searle, who is a refrigeration engineer masquerading as an electrician, installed underground wiring in September; the tub arrived by barge in late November; and the installer had it up and running on December 4.

"I put 'neighbourhood builder' in quotes because, although Michael lives only four miles away as the crow flies, it takes one-and-a-quarter hours to get from his place to ours by circuitous FWD mountain tracks. As you can understand, getting things done around here takes an inordinate amount of time. If items are needed – bolts or wire, for example – there's no way to run down to the shopping centre to pick them up. Unless one of our two neighbours happens to have them, we have to wait until at least the next week's mailboat for them to be sent out from town. Because of this, plus the fact that Michael is always working on half-a-dozen jobs at once, it took us three months to get the efficient wood burner installed in Jo's studio downstairs. My how we appreciated the warmth once we got it – and maybe that's the teaching here: You really get to appreciate how much goes into the amenities that make life comfortable.

"We went to India in September to lead our Himalayan tour and were away for almost six weeks, during which our friend Carol Dommet house sat and cared for the cats. The timing was good. It helped to put our wonderful life here at Te Wairua in perspective. Mind you, after our months of isolation in the bush, it was mind-bending to plunge into the tumult of Delhi! We had 16 participants from four countries on this tour, a bigger group than usual and a very compatible one."

As this letter makes clear, in our life at Te Wairua we were dependent on the help of friends. We took Rai and Kia with us on our supply runs to Nelson, but for more extended trips, we needed someone to house and cat sit, and over the years, we recruited a circle of people who were happy to enjoy the seclusion of the Marlborough Sounds for a few weeks. In addition to New Zealanders, these included friends from Australia and the US.

Neighbours like the Brennans and the Searles, with years of Sounds experience behind them, gave us invaluable advice on property maintenance, backed up with practical assistance. Both Michael Brennan and Derek Searle had mechanical diggers, which they were very willing to put to work on our access road to restore culverts and surfaces damaged in the periodic heavy rains. Sometimes they declined to accept payment for this work, and we had to find suitable thank-you gifts.

Getting routine help on the land, by contrast, was more difficult than expected. We had imagined there would be people living in the area who would like regular employment, but Sounds people were not of the 9-5 crowd. Although many were in need of cash, they valued their free time and their escape from routine. When we did find someone willing to work, there was the problem of their getting to and from our place. They could not come in by road, which meant they had to have a boat of their own or I would have to pick them up in our boat at one of the neighbouring bays, weather permitting.

From September 1996, Brian Plaisier started working fairly regularly for us. The Plaisiers were migrants from the Netherlands who had bought 100 acres of forested mountain top to start an eco-resort. They named this Tui Wilderness Reserve. It was about five km from us further out on Pelorus Sound, with stunning views in every direction. When we met, Brian was in his mid-thirties, his wife Ellen in her late twenties. During our first year at Te Wairua, Ellen had a daughter, Leona; two years later, son Liam was born; and in 2008, another daughter, Esmae, arrived. The family became our closest Sounds friends.

Immensely plucky, Ellen and Brian initially lived in a tent while he built a house. He followed that with a second house for paying guests, and as the years went by, he added more guest accommodations, as also aviaries for endangered birds, lizards, and insects in a collaboration with DOC. Brian had been a certified marine electrical engineer in Holland, but he did not take the qualifying exams in New Zealand because, he said, he wanted to spend his time developing the eco-resort, this despite the fact they were strapped for cash. The Plaisiers had a boat, and Brian agreed to come and work for us, on average one day a week, but he made no secret of the fact he regretted the time away from Tui Reserve. He and I had a similar robust sense of humour, and we enjoyed working together on the rugged land.

Jo to Cathy and Ralph Metzner, March 10, 1997:

> "We are very happy with a new upgrade of our water system, which involved the installation by John and Brian of

fancy new filters. They got it all in place, with the water flowing beautifully through the filters .... but no water was reaching the house. So they had to trace every foot of the pipe the half mile to the house, struggling through dense manuka and other undergrowth on steep, rocky ground. It took them three hours and the replacement of two rusted pipe connectors before the blockage was found. When they did find it, the pressure blew wads of mud and rust all over them. I was mightily amused when these two filthy, jubilant, cheering figures struggled out of the bush to drink a celebratory beer."

Jo and I shared with Ellen and Brian a determination that our land would never be subdivided, and, like them, we placed an open space covenant on our property with the Queen Elizabeth II Trust. This was a national trust created by an Act of Parliament to register privately owned land of conservation value as permanent open space and, where resources would allow, to assist the owners with fencing and other facilities to protect the land. In the case of Te Wairua, all the property was placed in trust with the exception of an acre stretching from the house to the seashore.

~ ~ ~

Everywhere I had lived in the world, after a period of acclimatisation, I wrote "Letters to the Editor." I had been back in New Zealand for little more than a year before I penned a piece to the *Otago Daily Times*, February 12, 1996:

"Dunedin can be proud of its Mayor for her good sense and courage in refusing to accompany the trade delegation to China. By challenging the policy of business as usual with the world's largest totalitarian regime, Mayor Turner has done all New Zealanders a service.

"Surely it is inconsistent for a nation which has taken pride in opposing France's nuclear testing to wheel and deal with a China that adamantly opposes international nuclear controls. China continues nuclear testing at will, dumping its radio-active wastes in minority population areas like Tibet and Islamic Sinkiang.

"When Nelson Mandela visited these shores, he congratulated us for our boycott of apartheid South Africa and spoke of how vital it was that New Zealand and other countries isolated South Africa's authoritarian regime. Why are we not applying this lesson to China, a country that brutally suppresses dissent and denies freedom of belief and worship? In a manner reminiscent of Nazi Germany, the Beijing regime is attempting to exterminate the Tibetans to provide 'living space' for ethnic Han Chinese. China uses convicts and other forced labour to manufacture low-priced export goods which undercut the products of other nations. The results can be observed on the shelves of almost any NZ shop.

"Boycotting China may be economically costly in the short run, but it is the right thing to do. Well done, Mayor Turner!"

With the copy of the letter I sent the Mayor, I added:

"My wife and I have the good fortune to spend a short time each year in Dharamsala with His Holiness the Dalai Lama. On our most recent visit last October, he was asked by a member of our group why the U.N. would not vote in support of self-determination for the Tibetans. 'Money,' he replied. 'The lure of the Chinese economy keeps politicians in many countries silent.' Bless you for swimming against that tide."

By this time, the Internet was gaining traction in New Zealand, but good old-fashioned mail was still our chief means of keeping in touch with our worldwide circle of friends. When we saw on NZTV a programme on Rupert Sheldrake's research on telepathic communication between dogs and humans, we wrote to let him know of his fame in our far corner of the world. (Rupert had guest-lectured in my classes at CIIS on his visits to San Francisco in the late '80s.) He wrote back from London, September 25, 1996:

> "Dear Jo & John, Many thanks for your letter. It was great to hear from you and to know you're in such a beautiful place. The photograph is stunning. I didn't know that this dog research had been on TV in New Zealand. It has certainly attracted a lot of publicity recently. The experiments are going exceptionally well.
>
> "By God's grace, we are all well. Jill is busy with her workshops, our sons are now six and eight and flourishing, and I am very busy with the research on pets and other projects outlined in my book, Seven Experiments that Could Change the World. I also have two books with Matthew Fox published this year, one called Natural Grace (Bloomsbury, London) and the other The Physics of Angels, being published next month by Harper Collins, San Francisco.
>
> "I'm going over to San Francisco later this week for ten days. We didn't go to Hollyhock this year, nor indeed to North America, but went to Ireland instead, where we had a wonderful time."

~ ~ ~

After years without contact, son Stephen surfaced unexpectedly in our lives in October 1996. From his mother, Jenni, who was still living in the US, I learnt that he was getting married, and she gave me an address for him in Smyrna, Georgia, warning that he was now calling himself Nik Eriksen. Jo's feeling was that I should not attempt to contact him, as she believed he would not respond. I decided, however, to send good wishes for the marriage and a wedding present of $500. In return, I received three wedding photos, and a note of thanks signed "Nik and Sherri." After this, he disappeared for another decade and a half.

— CHAPTER FOURTEEN —

Rekindling the Fire

"The creeks are the world with all its stimulus and beauty.
I live there. But the mountains are home."
– Annie Dillard

Jo to Carol Dommet, Wednesday, February 18, 1997:

"The Great Fishhook Adventure: A settler story that is
long but entertaining, the sort of story that makes regular people glad they stay on asphalt in cities. A few weeks
ago at Te Towaka Sports Day we met Jude Sonneland, the
District Nurse, who is based at French Pass. She asked if
she could come to visit us sometime, just to get to know
us, and we agreed enthusiastically. Yesterday she called
and suggested she come this morning, so we set a time.

"Soon after her call, John gathered his fishing gear
and the mailbag to go down to the wharf to fish while
he waited for the mailboat. The fish were biting, and
John caught a big one and then a little one, too small to
keep. Just at that crucial moment, he heard the first deep
rumblings of the mailboat, which then takes about five
minutes before it reaches our wharf. Perhaps it was the
feeling that he needed to rush a bit, but John grappling
with the young wriggling cod, speared his right thumb
with the hook. So there he was dressed in his settler finery
and fishing regalia, the sort of scene that tourists on the

mailboat think picturesque and perfect for their cameras and videos. Unfortunately, John and the young cod were attached to the hook deeply embedded in his thumb, which in turn was attached to the fishing pole. As you can envision, this called for two free hands just to hold the fishing gear and fish, but John also needed to be able to exchange mailbags. He did not want to be humiliated in front of all those people, and there was the small matter of pain every time the fish wiggled.

"The first I knew of the problem was a loud bellowing coming from below the house. I went out on the veranda and saw John and his rod. He shouted the pertinent details and said I needed to dash down to the wharf to do the mailbag exchange. So I dashed, not terribly concerned at that stage about John's thumb, but more concerned about the fact I was wearing a long wrap-around skirt. Early on in our days at Te Wairua, I was wearing it when I met the mailboat, unaware that the far end of the wharf tends to be windy even if it's calm elsewhere. On that occasion, I had uneventfully handed over the mailbag, waved to the onboard summer load of tourists and turned to walk back up the wharf. Just at that moment, there was a gust of wind, and I flashed them my entire posterior sans underwear.

"Nevertheless, yesterday, I dashed out onto the wharf just in time. I held my skirt. I waved but did not tarry, and then I rushed back to find John, who was crouched in the doorway of our ute with a knife in one hand and the fish attached to his thumb in the other. By this time, he had bitten through the line to detach the dangling fishing pole.

"Once again, not grasping the scope of the problem, I murmured sadly that we should try to save the fish. Perhaps preoccupied, John took this with considerable calm. We decided to walk up to the house to see if we could find some better tools. I kept thinking this was something John and I ought to be able to handle. I mean, we're settlers, and settlers sometimes face perplexing problems that we just have to deal with on our own. But once we got into the house, all I could do was cut off the end of the fishhook with wire cutters, and then we were faced with either pushing the hook all the way through John's thumb or cutting it out with a knife. Ick!

"By this time, both of us were shaking a bit, neither of us enthused about the sort of pain that was going to cause. The fish, by now, had slid off the cut hook and unfortunately passed into fish heaven. We spent the next few minutes with my pacing and John poised with a knife in his trembling left hand, trying to summon up courage. I fetched scissors of various sizes, razor blades, disinfectant, tweezers, and a mild herbal calming pill – which I took!

"This was not looking promising, so I finally suggested we call Jude at the French Pass Clinic to see if maybe she'd like to come for her visit sooner than scheduled. But alas, Judy was not in. I got her answering machines at the clinic and on her mobile phone. So we waited. John then dazzled me by going on with various chores. The pain was not too bad, he said, except when he caught the hook on something.

"Jude finally phoned an hour later. She'd been on call at Elaine Bay. She got to us at 4:30, and we joked that we had been so eager for her visit that we decided one of us should injure ourselves. The most comforting thing – to me but probably not to poor John – was it soon became clear that few settlers – real or neo – would have handled this situation on their own. It took Jude well over half an hour to get the hook out, and John got four shots of pain-killer in his thumb. It was only after he went down to the workshop and got a similar hook that Jude could see how this one was shaped. She had been trying to pull it out while I braced John's thumb, but finally, she had to push mightily before it poked through the skin. Feeling queasy? So was John, just a tad.

"Amazingly, John's thumb today is not very painful. It is a bit bruised, and there are two small gashes about half an inch apart, but you'd never guess he'd had a fishhook in it. Jude has done this many times in settler homes."

On Boxing Day 1997, we again had to call for Jude's help for the same patient, but with a more serious accident. Clearing a track through the bush with a chainsaw, I carelessly struck a small rock, and the saw blade rebounded onto my left knee, slicing it almost to the bone. Fortunately, it did not hit an artery, but blood was pouring from the cut. I dumped the chainsaw and raced for the house about a quarter of a mile away, concerned that I might faint from loss of blood. Calling Jo, I lay down on the concrete outside the back door with my leg stretched up a pole to reduce the blood flow. As Jo tied a tourniquet around my thigh, weka circled in the hope they could get blood.

Jo phoned Jude, and fortunately, she was at home. I lost track of time, so I have no idea how long it was before she arrived. She immediately went to work right there on the stoop, cleaning and sanitising the wound and injecting me with local anaesthetic before sewing up the gash and bandaging my leg. All three of us needed strong cups of tea before Jude departed with our heartfelt thanks. Although the stitching job did not look operation-room perfect, the knee seemed to be healing well until about six months later when it began to swell and ache. I guessed some dirt had escaped Jude's notice. When I accidentally bumped the knee one day, the old wound split partially open, and puss oozed out. I cleaned it, swished it out with disinfectant and pulled it together with a plaster, and it has been fine ever since.

~ ~ ~

No more gory stories, I promise you, but there is other illness to discuss. As I have mentioned, our first year at Te Wairua was a huge struggle for Jo, given her severe depletion of energy with CFS. Fortunately, early in 1996, we met Nelson journalist Melanie Thornton. She and her younger sister Fiona were also CFS sufferers, and on our visits to Nelson every six weeks or so, Jo and I began spending time with them at their central city cottage. Fiona was so ill that she was bedridden, and at the women's request, I served as a timekeeper to keep the visits short enough so the three did not exhaust one another.

It was from the Thornton sisters that we learnt of Tim Ewer, a GP in the village of Mapua about 35 km west of Nelson, who specialised in the treatment of immune disorders, including CFS. In September 1996, Jo began regular consultations with him. Step by slow step, he guided her back to full health. I wrote about his methods in my 1997 book *Other Ways of Knowing*:

> "In dealing with these intractable diseases, his approach is holistic. In obtaining a patient's medical history, Dr. Ewer gives careful attention to environmental, nutritional and psychospiritual factors, and as a diagnostic tool, he uses 'the person's own body as a biofeedback device' through a bioenergetic system of muscle testing. Treatment integrates what he describes as 'a variety of therapeutic approaches in order to help the person balance his or her physical, mental, emotional and spiritual self.'"

As a result of muscle testing, he suggested a modified diet for Jo, removing among other things, milk, sugar, and white flour. This helped her energy immediately. Tim prescribed herbal and flower remedies. On his recommendation, Jo consulted a past-life regressionist. She had a dentist remove her mercury amalgam fillings, and she undertook bowel detoxification.

Tim also gave me a physical examination, which revealed an irregular heartbeat. An ECG test and further examination by a cardiologist established that my heartbeat, though irregular, was steady and of no great concern. My blood pressure, however, was too high, and Tim put me on hypertension medications. He also recommended I consult John Black, whose field was Traditional Chinese Medicine. John treated me with acupuncture and herbs. With Tim's encouragement, Jo also started working with John. Here is her description of the experience:

"John is probably mid-forties, a small, wiry man, with dark shaggy bangs streaked with grey and a dark-flecked, neatish beard. In his consulting room, he goes barefoot and wears loose cotton pants and a singlet. He spent eight years living and studying in China. He speaks fluent Mandarin and has a Chinese wife, Zhifang, and a darling two-year-old daughter, Yulan, who spent some of her time with us in the little treatment room. John works out of his house, as many NZ medical practitioners do. In this first session, he spent well over an hour taking a thorough history, all of which he wrote down in Chinese! This was followed by a lengthy session of acupuncture and moxibustion. I like him a lot. He's got an easy sense of humour, and he's quiet, kind, and caring."

Jo and I both became regular patients of John, and the whole family became close friends. This included son Daniel, born in January 1998, and Zhifang's father and mother, who regularly visited from China until her father's death in 2011.

It was about the same time that Jo and I became patients of John Black that we began having regular massages from Anna Szefczyk Moore, who became another lifelong friend.

Anna had grown up in a severely dysfunctional Polish family in Adelaide and had come to New Zealand at 15 in 1970 with a Kiwi boyfriend a few years older, whom she married. In their 12 years together, they travelled back and forth between NZ and Australia and had three children, who ended up living in Queensland and Thailand. After studying massage therapy, herbalism and psychology in her twenties and thirties, Anna became a social worker and counsellor. She moved to Nelson in the 1980s, divorced her first husband and remarried. By the time we met her in the late nineties, she had returned to massage therapy.

~ ~ ~

I have mentioned my book, *Other Ways of Knowing*. This had its origins in the courses I had developed from the mid-seventies at the University of Michigan designed to jolt students into the realisation that contemporary organisational and technological developments could have disastrous outcomes, including eco-system collapse. It had been the focus of my work during an extended sabbatical leave from summer 1980 through summer 1982 when I held fellowships at the ANU, MIT and the Indian Institute of Advanced Studies. The writing had been put on hold during my years as President of CIIS, from 1983, but again the book was my focus during a leave period in the village of Naggar in the Himalayan Kullu Valley in 1989, a location chosen so I would be writing amongst people living by "other ways of knowing."

The core manuscript was complete by the time Jo and I returned to the US in January 1990, but I kept adding material as I sought a publisher. It was 1996 before that publisher finally emerged: Inner Traditions, a small independent press in Rochester, Vermont. Its editors encouraged me to add more personal material, and in 1997 they produced a meticulously edited and beautifully designed 260-page paperback entitled

Other Ways of Knowing: Recharting Our Future with Ageless Wisdom, the subtitle a contribution from Jo, who also gave me invaluable editing advice drawn from her 20 years of US journalism experience.

Inner Traditions said they kept their titles in print for as long as there were sales (few publishers do that), but they warned that they had virtually no promotional budget, so I would have to hustle the book myself. Consequently, it did not have an extensive readership, but the attention it gained amongst like-minded advocates of sustainability resulted in invitations to contribute in the following decade to innovative academic programmes in New Zealand, Australia and the UK

As soon as I received copies, I sent one to Geoff Park with thanks for the inspiration he had provided with his 1995 *Nga Uruora – The Groves of Life: Ecology and History in a New Zealand Landscape*. In response, Geoff invited me to join "The Basket," an informal group of writers, teachers and thinkers who gathered periodically for weekends at his Wellington house. He also recommended a 1996 book he thought I might enjoy with the intriguing title: *The Deep Sky Waits on the Outskirts of Town*. The work of another NZ ecologist, had parallels to my book, he said. The author was Annette Lees. When I attempted to buy *The Deep Sky*, I discovered it was already out of print, and it was 18 months before I could get my hands on the Nelson Library copy. As it spoke in a personal, lyrical voice, I loved it from the first few pages.

Then I became increasingly mystified. The family stories the author said she was told in her childhood were the same stories Dad had told Bronwen and me. Lo and behold, Annette was my second cousin, granddaughter of my father's younger brother, William. When I sent Annette a copy of *Other Ways of Knowing*, I told her how delighted I was to have discovered *The Deep Sky* and said I was struck by the parallels in our lives.

> "Besides the fact we were woven by the same family stories, our childhood experiences of exploring enchanted

places in nature awoke in us both a desire to gain practical ecological knowledge combined with a passion for the mystical qualities of the earth. I'm delighted to realise we were at work at exactly the same time on books that were the product of these shared sensibilities."

In reply, Annette sent me a copy of *The Deep Sky,* which she inscribed: "To John for returning a missing strand of family." There was one more twist in the tale: Leila, Annette's only sibling, proved to be a shamanic teacher!

~ ~ ~

The half dozen gatherings of "The Basket" in which I participated in the late nineties gave me an acquaintance with philosopher John Patterson, author of *Exploring Maori Values,* and eco-historian David Young, author of *Woven By Water: Histories from the Whanganui River.* It also gave me friendships with Joan Ropiha and Peter Horsley.

Joan, who is Ngati Kahungunu, had grown up in a traditional Maori family on iwi land on the Mahia Peninsula south of Gisborne, speaking only Te Reo Maori until her teens. Despite this, she had excelled at university and had taken advantage of her traditional background to write a brilliant M.A. thesis at Victoria University on customary Maori agricultural practices. When I first met her, Joan had a salaried position in Te Puni Kokiri/Ministry of Maori Development in Wellington but subsequently left that to return to her home marae to provide leadership on conservation issues. When I attended my first gathering of "The Basket," I took my drum and introduced the group to shamanic journeying. Joan had powerful journeys, which led her to reveal to me that she was *matakite,* a clairvoyant. Our friendship has blossomed in the years since, and she has joined me in "Spirit in Nature" workshops and as a co-leader on New Zealand tours.

When I first met Peter Horsley, he was on the faculty of Massey University, Palmerston North, teaching innovative interdisciplinary programmes in the School of Resource & Environmental Planning. A lawyer by training, in the 1970s, he had initiated the earliest Waitangi Tribunal hearings that resulted in the Treaty of Waitangi being recognised as a source of NZ constitutional law. It has since become a pivotal fulcrum for an emerging bicultural and plural society. By the nineties, he was a leading advocate of collaborative management by DOC and iwi and other community groups of sacred sites and similar lands important to cultural heritage. He was involved with numerous such initiatives along the west coast of the North Island, and he organised visits by my tour groups to some of them. He also invited me to serve as an examiner for several doctoral students at Massey, and when I visited the Palmerston North campus, he arranged for me to give talks to community groups. In the following decade, he became involved with US universities in study-abroad programmes, and he recruited me to lecture to the student groups he brought to NZ. Peter became and remains one of my closest friends.

It was on behalf of my fellow members of "The Basket" that I wrote a letter to the editor of *Forest & Bird* magazine on December 15, 1998, drawing attention to the absence of any mention of partnership with Maori in the previous month's issue visioning the Society's next quarter century.

"There was no acknowledgment that Maori should and will have a major role in shaping the ecological future of this country. Are we blind to the centrality for Maori of concerns about this land and its life-forms embodied in their self-definition as tangata whenua, 'people of the land'? We believe our Society will be guilty of both neglect and arrogance if we rely solely on the brief 150 years of Pakeha experience of New Zealand eco-systems to the exclusion of the 1,000 or more years of Maori experience.

It is from this experience that the ecological concepts kaitiaki (guardian), mauri (life force), wairua (spirit) and whenua (land as nurturer) have emerged. There is much here for us to learn. We believe the environmental future of New Zealand can best be prospered in relationship with Maori."

~ ~ ~

Preparing to leave the US for New Zealand in 1994, I had to dispose of most of my 3,000 academic books, but I took with me those I felt I would need to complete *Other Ways of Knowing* and to write a long-postponed book on an entrepreneurial family in West Bengal. In 1966, I had discovered that the Sahana family of Bankura District had a treasure trove of documents, most notably diaries from 1900-1960 kept by the then head of the family, Satya Kinkar Sahana.

The family were large landholders, rice millers and mine owners, and Satya Kinkar was the most interesting of all. In addition to being a successful entrepreneur, he was active in district and provincial politics; he regularly wrote for Calcutta political and literary journals; he published five books of essays, poems and religious commentaries; and in his fifties and sixties was a mainstay of the provincial Hindu Mahasabha, then India's main neo-fascist political party. He had charged his sons with the task of finding an author to write his biography, and they had no doubt I was that author when I showed up on their doorstep. They gave me all the diaries to take back to Calcutta for microfilming, and they promised me access to their other papers. It was a great find, building directly on the work I had been doing and opening up a number of new issues I was keen to explore.

My next leave in India was 1971–73, and in addition to fleshing out material on all branches of the Sahana family back to the eighteenth century, I expanded the research into neighbouring areas of what was then Bihar, where the Sahanas had acquired coal and mica mines as the railways expanded north-westward in the nineteenth century. I returned to Michigan feeling I had all I needed for a book. I published a lengthy article entitled "The Rural Parvenu," but when I went to New Zealand in 1994, I still had the book to write. The work on the land at Te Wairua, along with my workshop teaching and tour leading, got in the way, and I lost the ambition for a return to monograph writing. I am left with a feeling of guilt that I let the Sahana family down. In 2015, I gifted the research materials—a gold mine for a doctoral thesis—to the New Zealand India Research Institute at Victoria University in Wellington.

"For as long as one lives on the land or regularly returns to it, a fire burns there (*ahi ka*). But if one goes away and does not return, the fire goes out (*aki mataotao*)." This *whakatauki* is quoted by New Zealand anthropologist Michael Jackson, who, like me, went overseas for doctoral study and made an overseas career. In his 2006 memoir, *An Accidental Anthropologist*, he writes:

> "In all my years away, I had never repined for New Zealand, for the simple reason that I had never entirely abandoned the idea that someday I might return there to live. Mine was a voluntary exile. Yet this had not prevented the fires from going out, and I had done little to rekindle them. I had come home often, to be sure, stayed with my parents in Auckland, seen a few old friends, but on each visit felt more and more a stranger to the country where I was raised."

George Orwell, in his 1939 autobiographical novel *Coming Up for Air*, reflected on the experience of returning after many years to a childhood town he called Lower Binfield:

> "It's a queer experience to go over a bit of country you haven't seen in twenty years. You remember it in great

detail, and you remember it all wrong. All the distances are different, and the landmarks seem to have moved about. You keep feeling, surely this hill used to be a lot steeper - surely that turning was on the other side of the road? And on the other hand you'll have memories which are perfectly accurate, but which only belong to one particular occasion. You'll remember, for instance, a corner of a field, on a wet day in winter, with the grass so green that it's almost blue and a rotten gatepost covered with lichen and a cow standing in the grass and looking at you. And you'll go back after twenty years and be surprised because the cow isn't standing in the same place and looking at you with the same expression."

Returning to my homeland after an even longer period away, I faced the same question as Orwell and experienced similar discomfort at the answer.

"Can we get back to the life we used to live, or is it gone forever? Well, I've had my answer. The old life's finished, and to go back looking for it is just a waste of time. There's no way back to Lower Binfield .... All those years, Lower Binfield had been tucked away somewhere or other in my mind, a sort of quiet corner that I could step back into when I felt like it, and finally, I'd stepped back into it and found that it didn't exist."

In a letter to my old swimming teammate in Christchurch, Ian MacDonald, I lamented the fact that, like Michael Jackson, the fires had gone out for me, and, like George Orwell, I too had found "there's no way back to Lower Binfield:"

"I have to tell you that returning to NZ after so long away was an unexpectedly strange experience. I left when I was 24 and returned aged 59. At that time, I had been back only for very brief visits in the eighties and early nineties, and my immediate family was gone, my parents having followed my sister to the UK in the mid-sixties. Consequently, when I first came back, memories of my childhood, teens, and early twenties felt a bit unreal – like a disconnected clip from an old movie. Even visiting the places I lived, surprisingly, did not initially dispel this feeling of unreality because I experienced them as stage sets on which the old movie was filmed. Being in touch with people like you with whom I shared those years and who have memories of the same events has steadily made them more substantial. I do feel a bit like Rip Van Winkle, though – and I have the beard to match!"

Attending reunions gradually restored for me some continuity between my NZ youth and my middle-aged homecoming – reunions of my high school class and sports teams, rugby club, university History Department and Australian tour swimming team. I did not achieve the full integration of my two NZ lives, but now at least (in Orwell's words), "the past was sticking out into the present."

The first reunion I attended was in August 1998, a gathering at CBHS of the school's entering class of 1948. I described the experience in a letter to sister Bronwen:

"I went with considerable trepidation but was agreeably surprised to find a warm, gentle group of men. Remarkably little 'Jokey Bloke' stuff. I was struck by how positive these men are about their lives, expressing gratitude for the quality of the education we were given and our good luck in being born in a rich country in a generation that missed all the century's wars. I realise this may have been a skewed sample. Only one-quarter of the total class (70 out of 280) attended, and these most likely are the men who feel best about their lives. Nonetheless, the absence of cynicism was in striking contrast to the pervasive tone of the US academic world in which I spent most of my adult years. One of the most surprising things was how many of the men remembered Mum – and with affection. A number of them said they had appreciated how much she did for the school."

~ ~ ~

By the late nineties, Jo and I had an established pattern of visits to Nelson about every six weeks, interspersed with tour and workshop leading. We found Nelson a far more interesting city than Blenheim and had given up regular visits there. In Nelson we stayed in a motel in Tahunanui, and the motel owners, Viv and Lance Grant, became friends. They had won our hearts by welcoming our cats. We were, however, spending $300-400 for accommodation each town trip, so we decided it would make better financial sense to buy a Nelson house to serve as our base for the purchase of supplies for Te Wairua, visits to doctors and dentists and as our way station for tour departures and returns.

What we had in mind when we started the search was a modest place with two bedrooms in a cheap area of town, but not liking the houses we were shown, we started to look at higher-priced places. We found many Nelson real estate agents surprisingly casual about follow up, which made it difficult to get a lot done in the few days we had for house inspections on our six-weekly town visits.

Ultimately, in 1998, we found a place we liked, the front unit in a two-unit townhouse in Enner Glynn, an upscale Nelson hill suburb in the south of the city close to Stoke. When we contacted the agent to make an offer, we discovered we had been pipped at the post by another buyer. The realtor, however, said that the larger back unit was empty and might be available for purchase. He contacted the owner, a Kiwi businessman in Japan, who agreed to its listing for sale with chattels. Selling points were its quiet location behind the street-side front unit and its wonderful view west across Tasman Bay to the northernmost ranges of the Alps. A spacious place on three levels, it had three bedrooms with two bathrooms, and on the ground floor a double garage converted to an office, fully carpeted. We stretched our budget and bought it.

Taking occupation was seriously delayed by winter flooding in the Sounds, with major landslides closing our Te Wairua access road for six weeks. We finally devised a way to escape. Johnsons Barge came into our beach at low tide, and we drove our fully loaded ute up the ramp to squeeze aboard amid large containers of live salmon. The cats could apparently hear the fish and were goggle-eyed for the entire hour-and-a-half voyage to Havelock. From there it was a little more than an hour's drive to Nelson, and as darkness fell with the kittens exploring their new territory, Jo and I were eating pizza and drinking celebratory champagne on the deck of our townhouse as Guy Fawkes Day fireworks lit the sky.

We might not have been celebrating that evening had we known about the thousands of dollars we would have to spend on the house in the years ahead to remedy defective construction by its cowboy builder. Both our place and the unit in front were leaky homes. The owner of the front unit could solve the problem only by installing a new roof. We didn't have to go that far, but to stop rainwater pouring into the large downstairs office space, we did have to have our front deck rebuilt and re-tiled.

~ ~ ~

Meanwhile, there were troubles back at the ranch where Derek and Mary Searle were proving to be problematic neighbours. Derek's enthusiastic activity as an electrician without a license led to our narrowly escaping legal action by Marlborough Electric Power Trust. Derek had installed a circuit breaker on our power board, persuading us that this was an excellent way to prevent getting shocks from household appliances. The switch malfunctioned frequently and ultimately caused one of the electric meters to stop running. When we reported this to the power company, its inspectors asked for the paperwork on the circuit breaker. We had none, of course. They threatened court action but did not proceed. We did, however, have to pay several hundred dollars for a registered electrician to rewire the board.

Mary Searle created difficulties in a different way. She was an inveterate gossip who embroidered her elaborate "Tales of the Outer Sounds" with colourful fictions that all too often were negative. We had to learn to tell her as little as possible about our doings.

The Searles had already stirred the pot with their western neighbours, the Schuckards, by announcing their ambition to subdivide to create 12-16 relatively small sections for sale, each no larger than an acre. Some would be along our boundary, but the majority would be adjacent to the Schuckards. Ultimately, I realised the Searles' initiative was a major factor in Harry and Liz Leov's determination that road access not be extended to new property owners. When Derek and Mary told us of their plan, we said directly that we were not eager to see a village developed in the neighbourhood. In face of the opposition, they fell silent but continued to pursue the issue with the Planning Office of Marlborough District Council. They were ultimately granted permission to subdivide.

Our neighbours on the other side, the Bridgemans, sold their place to a Nelson developer, Charlie Harwood. We quickly earned his ire by requesting that his pre-teen son not hurtle around our tracks on their farm bike. Charlie, having discovered that ten meters or so of our access road crossed the boundary of his property, threatened to erect a fence to stop us using the road unless we let his kid ride on it. We were forced to concede, but then Charlie declared that he was planning to build a second house close to our property and visible from our house. Even though his property was small (perhaps two hectares compared with our sixteen), he also announced he would install tanks in which to raise *paua* (abalone). He became very angry when we told him we would oppose the grant of planning permits for both projects. Neighbours on his other boundary also expressed opposition to the second house, and DOC said his *paua* farm would be unacceptable because of the effluent that would be discharged into Apuau Channel alongside protected Maud Island. Charlie, cursing us all, pulled up stakes and left.

~ ~ ~

Our neighbours' "development ambitions" provided me with ammunition for an email I wrote to TVNZ in September 1997 in support of the Resource Management Act [RMA]. A weekly TV public affairs programme called "Assignment" had aired what I considered an unbalanced critique of the application of the RMA.

> "You did a disservice to your audience by tilting so heavily in favour of the critics of the Regional Councils' plans. At some point in the discussion, you could have posed the broader question of why New Zealand needs Resource Management Plans. The answer seems painfully obvious: To arrest the precipitous destruction and degradation of our unique natural environment – flora and fauna both – through inappropriate and unsustainable land use. It is widely recognised that as a nation we had to change our ways – and fast. Ironically, some of the worst damage has been inflicted by our farming and forestry practices and yet it was protests by these interests that you featured so uncritically.
>
> A second way in which you could have balanced the picture would have been to interview people who have

had positive experiences of the application of the plans. My wife and I fall into this category. Our property in Marlborough is in an area of regenerating and old native bush close to extensive DOC lands, including a refuge for endangered species. Within just the past four years, the requirement to secure Resource Consents has protected the fragile land and ocean here from one neighbour's efforts to build a commercial guest lodge on an unstable hillside and to bulldoze a road down to the beach across wetlands, a second neighbour's plans to subdivide to create a holiday village, and a third neighbour's desire to discharge effluent from a land-based paua farm into the clear water of Pelorus Sound. I should add that two of these three individuals are not local residents and none of the three is economically dependent on the land.

"To be reminded of the importance of the Resource Management Act, we need only look out our window at the huge scars on the steep hillsides on the far side of the Sound, soil erosion resulting from uncontrolled bush clearance, bulldozing and overstocking in 'the good old days.'"

~ ~ ~

When Charlie Harwood announced he was leaving, Jo and I breathed a sigh of relief, but the fun and games were not over. Charlie sold to a couple from South Canterbury: Susan Rapach, a former American who earned a living buying and selling houses, and Allan Thompson, who had made a small fortune by converting his sheep farm to growing currants for Ribena. On their first weekend at their Sounds bach, they invited us over on Sunday afternoon. We arrived about 3:00 pm to find them both drunk. Susan was seriously sloshed, and as she continued to drink she became unbearably loud. We left as soon as we could.

Allan had told us that Susan and he had not known each

other for long and, as it proved, theirs was destined to be a brief relationship. About two months after our first meeting with them, they had a drunken night-time row, and Susan called Havelock Police to tell them that Allan was threatening her with a firearm. The Blenheim Armed Offenders Squad was mobilised, and when they arrived by boat they found Susan with a rifle standing outside the bach and Allan barricaded inside. They confiscated the rifle and, at Allan's request, took him back to Havelock with them. Before they departed, a constable knocked on our door to tell us everything was now OK. This was the first we had known about the drama, and we were left feeling anything but OK!

With Allan gone, Susan went looking around the Sound for other drinking companions whenever she came up from Timaru on her periodic visits. She had a small runabout, and when she returned after dark from a drinking excursion, she would tie her boat to a manuka on the narrow strip of beach directly below her bach.

One night after she had done this, a strong sou'easterly blew up, and she decided about 1:30am she should move the boat to her other beach where she had a trailer with a power winch. She was already in her nightie, and she simply added a raincoat and jandals when she went down to the boat. She pushed it out and climbed aboard. The outboard motor would not start (later she realised she had forgotten to turn on the petrol). Caught in the wind, the boat was swept into the channel. Susan lost her bearings and had no idea where she had drifted by the time she sent out a mayday call on her VHF radio. It was picked up by Marlborough Radio in Havelock, and they were able to track the signal to Waitata Reach, the large body of water that leads to the mouth of Pelorus Sound and Cook Strait. By this time the wind had dropped, so the operator told Susan to "sit tight," and in the morning they would get a boat out to rescue her. Fortunately it was summer, so she was in no danger of hypothermia once she covered herself with a tarpaulin. I imagine she ultimately sobered up, and she remembered she had failed to switch on the petrol. When she did, her outboard started immediately, and she was home in bed shortly after daybreak.

Later in the day, she came over to tell us about her adventure. I left her talking with Jo, and in my absence she confided that she had been unsuccessful in persuading Allan to resume their relationship and go with her to the US to enter an addiction treatment programme. Jo told her that, whether or not Allan was willing to get treatment for alcoholism, she should do so. Susan was startled that Jo thought she was an alcoholic. She said she was talking about Allan's addiction to sex!

~ ~ ~

There is no justification for my feeling superior to Susan in regard to her boating mishap. In 2003, a few years after her misadventure, I made a serious misjudgement that resulted in our boat sinking in a southerly gale. The storm was forecast, and before it struck I should have moved the boat to safety on a trailer on the beach. Instead, I left it on a running line at the jetty. The wind kept rising through the evening, and I checked the ropes several times until by midnight the gale was so strong it was no longer possible even to crawl on the jetty.

At daybreak the wind had eased somewhat, but the sea was still rough. I was horrified to see the bay littered with foliage ripped from the surrounding trees. The jetty was not visible from the house, and I made my way down to it with great apprehension. I could hear sounds of thumping and metal grinding. The tide was exceptionally low, and there to my horror was the boat upside down with every wave smashing it on the rocky bottom beside the jetty. I saw that the stern rope had broken, and the boat had been flipped over. I felt sickened.

My task now was to get the boat out of the water. The Johnsons, I knew, had a crane on their barge, but I discovered they were away on holiday. I called Dennis Port in Elaine Bay. Dennis worked with a mussel harvesting company, and to my relief he was able to arrange for the largest of their mussel barges, "Innovator," fortunately working not far off, to come to our bay. It was a huge boat, and when the waves drove it against the jetty, there was an ominous splintering sound from one of the front piles. The impact almost knocked Jo and me off our feet, but the jetty held.

The crew tied ropes to the boat, which was pulled against the side of "Innovator." A crane was then attached and the boat was lifted right-side-up onto the barge. It lay like a great wounded fish on the bags of harvested mussels. Its super-structure and the outboard motor were destroyed. As the full extent of the damage became visible, an older member of the crew, a Maori man standing beside me on the jetty, said com-passionately: "You must be feeling pretty sad, seeing your boat like this. The boat probably means a lot to you." I was crying inside.

"Innovator" took the boat to Elaine Bay where Dennis put it on a trailer, and the following day I towed it to Havelock to be repaired. Fortunately, we had good insurance, and all costs were covered, except for part of the expense for the re-placement outboard motor. As it turned out, the one I got ran better than my old one. I was left feeling foolish at making the mistake that led to the boat's sinking, but to my surprise I dis-covered that a majority of our fellow settlers in Outer Pelorus Sound had suffered the same fate with their boats at one stage or another.

A year or two after my boat sank, a gale stripped off the canopy from the repaired boat. It was tucked away securely on its trailer on a corner of the beach, sheltered from both the prevailing nor'west and sou'easterly winds, but a severe gale blew up from due south and sent the entire canopy sailing into the bush. Back to Havelock for another repair.

CHAPTER FIFTEEN

New Ways of Looking

"Our destination is never a place, but rather a new way
of looking at things."

> – Henry Miller

In opting to live on a remote bush property in an isolated corner of New Zealand, it might seem that I had narrowed my
life, but in fact my activities in the last years of the twentieth
century and the first decade of the 21st were as diverse as they
had been during my time in Ann Arbor and San Francisco –
and the contrasts among them were greater. In addition to
leading workshops at Te Wairua and elsewhere in New Zealand, I taught in Australia, the US and the UK I supervised doctoral students in NZ, Australia, the US and Canada. I presented
at conferences in Australia and the US. I led tours in India,
Indonesia, Australia and NZ. I continued to write. And with all
of this, there was my deep engagement with land and ocean.

I loved the dramatic contrast between the absence of human activity and noise at Te Wairua and the giddy mayhem of
many of my Asian tour destinations.

Fax to Jo from Swinhoe St., Calcutta, October 17, 1997

"I'm sitting on the veranda at the Institute [American
Institute of Indian Studies], and I'm immersed in mu-
sic, horns, excited voices, and flashing lights. There are
Durga Puja pavilions with brilliantly illuminated goddess

images on each of the streets leading up to the Institute, and their drumming teams and recorded music vie to drown out all competitors. Meanwhile, truck-loads of ecstatic shouting young men, all with drummers, pass by every few minutes bearing images away to the Ganga for immersion.

"Earlier I went for a walk around the neighbourhood just after dusk and discovered that the former relatively modest strings of coloured lights decorating the pavilions have now become five-storey-high neon extravaganzas spelling out homage to the goddess amid moving cartoon-like images. Fantastic! (The person letting off banger after banger below me is less than fantastic!)"

Tours in India delivered other amusements. For my flight from Calcutta to Madras on this October 1997 tour, Indian Airlines had sold me a ticket for a morning flight that did not exist. I had changed the booking to a 5:30 pm departure, but my ticket still read 9:30 am. When I presented it at airport check-in, I explained to the clerk what had happened.

"He gazed at the ticket thoughtfully for some time and then with a broad smile said: 'SO, you missed your flight this morning.' 'No, I said that flight did not exist.' 'No, of course. That is a non-existent flight – but you missed other flights?' I was non-plussed, but as he had handed me my boarding pass and baggage checks for the desired 5:30 flight, I decided it should remain the great unanswered question."

Many years in India has taught me there are times when it's best not to argue. Later on this same tour, I ran into another situation when I thought I should honour this dictum.

Fax to Jo from Kovalam Beach, Kerala, November 7, 1997:

"We show up at Ernakulam Station in good time for our train to Trivandrum. The platform is strangely deserted. The train is running an hour late. The locals stroll in at an appropriate time for the revised schedule. It is hot and very humid, and we are looking forward to our reserved air-conditioned chair car accommodations. Train arrives. Porters express mild dismay. The AC chair car has been left off today – so poof go our reservations. We have to squeeze in wherever we can in a non-AC first-class carriage. I find seats in various compartments for all our group by cajoling other passengers into moving luggage off seats and persuading a couple of women that they can no longer sprawl across three seats each. I end up lying on a top berth with my back pack as a lumpy pillow. All seems right with the world, and I drift off to sleep.

"The ticket collector arrives and gently awakens me. He gazes mournfully at our collective ticket and informs me I have to pay Rs.450/- (about NZ$20) surcharge because we are travelling in the wrong class! Although AC chair class tickets cost as much as first class, that fare includes an AC surcharge and a reservation fee, which are now irrelevant because we are not in an AC coach and we do not have reservations here. So those portions of the fare must be deducted. That means we actually paid a base fare lower than first class. We are, in fact, travelling first class, are we not? So I must pay the difference. Impeccable Indian bureaucratic logic, you must agree!

"I grumble but pay up, secretly amused by the perfect Catch 22. My compartment mates discuss the issue with the ticket collector in a mixture of Malayali and English, pointing out to him the unfairness of the rules. Everyone says: 'What to do?' We all laugh, and the ticket collector goes off looking hugely relieved. My compartment mates adopt me as a best friend, find a seat for me with them down below, assure me that the NZ cricket team is not nearly as bad as I am insisting and generally share their life stories with me.

"We arrive at the next station. In comes a group of about 15 Swedes, fuming that their reservations in the AC chair car have vanished into thin air. What's worse, few of them can find seats because they don't know how to identify devious Indian techniques of expanding to fill six seats with three people. Their annoyance turns to outrage when a junior ticket collector informs them they must pay a surcharge. They angrily refuse. (Our compartment watches with steady attention as though the Mahabharata were being acted out for our travelling entertainment.)

Junior ticket collector retreats, and the Swedes declare victory. I chuckle silently to myself. Sure enough, two senior ticket collectors return with the timid junior collector. The unshakeable logic is explained to the Swedes. They explode. The train is late, they have been robbed of their reservations, they have no seats, and they are being told to shell out more cash. They say they will make a complaint to the head of the railway system. The senior collector says: 'No problem.' They should do that. In fact, once they have paid him the surcharge, they can claim it back from the head of the railway system. 'No,' the Swedes declare. 'They will demand that their entire fare be refunded.' 'No problem,' says the ticket collector, but now they must pay the surcharge or he will have to add a 'ticketless travel' fine. (Our compartment is riveted. The Mahabharata is reaching a climax.)

"The 'ticketless travel' bit pushes the Swedes right off the edge. They declare they will leave the train at the next station and take taxis to Trivandrum. They figure it is only 140 km from there and that should take them little more than two hours, unlike the train which is going to take another three-and-a-half hours. (I wince at their arithmetic. On our tour, we have been averaging 30-40 km per hour in our taxis and bus.) The senior ticket collector lamely assures them that if they pay up and stay they almost certainly will get seats soon. They dismiss him as an ass and say they are leaving and will demand their money back and an apology from Mr. Big of Indian Railways. The senior ticket collector leaves.

"The junior collector, now relieved of responsibility, cheerfully assures them they can probably hire a small bus for all the party at the upcoming Podunk railway station – where, in my view, they will be lucky to find as much as a scooter rickshaw. They duly leave, looking pleased with themselves. Plenty of seats become available from that station onwards!

"As our journey resumes, some of my Indian travelling companions ask: 'Why all this fuss about time?' They say they were perplexed by why the Swedes were upset by their calculation that the train would take at least an hour more to reach Trivandrum than the taxis they thought they could hire. 'We Indians have all the time in the world,' said one of them. 'You either spend an hour on the train or you spend it somewhere else. What's so upsetting about one place over another? Did the Swedes have some place they urgently had to be?'"

In Madurai during this 1997 South India tour, I bought a beautiful bronze statue of Nataraj, the dancing Siva, to be shipped back to NZ. It was almost two-months later before it arrived at Te Wairua, and we had to decide where and how to install this meter-tall dynamic figure. We chose a position on the edge of the garden squarely in front of the house. With Brian Plaisier's help, I built a platform of large rocks and cemented the base of the statue to this. As night came, the concrete was yet to harden, and Jo and I were concerned that inquisitive possums might knock the statue over, so we decided to take shifts to sit through the warm summer night on possum watch.

What we didn't expect was that a possum would befriend us. It was a small grey possum, a female we were later to discover, who came during Jo's first watch and stood up with her front paws in Jo's lap as though she was inviting Jo to pet her, which she did. When I came out to replace Jo, the possum did the same with me, and she stayed with us all night.

Later in the week, the same possum appeared on our verandah one evening with a small baby on her back. Our family obviously had two new members, and we gave them the names Minnie and Clive. Of course, suckers as we were, we fed them and, as any family member would, Minnie came into the house – via the cat door! Strangely she always left Clive outside. The cats were not amused when she began helping herself from their bowl of food on the kitchen floor, but they did not attack her, simply sitting glowering at her. She was in no way fazed by their presence. We would pick her up to put her outside, holding her under her front "armpits" so she couldn't scratch or bite us. Meanwhile, she tried her best to wrap her prehensile tail around door handles.

Each Christmas, masseuse Anna gave us with a card two silver-paper-wrapped chocolate Santas, which we put under the Christmas tree. One morning, after Minnie had joined the family, we found under the tree two neat piles of silver paper with the chocolate Santas gone. Not the work of the cats, we decided!

In regard to the general "possum problem," we never did shoot, trap or poison. We killed no possums. Under the terms of our QEII Open Space Covenant, we were committed to "possum control," and we were concerned that the periodic inspections by the Trust's field officers would reveal our neglect. Not so. Miraculously, our bush suffered considerably less possum damage than that of our three neighbours, all of whom applied one or more of the approved methods of slaughter. Our first QEII inspecting officer observed: "Whatever you are doing with the possums, it's really working." This positive judgment was echoed by Trust officers in subsequent years and by DOC rangers who visited Te Wairua.

We suspected there might be a scientific case to be made for letting possums be. Threatened species, we had read, often breed at double their normal rate. Secondly, dominant males on a territory will keep other possums away, and we certainly had several dominant males.

Our possum control strategy was one that would have been ridiculed by most of our fellow New Zealanders had we publicised it. We talked to the possums, telling them they were welcome at Te Wairua if they exercised restraint in their feeding in the bush. Similarly, we talked to the wild deer and pigs, assuring them they would not be hunted on our property as they were on neighbouring lands. Once the deer got to know us, they grazed contentedly on our lawns at night. We put high fences around our vegetable gardens to keep them from grazing there.

Before we assured the pigs that they were safe from hunters, they rooted on our lawns, but they stopped doing this once we offered them sanctuary at Te Wairua. Unfortunately, after a couple of years, a rogue hunter came on to our place from the Leov farm, and one night soon afterwards the pigs dug up our small back lawn. We apologised for our failure to protect them and assured them we would do our best to prevent a repeat. They never touched our lawns again.

~ ~ ~

By 1997 I had had almost 40-years' experience of travelling in India, so situations such as that with the train reservations were familiar. I had had the same length of experience in Australia but it was of a restricted area: the heavily populated south-eastern corner, the part of the country most like NZ. Fortunately, in January 1996, I had gone to the annual Australian Transpersonal Conference [ATP] in Sydney to lead a workshop on Maori shamanic practice. The presenter who followed me was Diana James, an anthropologist who had just left the Australian outback after living 20 years on Pitjantjatjara Homelands south of Uluru. A fluent speaker of Pitjantjatjara, she had been adopted as a daughter by an influential Aboriginal family, whom she had assisted in starting a tour business called Desert Tracks. Diana and I became good friends, and for a number of years from the late nineties we collaborated in leading tour groups to the Homelands under Desert Tracks' auspices. I learnt a great deal from all the tours I led, but from none more than these to the Australian Outback.

After the ATP Conference, I drove down to Canberra in a rental car to spend a day or two exploring old haunts. Somebody at the conference had told me the National Art Gallery had an exhibition of sacred art from India. It was fine, but something quite unexpected moved me much more. When I came in the grand entrance to the gallery, there, right in front of me, was an Aboriginal Memorial. Occupying the whole of a large hall. It consisted of vertical, hollow tree trunks (perhaps 100 of them, I did not count), anything from 3-8 feet in height, all exquisitely painted and, in some cases, shaped at the top. This is the traditional form used by Arnhem Land tribes to preserve the bones of their most honoured dead. The trees are naturally hollowed by termites. (The 'caskets' in the museum had no bones.)

This memorial was commissioned in the 1970s to commemorate all aboriginal women and men who have died defending their lands since 1788. The artists are named, along with their tribes, and the caskets are arranged in the geographical order of the tribes along a stone pathway, twisting in replica of the great river that flows through their lands.

I walked onto the pathway among the caskets and was immediately plunged into an energy field more powerful than anything I can ever remember experiencing. It was like walking into a high voltage field. I shut my eyes and felt I was surrounded by spirit presences. I wanted to sit down right there and just BE ... but my polite, gallery-going white self wouldn't permit it.

I kept coming back to this memorial over the next two hours, and each time I was caught up in the same force field. All of this told me that the work Jo and I were doing at Te Wairua – or, more correctly, the learning we were attempting – was the right work for us. Along with our efforts to build contacts with Maori teachers.

~ ~ ~

From the late nineties, Jo chose to concentrate most of her activities closer to home. She and I shared the workshop organisation and teaching at Te Wairua, but she travelled with me only occasionally. She loved being at home alone to enjoy the land and the critters, to walk with the cats, meditate, write, garden and create art.

Outer Pelorus Sound is subject to frequent wild storms, with gale-force winds and torrential downpours. These would turn the creeks into raging torrents, leading to the blockage or displacement of our water intakes. In my absence, Jo would have to wade into the main creek once the water level had subsided somewhat and reseat the pipes. The faxes back and forth between Te Wairua and my far-distant tour locations often contained discussions of water-system problems. I always tried to find for the faxes more entertaining topics.

"Here's a funny for you, a notice on the milk carton at my Wellington motel: 'Keep New Zealand beautiful. Flatten before disposal.' Different subject: Don't fly into Australia with hard-boiled eggs. Bad move. I got hauled into the Agriculture Quarantine pen and stripped of my eggs with an unsmiling rebuke: 'These have to go.' The muesli passed muster, and the drug beagle also gave me an OK, along with a wag and a lick on the hand. He could have had the eggs!

And from Kerala:

"The fire instructions on my room door here at the Casino Hotel have a big red dot saying: 'You are here.' But (small shit) the dot is on the wrong room. In addition, the evacuation arrows for the hallways are in two different colours running in opposite directions. There is no clue given as to what the colours mean. I have decided in case the fire alarm goes, I will run first to my assigned dot and then dash off madly from there in both directions! That should fool the fire god."

Closer to home, I wrote of a visit to Kaikoura's Takahanga marae:

"It is beautifully decorated in a modernistic style similar to the marae at Te Papa in Wellington (one of the same artists was involved). The location is spectacular on a plateau looking out over the ocean and with the 9,000-feet plus Seaward Kaikoura Range as a backdrop. The wide lawns and gardens – lots of roses and peonies – running from the front of the buildings towards the sea are dotted with fantastic tall-tall-tall wooden and stone figures and archways, fantastic in the fantasy sense of the word. It is a magical place, and we got to sleep in the whare nui among all the spirit sculptures.

"We were given a beautiful formal welcome followed by the requisite cuppa and bikkies. Lorraine Hawke, one of the founders of Whale Watch, talked to us for an hour or so after the cuppa, giving us the ancestral stories of the local hapu and its intimate relationship with whales and other sea creatures. As I should have realised, it is really the sea creatures who are the kaitiaki (guardians) of the humans. The humans are simply reciprocating for the care the sea creatures have always given them. We were very moved to learn that Whale Watch boat captains monitor the breathing of the whales and will not go close to any whale that is agitated for whatever reason. They get to know individual whales, and some whales that are initially agitated may take as much as two years before they signal their readiness to be 'visited' by swimming over to one of the boats and rubbing against it. Lorraine made it clear that she and some of the others working with Whale Watch have a consciousness connection with individual whales. It was a wonderful talk."

~ ~ ~

As her health improved, Jo resumed her fabric art. She found special inspiration in the World of Wearable Arts, an extravaganza staged annually in Nelson. By the time we discovered it in 1997, it was already in its tenth year and had gained international recognition. Jo wrote in her journal:

"The show was simply breath-taking. It was staged on a long ramp that ran down the centre of the hall, which is normally used for in-indoor sports such as basketball. Half-way along, the ramp expanded into a circular area where various props and performers came up from some subterranean area, much to the audience's surprise. Other performers entered from either end of the ramp, so one had to keep lively looking from side-to-side to see what novelties were emerging.

"There were about 150 entries, some of them so utterly breath-taking and extravagant that words fail. But one of the neat things about the show was that it was not a matter of the models parading one by one. There were nine categories, each choreographed and often with about 50 dancers, also in amazingly beautiful costumes, zipping in and out between the models who also danced and moved according to how their costumes could best be shown. Depending on the category, some of the costumes were made from recycled materials – old tyres, plastics, used computer parts or pipes and wires. Others were all natural materials. One category was for silk, another for porcelain. Some are exquisitely beautiful; others are whimsical and funny. Many of them looked medieval – lots of flowing gowns and immense head-dresses; knight-like figures in armour. Mythical creatures.

"Last year's grand-prize winner was featured early in the programme. The lights were dimmed and when they came up again, there in centre-stage was this towering thing, cocooned in white silk. Two dancers circled in opposite directions unfurling the fabric to reveal a creature about ten-feet high, which stretched out its wings of batiked silk. It was a combination of a dragonfly and fish and called Dragonfish. Oh my, it was incredible!

"There was so much else about which I could write: costumes for old people; the children's section, with dream sequences in which the child models were accompanied by fairies and leprechauns; and my favourite: Kiwiana, costumes inspired by the 1950s and 1960s. I just about split a gut laughing. It was wonderful to see our sometimes pretentious and defensive little nation parodying itself!"

With her fabric art, Jo had worked since 1990 with individual customers, creating on commission one-of-a-kind vests, jackets and coats. Now the World of Wearable Arts show emboldened her to offer her creations for sale in stores. I undertook to be her marketing manager, and I found two boutiques in Nelson willing to sell her work. On a trip north to lead a workshop, I was able to add a central Auckland store as an outlet.

~ ~ ~

I went again to the Australian Transpersonal Conference in April 1998, this time in Adelaide, and before the conference started I had fun exploring the central city. I wrote to Jo:

"I must say it has a lively café scene and, in what the guidebook says is 'the Bohemian section,' even cosmopolitan me was wide-eyed at a figure walking towards me yesterday morning: a broad-shouldered six-foot-six (or thereabouts) Aboriginal man wearing tight, tight magenta pants, white knee-high boots and a skin-hugging T-shirt in some other brilliant colour my mind could not register. Oh my! I thought of plopping him down in Blenheim. In San Francisco he'd be a huge hit."

The special friendship I made at this conference was with Warrnambool artist Bruce Vinall. Among other things, this led to my service on his La Trobe University doctoral committee. His dissertation was on transformational art – "Paintings as Maps of Consciousness" Warrnambool and I travelled to Melbourne in August 2002 to view an exhibition which was the visual part of his thesis. A year or two later, he attended one of our Te Wairua workshops, and in exchange he gave us his magnificent painting, "Wild and Delicate," which enjoys pride of place above the entrance stairway in our Nelson house.

In June and July 1998 I returned to the US for five jam-packed weeks to promote my book, which had been selling well enough to require a second printing already, and to give a series of lectures and workshops in California, Colorado, Indiana and New York, combining this with a visit to Alastair, Debbie and their sons in Owings Mills, Maryland.

A very busy year was rounded out with leading a two-week August tour in Bali and Lombok. I described some of its delights in a letter to an American friend:

"The Balinese are amongst the warmest people I know anywhere. They win hands down as the world's best smilers and they are incredibly mindful. As you can imagine, staying at a Balinese hotel is a very special experience as a result.

"Bali is most famous for the amazing frequency of colourful Hindu-Animist rituals. The first evening when I went for a stroll among the little shops on the street near our hotel, I suddenly found myself in the midst of musicians and costumed dancers, accompanying a Barong, a 'scary' creature from traditional folk theatre, a sort of Chinese dragon with a huge hairy and toothy bear face. The Barong was dancing in and out of the shops on its four human legs, chasing away evil spirits in preparation for the festival of the goddess Saraswati.

"A few days later, our visit to the inland town of Ubud happened to coincide with the annual purification of the major temple. Two evenings in a row, there were processions down the main street of musicians leading hundreds of people in ceremonial garb, bearing richly ornamented ritual umbrellas above giant animal images and carrying to the temple colourful offerings of fruit, flowers and sculpted bamboo.

"On Bali's neighbouring island of Lombok, we spent four days at my favourite beach, Sengiggi – white coral sand with an inner reef only a few yards offshore. I floated around with my snorkel and goggles over the luminescent blue, purple and pink coral amongst an array of fish of every brilliant tropical hue, ranging in size from fingernail to arms-length. Breathtaking colours."

A highlight of this tour was a meeting at her home in the Balinese capital, Denpasar, with Dr. Luh Ketut Suryani, a friend of our NYC friend, Freda Birnbaum. Describing the meeting in a fax to Jo, I wrote:

"What a gem! She is in her late 40s, I would guess, a wise and wonderful combination of western psychological knowledge and Balinese spirit-healing knowledge, all wrapped in an energetic Earth Mother. She is the author of two books on Balinese culture (refuting Margaret Mead and Clifford Geertz!) and one on Balinese meditation – well, her method – which I am bringing home. She works with *balians* as respected co-healers. She is a social activist, was an outspoken opponent of Suharto's regime (was under police surveillance) and now of Habibie's window dressing. The group was mightily impressed and moved by her – me too!

~ ~ ~

On my return to NZ, Jo took her first voyage on the mailboat to meet me in Havelock so we could have a day together in town. The cats were on their own for 24 hours, and Jo described her difficulty in leaving them.

"The mailboat was really neat. I was nervous about getting on it, leaving the cats, etc., so the countdown till it came was unexpectedly stressful. I had hoped to creep down to the wharf sans cats, after umpteen cuddles and discussions with them about what was happening. I sneaked out of the house with the mailbag, backpack and a small overnight bag, locked the door (a bit silly as I don't bother to lock three other doors!) and strode down to the wharf before I looked around. Right behind me was Kia, and here came Rai rushing down the driveway howling. So we three sat on the grass and cuddled some more, and then I heard the distant roar of the approaching mailboat.

"It is big, a red-and-white double decker flying the NZ flag. It can seat 75 inside, with ample room also for people to be out on top, back and front. There are never that many people aboard; 40 is the max I have seen in the summer. This time there were maybe 20, most of whom were out with their cameras to record my coming aboard. I felt reassured waving to the captain, Ken, who is a warm, friendly man, unlike the previous captain. Ken pulled the boat parallel to the front of the wharf, and I swung my bags over to the young assistant. Luckily, the tide was high, so I could easily grip the handrails and jump down a foot or so onto the boat. And then we were off.

"I turned around, and there was Rai sitting on the dock watching me go as Te Wairua rapidly receded in our wake. Tears flooded my eyes, and I found myself bellowing 'I'll be back' over the considerable engine noise. The young assistant murmured something about it being hard to leave for a few weeks and asked – intrusively for a Kiwi, but I liked it, of course – how long I'd be gone. I composed myself enough to choke out a wavering reply that it was just 24 hours, but that I had never left the cats on their own. We laughed.

"Made my way inside. Dumped my stuff and took a window seat. Went up to pay Ken, who was talking with a Kiwi couple my age on holiday, I assume. They certainly weren't settlers, who tend to have a distinctly rugged rural look and whose conversation generally is limited to weather conditions. The captain asked after my cats, who usually accompany me to the wharf on mailboat days. I said it was hard to leave them even for 24 hours, and Ken said he'd never leave his cat that long. The four of us talked about the upscale vet-recommended diet we all feed our cats, and I knew I had fallen among non-settlers.

"Went up top to sit in the sun and wind as the boat went past the Searles and Schuckards places. I could look down the first inlet to the right and see our farm road leading precipitously over mountains to Te Towaka, the Leovs estate. It was a brilliantly clear, sunny, blue-skied, calm day, and I felt deep pleasure in this rare place I have come to live.

"I knew that after our place there were but two stops to drop off mail. I was eager to see other settlers get their mail, so I went out onto the stern to see who might be waiting as we slowed down to enter Hallam Cove, another lushly forested, utterly wild nook of the sounds, and here was a grizzled guy about John's age grappling with oars in a rowboat!

"Settler George manoeuvred himself alongside the mailboat towering above him, grabbed the side and pulled his boat along to the stern. Then the assistant dropped a box of groceries and the full mailbag into the rowboat and leaned way down to pluck out George's bag of outgoing mail. Meanwhile, George is peering up at the captain, and they're having a quick conversation about fishing. George is your achetypical settler, straight from central casting: worn, rugged clothes, gumboots, a boat that has seen a decade or two of hard use. He has skin like leather, he's missing a couple of teeth, and he grunts out a sentence or two in response as he sits casually holding his oars and the side of the mailboat.

"I was most unsettler-like. I positively gaped. It was the calmest of days, but John and I have often gotten our mail in the midst of gales, some so strong we've had to hold on to keep from blowing off the wharf. Sheeting rain is also not uncommon. I gasped to the assistant: 'George must have one hell of a time with the weather.' 'Oh yeah,' said the assistant with feeling. Never again will I complain about meeting the mailboat on our wharf!

"Then we chugged out of Hallam Cove and crossed the Sound to Brightlands, directly opposite Te Wairua, five miles to the South. From our boat, I've seen the distinctive lines of their big mussel farm floating in front of their property, but never that close. There are long rows, one after the other, of big black buoys floating about three-feet apart, and the mussels grow underwater on ropes that go down in loops about ten meters, hooked up from one buoy to the next.

"I was pleased the Captain took the mailboat close to a barge to watch the seeding of mussels onto bare ropes that had just been harvested. Later we stopped by another barge to watch the men harvesting mature mussels and sorting them on a long conveyor belt that ran along one side of the barge, – hard, hard work at a fast pace. It's a quintessential Sounds scene, and I was right there with all the other tourists, thoroughly engaged. One woman turned around after getting her fill of pictures, and our eyes met. We smiled at each other, and she mouthed to me: 'What an awful job.' And we laughed as we made our way back to our seats to continue the peaceful journey.

I boarded just before two, and just after four we started making our way into the narrow shipping lanes to tiny Havelock, population 400. It is a central port in these isolated parts, so there is a goodly number of fishing boats, mussel barges, yachts and settler boats in the marina This is where John and I have had adventures docking our boat, though we are much better now and for a long time now I haven't screamed: 'Jesus Christ! You're going to hit that post!!'

"Naturally, I was up at the window excitedly trying to find John. In good Californian fashion, I found myself yelping aloud with delight when I saw him. He makes a damn good sorta upscale settler photo. He's got this great felt outback hat I've always loved, jeans, a thick sweater and an outwardly calm demeanour as he spotted me and started waving back. He got warmly greeted by the Captain and assistant, who were surprised to see him standing there, and I passed my luggage over the railing to him as he stood on the wharf as we berthed. Then a long hug and a passionate kiss."

~ ~ ~

Diana James and I collaborated on our first tour to the Australian Outback in October 1999, and I approached it as a personal vision quest. I was aware that as soon as we reached the Aboriginal Homelands, local elders would be our guides. This would enable me to be silent most of the time, which is the way I like to go into the bush – silent and fully present to whatever chooses to reveal itself.

As we journeyed south from Uluru towards the Pitjant-jatjara lands, we were alerted by our guide, Hussein Burra, to the uncertainties created by important "Men's Business" in progress nearby. The knowledge that traditional rituals were underway just over the horizon set a powerful background for our time in the desert. We were connected to what we could not know directly by the elders who went back and forth between the initiation and our camps.

Walinynga (Cave Hill) was a powerful first destination, with the awareness we were camped alongside a Dreaming site into which we should not venture without guidance. Dressed for the occasion in cowboy hat and bare feet, Law Man Stanley Douglas (a Sergeant in the South Australian State Police as well as a guardian of Pitjantjatjara sacred tradition) joined us immediately on arrival. I was thrilled when he launched right in with the story of the Seven Sisters and Wati Nyiru, he of the uncontrollable double penis. As I wrote to Jo: "As soon as he had his cuppa and a biscuit in hand, Stanley started telling us stories of the Dreamtime ancestor animals and other spirits as matter-of-factly as a Sounds neighbour who has dropped by for tea might recount the latest local gossip." We learnt that Wati Nyiru chased the Seven Sisters all the way from the West coast of the continent and back again. Stanley is just one of hundreds of local guardians of a Songline that runs unbroken for thousands of kilometres.

Stanley talked on and on as the dusk gathered and drizzle began to fall, and I glimpsed a very large bird with a long, stalk-like neck flying behind him. Over dinner I described it to him, and he said there was no bird like that in these parts. Next morning, however, as he farewelled us, there it was, a Pacific Heron. Stanley said we had brought it from New Zealand, along with the rain. For me, the land itself and the animals who choose to show themselves are some of the most powerful spirit teachers. The heron confirmed for me that we were "on the path," and this was reinforced by the colossal electrical storm and deluge at midnight on this first night, a rare event in this arid locale.

Being led by Stanley and the other male elders to the caves and the water hole at daybreak on the second day at Cave Hill was a moving experience. Here was the Seven Sisters Dreaming «made flesh» (or rock, if you prefer), the land carved and shaped by the Creation Ancestors. In the caves, I felt the presence of the spirits to whom Stanley called to herald our coming. Here I saw for the first time Aboriginal rock paintings of which I had read so much, and, unlike those in Kakadu, these are still repainted regularly. It was awesome to stand in the presence of a living spiritual tradition that stretches back unbroken forty or sixty thousand years.

In preparatory reading I had learnt that Aboriginal Australians understand the world to be the product of consciousness, a great Dreaming. In the Beginning, Ancestor Spirits walked the land with a song and gave all things their life form.

To keep the Earth vibrant and healthy, every generation of humans must periodically re-enter the Dreaming – a sacred parallel dimension of time and space – by travelling the Ancestral Songline and recounting the creation stories in painting, poetry, song and dance.

This feeling of awe at ancient continuities was reinforced for me throughout the week: By the grinding stones and silky smooth grinding indentations beside the rock holes. By the shards of ancient rock tools found along the hill margins. By the singing and dancing of the Ngintaka Tjukurpa (creation story and law) and our journey on that Songline to see the Ngintaka's shape-shifting in stone. By sitting in the circle of men beside the Atal rock hole to hear old Mick's account of his naked childhood in that very place; his family's encounter with their first white man and his "huge angry dog" (camel); and the spear battle that left teenage Mick seriously wounded and his father jailed. Awe at the ancient continuities was most powerfully reinforced by the accounts from both Stanley and Lee Brady of their recent encounters with the elusive "wild people," who are still living naked in the old nomadic ways in that desert. Or was it spirits of which they spoke?

Lee Brady, who joined us a few days into our journey, was a very big man in both physique and personality, with excellent English and a great rolling laugh. He led us one day on a round-trip of about 50km, travelling the Ngintaka Songline in the transporter accompanied by a dozen-or-so Anangu (local Aboriginal) men and women, who sang the story appropriate to the stage we were on to an accompaniment of click sticks. The end of each stage was marked by a rocky feature in the landscape where the Ngintaka Man performed a particular Dreaming (act of creation). We piled off the transporter at each of these, and the Dreaming was re-enacted with song and dance, often with all of us roped in for a second performance. Back on the bus and off to the next outcrop, boulder pile or cave with paintings, all the time with chanting and stick clicking.

Very soon we were in an altered state – a real shamanic journey – and it's no wonder the animals started to appear: first kangaroos, then a dingo, a young Ngintaka (Perentie Lizard, just four feet long), a brown falcon, crows, minahs, goanas, a large King Brown Snake (very poisonous) and a Spiny Devil (the most exquisitely decorated eight-inch lizard).

On another day, along the road to the witchetty grub hunt, an emu and his babies tried to outrun the bus. And then there was a full-grown Perentie lizard (probably seven feet in length), which Lee stalked, hypnotised and killed to give us an evening campfire feast. As Anangu said: "Who could be surprised we got rain?"

I was struck by the common core of shamanic practice worldwide. An example of this was Lee's story (told while painting us for dances) of his two spirit guardians, who come to alert him to danger. His description of the forms in which they manifest could have come from any of the world's shamanic traditions. Another example was what I learnt of *Ngangkari*, Anangu traditional healers. The different ways in which they gain their healing vocation, their diverse "specialties" and their soul recovery journeys are all classic shamanic patterns.

A third example was the shape shifting, another core feature of shamanism. This, of course, is central to the Dreaming stories. The shape shifting of the Ancestor Spirits is given form in the landscape, as also when their Tjukurpa are danced. I was struck by the ability of the Anangu elders (men and women both) to shape shift. Apparently aged and creaky, with incredibly spindly legs and bony bare feet, they magically transform into lithe, rhythmic dancers. Even more magically, the men from our group were transformed when we danced. This may not have been very apparent to the watching, singing women, but if they could have seen how sadly bad we were during our rehearsals (me worst of all, by far), they would have agreed that our final performances were shape-shifting miracles! Personally, I had the mysterious experience of being thoroughly energised by the body painting and the dances, when I had started out at the rehearsals feeling so tired that I doubted I could get through it.

There were the desert oaks, shape shifting from their aquifer-seeking, pencil-slim, youthful form to their expansive maturity. The final shape shifting was that of the frogs at the base of Uluru on our last evening. Who could imagine that such creatures were capable of combining beautiful music with what sounded like the bleating of sheep and an accompaniment of click sticks?

Shamanism is nothing if not practical. It embodies the survival techniques which brought thousands of generations of our ancestors successfully through the millennia. It was impressive and humbling to observe the depth of ecological knowledge and bush skills demonstrated by the Anangu, even in the limited time we had with them. They moved with such ease from story-telling and singing to practicalities like weather forecasting, bush tucker gathering and fire lighting with soaking firewood.

We were grateful for these practicalities at tour's end. At daybreak on what had been scheduled as the second-to-last day in our bush camp at Atal, we were woken by the three female elders who were camped with us to say we must pack-up immediately and head for Uluru. Heavy rain was on the way, and if we did not move quickly we might be stranded by flooding. We were travelling in three vehicles: a kitchen truck, a troop carrier and a large ute driven by Diana. After heating a kettle for tea and coffee for the rest of us, the kitchen crew headed for the settlement of Amata to get set up to greet us with lunch. As soon as we had packed and tidied the camp, the rest of us followed in the two other vehicles.

Through the hills between Atal and Amata, we travelled on narrow sandy tracks, and we had gone no more than 10 km when the troop carrier got stranded, sinking to the tops of its very tall wheels. Fortunately, Diana in the ute was on a parallel track which held up. Our drivers declared that the only way to extract the troop carrier was to dig down around the wheels and load in brush to restore some traction. They cautioned us not to use mulga branches as these broke into hard sharp spikes that could puncture the tyres. Fortunately, there was also willow where we were.

Cold rain was falling steadily and there was no shelter. We blessed the Anangu women who lit a fire despite wet wood and got a billy boiling. After brush gathering, Diana and I set out in the ute to see if we could find anything more substantial to provide grip for the transporter wheels. At a small group of apparently deserted houses, we found some sheets of corrugated iron and an aluminium screen door that seemed to have been discarded. Some progress had been made on the digging by the time we got back to the stranded vehicle, but we also found our most senior tour member, Michael Lesparre aged in his late 70s, shaking with hypothermia. We got him into dry clothing and packed him into the ute with the engine and heater running.

It took eight hours of digging before the wheels on the transporter had been cleared sufficiently for Diana to attempt to pull it out with the ute. After a few goes, she got it free, but frustratingly the corrugated iron punctured a tyre on the transporter in the process, and it had to be jacked up for the wheel to be changed. Then both vehicles could head for Amata, leaving behind dented iron and a crumpled screen door. As it proved, the screen door, rather than being discarded, had just been purchased by Lee for a house he was building. He was slightly peeved when he discovered it bent and worthless.

The transporter had transmission trouble, and it was after dark before we reached Amata, where the cooks had commandeered the school as our refuge for the night. After showers and a change to dry clothing, we became a noisily cheery bunch telling one another exaggerated stories of desert heroism. The following day, one of our group had a birthday, and guide

Hussein baked and iced a cake for him right there in the school kitchen.

~ ~ ~

Jo and I had used a fortnight's holiday in July and August 1999 to scope out a possible tour in Far North Queensland [FNQ], and we decided to develop a Tropical Australia Tour which would combine FNQ with travel in the Northern Territory. After the Outback tour, I flew to Darwin in early November to visit Kakadu National Park to choose locations for this new tour. I had been attracted to Kakadu by a hauntingly beautiful National Geographic documentary film, "Australia's Twilight of the Dreamtime," which chronicled the threatened way of life of the Aboriginal Gagadju people of Kakadu. Kakadu proved to be magnificent, and I fell in love with it and its spectacular animals, with which I had some beautiful meetings even on this first short visit. I wrote Jo about one encounter:

> "A lizard (it proved to be a Spotted Tree Monitor) about two-feet long with wonderful blueish-grey mottled skin and a brilliant blue tongue, slithered away from me through the grass and stopped at the bottom of a slim tree. As I came closer to have a good look, it ran onto the tree and disappeared around the far side. It was just a couple of yards away from me, but by the time I got to the tree it had vanished. I searched and searched, all the time telling it (out loud) what a magician it was and how much I would like it to show itself to me. Also that I loved it and would never hurt it. Then it appeared, again like magic, high up the tree, and once it saw I had seen it, it came steadily down until it was right beside my waist, leaning out towards me and staring with its bright blue eyes into mine. We spent a minute or two in conversation

before it went off calmly through the grass. Boy, that left me exhilarated!"

When later I took tour groups, they were equally entranced by Kakadu.

— Chapter Sixteen —

2001

"God is the wind that touches everything."
– Malawi proverb

In 1998, Jo had begun creating mosaics. Whimsically, her first were on the concrete base and pipe of a new rotary clothes line I erected on the back lawn, and this delighted her so much that before long, almost every pipe and concrete surface on the property was ornamented with a mosaic. The most spectacular decorated the spa pool base and the stepping stones to this from the house. That led to her fashioning mosaic stepping stones for sale at garden centres.

With marketing Jo's garments and mosaics added to workshop and tour leading and work around the property, my days were full, but I still found time to write. After *Other Ways of Knowing* went to press in 1997, I wrote a major article on "The New Zealand Maori Renaissance" for *Lapis*, the journal of the New York Open Center, and two years later, in 2000, a shortened version was published in *Resurgence*, a UK journal edited by Satish Kumar. Satish, a former Jain monk, was a leading figure in the spiritual Deep Ecology movement. He had visited me at CIIS in the late 80s when he was preparing to found Schumacher College in Devon, of which he became Director. Inspired by the legacy of E.F. Schumacher, author of the path-breaking *Small Is Beautiful: A Study of Economics as if People Mattered*, the College developed holistic education courses for people concerned with social and environmental issues.

As a result of my *Resurgence* article, Satish invited me to teach at the College, and together we devised a three-week course for May 2001 on "Shamanism & the Natural World." On my recommendation, my former colleague from CIIS, Angeles Arrien, anthropologist and Basque shaman, was invited to teach the third week of the course. Satish recruited Jonathan Horwitz of the Scandinavian Center for Shamanic Studies in Copenhagen to teach the second week, and I would lead off in the first week.

2001 was an immensely busy and rewarding year, even though it produced some major disappointments and sadness in the family. I began by leading a South India tour in late January and early February and was back in NZ just in time to teach with Peter Horsley in a US-based International Honours Program [IHP], which took outstanding American students around the world each year studying Global Ecology.

In April, Jo and I left for Schumacher College. We arrived in Devon at the height of spring, with trees bursting with blossom and fresh green leaves and the woods carpeted with bluebells. We fell in love with the area and with Schumacher College, which was housed in a restored medieval building of grey stone on Dartington Estate. Jo and I were given a comfortable self-contained flat.

Disturbing news awaited us. After a hectic workshop schedule that had had her travelling back-and-forth across the US in the early part of the year, Angeles decided she should rest, so she apologised to the College that she would not be coming to teach. The front office was waiting to ask me what was to be done. Not unreasonably, they felt let down by Angeles – as did I. It was decided that I should teach both the first and third weeks of the course, with Jonathan teaching the second week as scheduled.

As can be imagined, the students were upset by the news

they received on arrival. Of our trio, Angeles was the indisputable star, an author with an international following. There was no question in my mind that it was her name on the marquee that had filled the course to capacity. Some students decided to withdraw, and their fees were refunded. The great majority stayed on, but there was discontent.

This was not an ideal situation for teaching, and I made matters worse with my efforts to meet concerns expressed by the College Administrator and the Programme Officer that the course not be purely experiential, as the only other shamanic programme hosted by the College had been. They wanted me to insure our programme included academic material. In order to do this, I modified my normal workshop content to include more lectures on traditional shamanism. This was not well received by some of the students.

Jo and I had originally planned to explore Cornwall during the week Jonathan would teach, and to return to the College to sit in on Angeles' week. We decided to proceed with the Cornwall expedition but reduce our time away slightly so I could sit in on the final two days of Jonathan's class before I resumed teaching. We took a rental car and had a wonderful time wandering the beautiful Cornish countryside and rugged coast. In particular, we hunted out sacred springs and stone circles and found ample evidence that pantheism was alive and well in contemporary Cornwall.

Returning to Schumacher College, I joined Jonathan's class as planned and was struck by how similar his shamanic techniques were to my own. This should not have surprised me, given that he had also trained with Michael Harner. I was rather envious of the close rapport he had established with the students, and I was in for a rude shock when I took over the class. A spokesperson informed me that the group had decided to run the programme themselves in this final week. Frankly, I had trouble letting go and agreeing to this. The excuse I made to myself was that I was being paid to fill in for Angeles, but in retrospect, it is obvious to me that I like to be a leader. The students and I negotiated a compromise where they would run their own show for most of the week, and I would close out the programme on the final two days.

As a footnote, I should observe that I was never invited back to Schumacher College. When a year or two later, I offered to organise another shamanic course, I was told that my teaching had not been given favourable reviews by a majority of the students. Their criticism? I was "too academic!"

~ ~ ~

Although things had not worked as well as we had hoped, Jo and I left with great fondness for Schumacher College, the exquisite Dartington Estate and the lovely nearby town of Totnes. We were headed now for the Findhorn Community in Scotland, where we were leading a "Spirit in Nature" workshop from June 16.

We had kept the rental car and had a fortnight to drive virtually the length of Great Britain. It was a splendid journey, almost all of it in fine weather, and it gave us rich memories. These were often a mix of the beautiful and the droll. Take, for example, our first stop in the small city of Wells. In addition to the cathedral, Britain's earliest in the Gothic style dating from the twelfth century, the city presented the unexpected delight of a Morris Dance Troupe performing in the main square, with the heavily perspiring actor Martin Clunes struggling to keep pace with other much fitter troupe members.

Our Wells B&B was considerably larger than the average establishment, with perhaps a dozen bedrooms. To Jo's delight, we were booked into one that promised the overnight companionship of a cat – and indeed, the cat arrived to settle in its own bassinette as we were preparing for bed. In the morning, we were amused by the contrast between cages of garrulous parrots in the entry foyer and the silence of the humans around a large oval table in the breakfast room. Our good morning greetings were scarcely acknowledged, and our requests for the toast, butter, and marmalade to be passed seemed to be regarded as an intrusion by some of our fellow guests.

From Wells, we travelled north through the West Country, keeping well away from London and its heavily populated surroundings. We stopped for two days with sister Bronwen and brother-in-law John Robinson. Both doctors, they had worked in the Cheshire County health system since 1966. They had a lovely house, Padeswood Lodge, in the Welsh hills, 30-minutes west of Chester. My parents had moved from New Zealand to live out their retirement in Chester to be close to their daughter and one set of grandchildren. They had died in 1991 and 1992, and I felt their absence painfully on this, my first visit back since their deaths.

From North Wales, we ambled through the Lake District, visiting my ancestral Braithwaite town of Kendal, before driving up the west coast of Scotland as far as Fort William. From there, our journey took us via Loch Ness to Inverness and on to Findhorn, 42 km east on Moray Firth.

As we approached Findhorn, we were in for a surprise. Bells and lights signalled a closure of the road as a huge B52 bomber came in to land on a runway just on the other side of the fence. In all the literature I had read about the exceptional gardens established on sandhills by the Findhorn founders and the lovely ecovillage built by the community to replace the old caravan park, there was not one mention of the fact that Findhorn was located cheek-by-jowl with an active NATO airbase. Every half hour or so, a huge jet roared overhead at a low level, momentarily drowning out every activity in the community.

Airbase or not, there was no question that Findhorn was a lovely place, physically and in spirit. It was perfect for our weeklong exploration of "Spirit in Nature," and we had an excellent workshop group of 12 drawn from across Europe.

The high point of the week for me was an incident involving a Dutch group member, Jobs, and her kindergarten-aged daughter, which I continue to recount to my workshop groups as possibly supplying the answer to one of the most common questions about shamanic journeying: "Is what a person experiences on a shamanic journey simply imagination?" One evening early in the week, I led the group on a fairly standard shamanic exercise: a journey to the land of the dead. The next morning around breakfast time, Jobs rang home, and her little daughter took the phone with great excitement. "Mummy," she said, "last night, I saw you flying with dead people."

I should add that Jobs could not have seeded this idea in her daughter's head with some prior description of shamanic journeying. This was her first phone call to her family since arriving in Findhorn, and until she came on this trip, she knew nothing about shamanism. In fact, she had signed on for our workshop, mistakenly assuming that "Spirit in Nature" would explore the techniques the Findhorn founders had used to get spirit help in creating the renowned gardens!

~ ~ ~

On our return journey from Scotland, we travelled on the Caledonian Express, an overnight flyer from Inverness to London. We had reserved a double sleeping compartment, but discovering it could be converted to two singles, we did that to give Jo a night free of my stentorian snoring! We left Inverness in the early evening and had picture-perfect views of the Highlands in the long summer gloaming. My most romantic memory, however, was after dark in Edinburgh, looking up sheer cliffs to the floodlit ramparts of the Castle.

It was mid-winter 2001 when we arrived back home in NZ to discover that the Marlborough Sounds were still suffering from the severe drought that had started the previous summer. The effects were aggravated for Te Wairua by the fact that the large plantation (perhaps 25 hectares of conifers) uphill from us was being harvested by a timber company. The major creek from which we took our water came through the plantation, and because the timber company was illegally dragging logs through it, its flow was not infrequently reduced to a trickle. On those occasions, I had to rescue tuna (eels) and kokopu (small fresh-water fish) by relocating them to pools deep enough to survive the reduced flow. Caring for Te Wairua in our absence, friend Laura Sessions had had to mount rescue missions for hungry weka, many displaced from the plantation. She kept water bowls filled around the property and laid out daily feeds of rice, which attracted as many as 30 birds at a time.

Homecoming was saddened by the news from Nikki that her husband Hank had died. He was a Vietnam War veteran whose lungs had been affected by deadly Agent Orange, the defoliant that US forces had poured onto the Vietnamese, Cambodian and Laotian countryside in an effort to deprive enemy combatants of protective cover. The effects were fatal for hundreds of US veterans like Hank and for millions of Southeast Asian civilians and military.

~ ~ ~

I was woken soon after daybreak on September 10, 2001, by a tearful Jo standing by the bed wailing, "Terrorists are attacking America." She, as usual, had woken earlier than I and had turned on the radio to the news of airplanes crashing into the World Trade Center in New York and the Pentagon in Washington, DC. We spent the day rivetted to the TV as it broadcast, again and again, appalling images of people falling to their death from the flaming World Trade Center and the unimaginable collapse of its twin towers. We were certain the administration of President George W. Bush would leap immediately to a retaliatory military response, making a bad situation worse. A few days later, I emailed friends around the world "Reflections penned in sorrow and apprehension, Te Wairua, Pelorus Sound, New Zealand, September 16, 2001."

"APPROPRIATE RESPONSES TO THE SEPTEMBER 11 ATROCITIES OF A SECURE, SELF-CONFIDENT, AND COM-PASSIONATE AMERICAN LEADERSHIP

"1. Reappraise and strengthen US intelligence-gathering apparatus and security systems.

"2. With international cooperation, hunt down and bring to the bar of justice all involved with this heinous con-spiracy. This to be done with due process of law, thereby providing a model of restraint to other nations facing security threats, e.g. Israel and the Palestinians, Russia and the Chechens, Macedonia and the Albanians.

"3. Explain carefully to the American people that terrorism cannot be countered with conventional military force. The analogy of the needle in the haystack will be useful. If the haystack is set alight, it will be the hay, not the needle, that is destroyed; innocents killed rather than the guilty. The objective is the reduction of violence, not its escalation.

"4. Apply massive Federal resources to assist individuals, families, communities, businesses, and other organisa-tions to heal and rebuild.

"5. Move calmly to restore global economic confidence.

"6. To signal that the US values international collabora-tive efforts to find solutions to global problems, affirm American support for the Kyoto accord on climate con-trol, the treaty controlling biological weapons, etc.

"7. Acknowledge the role of the arms industry in the world-wide culture of violence and mobilise American opinion against US participation in this lethal trade.

"8. Acknowledge that the pervasive movie and TV images of violence poison consciousness around the world and mobilise American opinion against this toxic Hollywood export.

"9. Intensify efforts to assist the poor and needy through-out the world, including the millions of refugees, by stepping up US support for Non-Governmental Organizations dispensing aid.

"10. Recognizing the vulnerability of high technology and the centralised bureaucratic systems associated with them, give large-scale Federal funding to apply the alternative technologies that already exist in fields such as transportation, energy, building design and decentralised workplaces.

"11. Fund educational programs to create a deeper American understanding of Islam and the profound concerns of Muslims about America's role in the world.

~ ~ ~

In February 2002, I received an email from David Wright in Sydney:

"John. Just finished reading your book, Other Ways of Knowing and can see real opportunities for communication. Am now working in a cross-disciplinary group at Uni of Western Sydney [UWS] where issues you discuss are part of our content and process. We have students working on research degrees round shamanic practices and the such-like. Have also staff and students who have had significant contact with CIIS. We are a fringe group in Australian academia. We relish the opportunity to work with people such as yourself."

An exchange of correspondence over the following weeks led to an invitation for Jo and me to participate in a postgraduate residential school at the Hawkesbury campus of UWS, July 24-28, 2002. As a Scholar in Residence, I would address a plenary session and advise individual research students on their dissertations. Both Jo and I would also contribute to small group discussions.

The spacious UWS campus at the foot of the Blue Mountains in Richmond, NSW was a former agricultural college, and the hut Jo and I were given sat on a concrete slab that seemed to suck in the cold of the mid-winter nights. The days were bright and warm, however, and the intellectual vigour of the Social Ecology Programme we had joined was infectious. The Programme was led by the brilliant and irrepressible Professor Stuart Hill, an expatriate Englishman who had started his academic life as a Zoologist but had blazed a trail from Natural Ecology to a defining role in the new field of Social Ecology "to integrate the personal, social and environmental." He had gathered around him at UWS a lively group of similar disciplinary mavericks, and their statement of purpose gladdened my heart: "An emphasis on equity and social justice, personal and collaborative action, imagination and learning from nature and history."

Jo and I had a wonderfully stimulating week, and I continued to work with the Programme for a number of years as a member of doctoral committees. I also contributed a chapter entitled "We Are Not Alone, The Shamans Tell Us" to a book published by Programme members in 2011, *Social Ecology: Applying Ecological Understanding to Our Lives and Our Planet.*

~ ~ ~

In the spring of 2003 (the Northern Hemisphere spring), I was back in India to lead another tour group in the Himalaya. My arrival in New Delhi close to midnight – international flights typically arrive in and depart from India in the middle of the night – gave me proof (as I wrote to Jo) that "India is still India."

> "At India International Centre [IIC] a porter took me to my room on the third floor but couldn't persuade the key to open the door. He then proceeded to pound on the door, presumably to flush out whatever rascal had stolen my room at 12:30 am. When he started to shout, I managed to get him to check the key to see if it was the right room, but that proved inconclusive, as the number on the key had been painted over indistinctly. He resumed the assault on the door but finally agreed with my suggestion that he check again with reception. As he headed in that direction (leaving me and my bags outside the battered door to face whoever might emerge angrily), there materialised in the corridor a small bedraggled person. This angel, whom I can only assume was a sweeper, took one look at the key and guided us straight to the correct room. Ah, India!"

The next morning I was out walking in Lodi Gardens, which border the grounds of IIC and are favoured by New Delhi's middle-class for brisk morning walks. A monkey's behaviour startled me.

> "I was ambling across the grass, avoiding the big crowds of intense Sunday-morning striders on the sealed paths, when to my amusement, I noticed a monkey sitting comfortably on a bench, looking very relaxed. I ambled over in that direction, though keeping a cautious distance, especially as it was a male. As the monkey was sizing me up, a small Indian woman in shorts striding by on a near-

by path caught his attention. He climbed off the bench, ran up behind her and grabbed one of her legs. She had not seen him coming and was startled out of her wits. Her scream made him let go briefly. He then embraced both her legs and looked as though he was about to climb up her shorts. She shouted and tried to push him off, and he let go only when I ran towards them, also shouting. The woman said to me, 'Why did he do that?' I had no answer. When monkeys go bad, perhaps? Or monkey lust? 'It's just India, madam,' I should have said."

"Over breakfast that same morning, I found a story in the day's newspaper that was replete with Indian logic. Headline: 'Bharatanatyam: a Bulgarian Odyssey.' 'Liliya Toneva from Bulgaria recently performed Indian classical dance at Lily Pool Lawns of Hotel Ashok as part of the World French Language Day.'

"I lunched in the IIC Lounge. The room was ringing with the loud cheerful voices of an animated Sunday crowd, and my glass table was vibrating so much from the sound I could scarcely read the new card thereon. It said: 'Members will kindly speak in low tones for the comfort and convenience of their neighbours.' 'Right on,' I was tempted to shout.

"In the upstairs Dining Room, there is another new notice, which is treated with the same measure of respect: 'Members will kindly switch off cell phones when entering the dining area.' Not on your life. Who in India would want to miss the opportunity of shouting repeated 'Hellos' at the top of one's lungs in a crowded dining room?"

~ ~ ~

India could surprise with its efficiencies as much as with its inefficiencies, as noted in my account of our tour group's departure from Delhi by train:

"What was mindboggling for me was the quality of Executive Chair Class. The seats were well-padded and comfortable, and the reclining mechanism worked. The windows were large and clean. Most amazing of all was the service. We were first offered complimentary newspapers and magazines. Then a choice of tea or coffee. Then a full cooked breakfast, with more tea or coffee. All complimentary. The toilets were kept clean, and there was a good supply of TP. Moreover, in four-and-a-half hours, we had only two stops on the 270km journey to Jalandhar, and we arrived almost on time."

It was not the quality of the Executive Chair Class that caught the attention of my tour group members, first-time travellers on Indian Railways. At New Delhi station, they enjoyed the amazing sights and sounds of the crowded platforms, if not the odours. They were very impressed later by a notice in the train telling them that New Delhi station, with some mindbogglingly large number of passengers in the millions per year, is the world's busiest railway hub.

Our subsequent three weeks of travel in the Himalaya gave us the chance to experience every range of efficiency and inefficiency, so we were well prepared for what we confronted on our final day when we flew back to Delhi from the small airfield at Kangra.

"We were shepherded into the security area for a rigorous body search and baggage inspection. Then, as we waited in the tiny departure lounge, the group was presented with the gift of one of those totally absurd, side-splitting Indian happenings. We had been surprised at how much high-level police brass was assembled in the airport parking lot. As time passed, they were joined by close to 100 men and women carrying marigold *malas* and huge blown-up photos of a man, woman and boy. It transpired that these were photos of the newly elected Congress Party Chief Minister of Himachal Pradesh and family, who were just flying in from Simla for some ceremony at Dharamsala. The crowd was the welcoming party.

"Led by the District Officer, all 100 suddenly came pouring through our waiting room and out onto the tarmac, excitedly preparing the garlands and arranging the photos for full effect. Of course, all the careful security checks to which we had been subjected were now pointless as none of this milling throng was checked in any way – and they kept running backwards and forwards through the wildly beeping security sensors. My group was in stitches.

"After about 30 minutes, we were shepherded to our plane, wending our way through the hyper crowd on the runway, and we were in our seats when the CM and party were landed by helicopter. They emerged to wild shouts of acclamation. The *tamasha* was in full swing as we took off over the crowd."

~ ~ ~

For six years from 2001, I served on dissertation committees for doctoral students of the Union Institute, Cincinnati, Ohio, a university providing external degree programmes for older adults across the US and Canada. How I came to be appointed to Union's adjunct faculty, I cannot recall, but I enjoyed this opportunity for ongoing involvement with doctoral research and for providing feedback on thesis writing. Participation in dissertation exams also gave me several trips to the US. Jo accompanied me on one of these in the summer of 2004, and after I had performed my duties as examiner in Boulder, CO, she flew to Iowa to visit her friend, Nicky Mendenhall, and I went to the Michigan Upper Peninsula to see Nikki and her two sons, Phillip and Tyler, and then to Maryland for a brief stay with Alastair and Deborah and their three children, Mark, Bennett and Cole, in their beautiful 1805 house in the Baltimore outer suburb of Eldersburg.

Alastair's company GloboMax had been bought by an Irish company in Fall 2003, and when I visited, his position had been eliminated along with most of the upper management. He had accepted an appointment at LifeBridge Health as Manager, IT Applications. LifeBridge comprised five Acute Hospitals in the Baltimore area plus another 100-or-so physician offices. They also owned other clinical businesses, such as Express Care, which consisted of a number of Emergency Walk-in Clinics around the Baltimore area. Alastair still held this position 20 years later, by which time he could report that they had 5,500 online users daily and were processing about 3 million transactions a day on their system.

~ ~ ~

Waiting for us on our return to Te Wairua in July 2004, Jo and I found a letter from Joanna Macy, which brought back a flood of nostalgia for the Himalayan village of Naggar, where we had spent the better part of 1989 on sabbatical leave from CIIS as I was writing *Other Ways of Knowing*. The house we had rented adjoined the estate of the Russian painters and mystics Nikolai and Helena Roerich, who lived in Naggar from 1928 until Nikolai's death in 1947. We discovered that Nikolai's memorial garden, where his ashes were interred, was choked with long grass and other weeds, and Jo worked for many months to restore it, in the process earning the gratitude and friendship of the estate custodian.

Joanna Macy, from Berkeley, CA, June 8, 2004:

"I'm back now from two months in Sri Lanka and India and am eager to tell you how much Fran and I were thinking of you both. Were your ears burning in late May?

That's when we were in Himachal Pradesh and then Delhi.

"We went first to Kangra, but the heat was intense, and we chose to move to cooler Kulu. That's when our thoughts of you went into high gear. Remembering your happy references to Naggar, we proceeded to go there for the first time. And we fell in love with the place.

"What a world you dwelt in back there in 1989! To us newcomers, it seems to be still unspoiled. Except for a group of Russian painters, there were hardly any pale-skinned tourists. The annual mela was underway, with everything from a man-powered Ferris-wheel to a volleyball tournament by the Tripura Devi temple and roulette tables and palanquins with goddess masks processing with drums and great curved horns. Sometimes the palanquins, as we noted by the hilltop Krishna temple, have a mind of their own, making it hard for the bearers to carry them where they don't want to go.

"We walked our legs off – through village streets, over to Roerich's place, up into apple orchards, south through deodar groves to the village of Nashalla. How could you bear to leave that Eden? Where did you live? Tell us. I tried to find a cyber-café (line down) to ask you while we were still there. Do I recall correctly that you, Jo, were performing some function for the Roerich Museum? We spent sweet hours there and would love to know. A number of Fran's Russian colleagues in environmental work adore Roerich and have brought us fine books of reproductions."

— CHAPTER SEVENTEEN —

Travels & Travails

"Every journey has a secret destination of which the traveller is unaware."
                                    – Martin Buber

On December 26, 2004, a monster underwater earthquake off Sumatra generated a tsunami that devastated coastal areas in Indonesia and Thailand and swept westward across the Bay of Bengal to cause similar havoc in Sri Lanka and South India. I had a tour to South India scheduled to start little more than a week after the disaster, and naturally I was uncertain whether to proceed. I checked with a friend in Chennai, Ranjith Henry, himself a tour operator, and he assured me that roads along the Tamilnadu coast were open, and most hotels were operating. My tour group members were eager to go ahead, and that's what I decided to do.
To Lisa Shaw from Te Wairua, February 28, 2005

"I reorganised the first week of the tour because of the devastation at our first scheduled destination, the beach village of Mahabalipuram, where our intended hotel was badly damaged. Instead, we started with two days in Chennai, which gave us an opportunity to get briefings on the relief situation from a local Tamil friend, Ranjith Henry, who works with Fair Trade groups and eco-tourism, and from the relief coordinators of CARE.

"The picture that emerged was that both government officials and social service NGOs had gone into action promptly disposing of bodies and restoring services (water, sewage, transportation, etc.) to ensure there was no outbreak of contagious diseases. Also, a good job had been done all along the coast in providing emergency food, water and clothing, and temporary housing was being rapidly constructed for displaced villagers. The CARE people considered the greatest immediate need was trauma counselling, and they were recruiting and training Tamil-speaking counsellors. Large sums of money for relief were available from government departments and private donors (national and international), but there were reports of inequitable distribution, with dalits (untouchables) being neglected, as is so often the case in India. From what I heard as we travelled in the following three weeks, I would judge the official Indian figures of dead and missing (together a total of around 13,000) is probably too low.

"From Chennai, we travelled 100 miles down the coast to Pondicherry. We stopped at a number of places along the way, including Mahabalipuram, to look at the damage and see some of the resettlement camps, most of which appeared relatively substantial and well laid out. What we observed here, as also in the Pondicherry beach village in which we volunteered, was the dramatic difference coastal topography made to the tsunami's impact. Alongside an area where boats were smashed, trees uprooted, cottages gutted and paddy fields swamped in salt water there could be a totally untouched area. The most obvious protective features were sandhills and sea walls, but we were told that variations in the gradient and contours of the offshore seafloor also made a huge difference. The saddest thing to observe in the damaged villages was that the poorest families were almost always the worst hit, because their houses were built of the least sturdy materials."

One of the active NGOs was Auroville, a New Age international community a few kilometres north of Pondicherry. When we reached Pondicherry, our group decided to assist for a day with the Auroville relief effort.

Fax to Jo from Anandha Inn, Pondicherry, January 15, 2005:

"Tuesday we were away from the hotel at 8:15 to do our stint of Auroville tsunami relief work. Close to 100 volunteers – people from all over the world – assembled at one of the Auroville communities, and we were bused to a fishing village about 8km up the coast. Although the tsunami was two weeks ago, the village was still piled with debris from cottages (of which about one-quarter were destroyed), broken boats, uprooted trees, tangled net and rope segments, thatch, personal possessions, etc. We were provided with rakes, mattocks, leather gloves and (for those who wanted them) light masks. These for the dust; there was no smell.

"We continued work started by previous days' volunteers, separating the burnable trash from the plastic and other non-burnables, and then hauling the burnables on tarpaulins to piles on the beach, which were set alight. The non-burnables were buried in a big hole. In the blazing sun and working on sand, it was hot, dusty, and tiring. We were well provided with water and (late morning) bananas, biscuits, and tea.

"I have to say the experience had a somewhat surreal feeling. For one thing, there was no real opportunity to connect with the people who had lived through this appalling horror just three weeks before. The village, which had perhaps 50-60 houses before December 26, was empty except for a handful of men sitting on the smashed hulls of fishing boats, some old women and pre-teen girls wandering about or squatting in the doorways of their damaged cottages and a few male youths, who were the only ones to lend a hand occasionally with the clean-up. I have no doubt the villagers were traumatised. They were like sleepwalkers. I don't speak or understand Tamil, so I couldn't ask them questions or even tell them how sorry I was. In this village, 10-20 people had been killed (the accounts varied) and half the houses had been reduced to ruins. Adding to the surreal quality was the backdrop of a beautiful golden sandy beach and a calm blue sea.

"Arriving in the village felt like coming upon a highway crash after the ambulances have removed the dead and injured but with the stunned survivors still sitting on the roadside amid the remains of their vehicles. You can only guess at how awful the experience was and, however much you sympathise, you cannot help with the emotional pain.

"On a lighter note, two young guys from Auroville who were working with us (one from France, the other from the US) had been surfing on the tsunami morning. The sea was flat, so they were delighted when they saw this big wave rolling in. They both caught it and then discovered it was a wave like no other they had ever ridden. One of them finished halfway up a coconut palm and the other was deposited in a paddy field a couple of hundred yards inland. Neither was injured, and even their surfboards survived! Imagine how they will dine out on that story for the rest of their lives.

"We worked until about 1:00 pm when we were bused back to Auroville and fed a great vegetarian lunch. I must say it is a very well-organised effort. Speaking with Jesus Ciriza at Colours of Nature the following day, I discovered there are already plans in place to provide training opportunities in technical skills for young people from the affected villages. I gave a Rs.6000/- donation (about NZ$200)."

~ ~ ~

Jo delivered an immense surprise for my 70th birthday in July 2005: two albums of photographs and messages of congratulations from family and friends around the world. Over the preceding months, she had solicited tributes and photos from various stages of my life and assembled them into the two wonderful albums. She had managed this so secretively that I had had no hint of what she was up to. I had even failed to notice that every Tuesday afternoon since May she had found ways to beat me to the mailboat and sort out the birthday letters from the mailbag before I could see them. The albums were (and remain) a superb gift.

In August 2005, I joined Jean Houston and Sohail Inayatullah in leading a ten-day "Social Artistry" conference on Fraser Island on the Queensland Sunshine Coast. The previous May as a result of my week at UWS three-years earlier, I had been invited to a preparatory gathering in Brisbane organised by Social Artistry Australia, a fledgling organisation inspired by Jean's writings. Jo accompanied me to Fraser Island, and we were awed by the setting for the conference: a luxury resort on a golden-sand beach with a backdrop of forested hills laced with walking trails. The size of the resort made it easy to forget how wild Fraser Island is until one saw dingoes padding along the beach and unconcernedly through the complex.

We were glad I had resisted the efforts of the hyper conference organiser to fill my every moment with conference activity. Even so, I had been unable to persuade Caffeinated Kathy (as Jo and I nicknamed her) that scheduling activities each day from 6:30 am to 10:00 pm was over the top.

Jean Houston, a charismatic personality two-years younger than I, had been publishing books since her twenties, and by 2005 she had 15 titles to her name. A leading figure in the Human Potential Movement, she described her role as "developing leaders for a new world." By 2005 she was touring almost non-stop, teaching worldwide with her associate, Peggy Rubin. Sohail Inyatullah, a Political Scientist originally from Pakistan, taught at Sydney's Macquarie University and was co-editor of the *Journal of Futures Studies*.

Jean had coined the term "Social Artistry," which she defined as "a new model for leadership." In this new millennium, she said, "we must use what we know to educate ourselves for the next civilization, the one that exceeds our expectations. In a sense, what is needed is training for the unknown and inexplicable." Although participants came from the Philippines and the US as well as New Zealand and Australia, the total enrolment was only 65, which was a major disappointment to the organisers. Nonetheless it was an inspiring week. Responding to the stimulating drama of Jean's and Peggy's teachings, role playing and other exercises, the group was a joy to work with.

From Fraser Island, Jo returned home, while I flew to Alice Springs to lead another Outback tour.

~ ~ ~

In April 2006, I had a tour scheduled to the Indian Himalaya, and Jo decided to come with me. Nicky Mendenhall, with whom Jo felt especially close, had signed on for the tour, as had my niece, Rachel Robinson. A few days before we were to fly out from Nelson, Jo went for a routine mammogram. To our dismay, the x-ray revealed a lump in her right breast, and tissue was taken for a biopsy. The results would not be available immediately, and after consulting a surgeon, Jo decided to go ahead with the travel. I was very glad we would be back in India together, but I worried about the possible consequences for her of delaying treatment should the biopsy reveal cancer.

We were in McLeod Gang, a week into the tour, when an

email arrived from Tim Ewer with the bad news that the biopsy had revealed metastasised cancer. It seemed such a cruel blow that, just when Jo felt she had worked her way back to health from CFS, she now faced cancer. Niece Rachel offered to accompany her if she wanted to fly back to NZ immediately for an operation, but she decided to continue with the tour for the remaining fortnight. Nicky was giving her close support and was a tower of strength for her.

As soon as we were back in Nelson, Tim Ewer arranged an MRI scan for her in Christchurch to ensure there was no infection in her left breast. After this, she and I flew to Wellington to consult Chris Adams, the surgeon who would reconstruct her breast after Nelson surgeon Graeme Skeggs performed the partial mastectomy. Chris told Jo he could use tissue from her stomach for the reconstruction, giving her a tummy tuck at the same time. Jo quipped, "This cancer thing just gets better and better!"

She had surgery at a small private hospital in Nelson on May 16 to remove her right breast and surrounding tissue, including lymph glands that were infected. This was followed immediately by the breast reconstruction. She was in hospital for a week, and said she was feeling very good when I came to take her home. As she was packing the last of her things, she was paying no attention to the hospital PA system, but I was dismayed by the music that was playing. It was Annie Lennox singing "Into the West," the final funereal track from "The Lord of the Rings" movie trilogy.

"Lay down your sweet and weary head
Night is falling
You have come to journey's end.
Sleep now and dream of the ones who came before.
They are calling from across the distant shore...
What can you see on the horizon?
Why do the white gulls call?...

A light on the water
Grey ships pass into the west."

It seemed to me a bad omen.

A biopsy on tissue removed during the operation revealed a more extensive spread of the cancer than had been expected, and a six-week course of chemotherapy was recommended. Jo began this in late June, and it made her horribly ill. We stayed in Nelson for most of this treatment, blessing our 1998 decision to buy the house in town.

Chemo was followed in October and November by five weeks of radiotherapy in Christchurch. In our search for accommodation in the city, I posted a request in the newsletters of both the CBHS Old Boys' Association and the Canterbury Varsity Rugby Club. The latter brought an offer from Jim and Nancy Stewart of the use of their townhouse in Beckenham. Jim had been an inspirational captain and coach of my Varsity senior rugby team. He had gone on to become Vice Chancellor of Lincoln College, and his service had been rewarded with a knighthood. Sir James and Lady Nancy Stewart now lived in retirement in the North Canterbury town of Amberley. Their small Christchurch place was perfect for Jo and me, and we had a lovely five weeks in the city, despite Jo's daily radiation treatments.

Halloween produced unexpected amusement. From Jo's journal:

"When the first kids knocked on the door, John was talking on the phone with Gail Donovan, and all three of us were sharing a joke. Laughing, bald-headed Jo opened the door to dole out the lollies, forgetting to put on her head scarf. There stood a girl of about eight in some sort of costume and her mother. They took one look at Jo and started laughing, too. They apparently thought she had specially donned a bald skullcap for Halloween to amuse them, which made Jo laugh harder at their delight at her supposed creativity. Afterwards John told Gail, and she said, 'Yeah, and if they only knew how much effort Jo went to to get that look for them!' We almost fell down laughing when John added, 'Oh, my God, wait until it hits that mother that she was laughing at a person with cancer!'"

~ ~ ~

We returned home in mid-November to find that Te Wairua had just been battered by a succession of storms that had dumped eight or nine inches of rain. Our main creek was flooding across the access road, and the culvert was so completely clogged with boulders, gravel, and mud it was difficult to see where exactly it ran under the road. All the intakes to pipes that brought water to the house had been swept out of the stream, and I had to get to work immediately laying an alternative small-bore pipe to give us drinking water. It took Jo and me more than a week of hard labour with crowbar and shovel to clear the culvert and restore the main water supply.

Throughout the year, Jo had received messages of sympathy and encouragement from friends around the world, and in a letter at Christmas she combined her thanks for their support with an invitation for them to join in funding projects in India.

"In the last seven months as I have been undergoing cancer treatment, John and I have been on the receiving end of countless supportive emails, cards, phone calls and gifts, and now, with your help, we'd like to try to give back a bit of what we have received.

"As some of you know, we have been financially aiding projects in India for years, including supporting three Tibetan refugee families at Tashi Jong community in the

Indian Himalayan foothills. Because of the generosity of others who have joined in this effort, our Tibetan goddaughter Pema Dekyi has just successfully completed three years of nursing school at a top-notch institution, something that was light years beyond the reach of her refugee family. She is now back at Tashi Jong helping her mother, Dawa, the community nurse. She plans to work soon in a government hospital in New Delhi to upgrade her skills and gain much-needed experience. As a bonus, she has inspired two other equally poor young women at Tashi Jong to aspire to nursing school, and John and I are part of their financial support team as well.

"Currently we have five projects in India we think are highly worthy of support:

At Tashi Jong, we want to establish a fund to enable some of the community's young people to enter the excellent vocational training programmes provided by the Tibetan Government in Exile. These are youths who are not scholastically inclined or gifted enough to qualify for scholarships to universities. Until they gain technical skills, they will have little or no opportunity to find employment in their adopted country.

Tashi Jong also has an urgent need to expand a classroom and playground for boys enrolled at its Kampagar Monastery School. At present 70 boys are training, with 10 more joining the school each year. The current facilities are too cramped to accommodate this many children.

When we were in India in April, we took our group to the Tibetan Children's Village in Dharamsala, which runs a network of schools throughout India for thousands of refugees still pouring out of Chinese-occupied Tibet. All the children are orphans or are from poor families still in Tibet thousands of miles away. Our tour group members brought with them suitcases full of used and new clothing for the children. The 'house-mothers' who care for the toddlers and infants immediately came to gather up clothing for their charges. We were told that clothing was in very short supply for children in these age groups. We are hoping to raise funds to assist in this area.

In the past, some of you have helped support our friend Satya Misra, who runs a school in eastern India for underprivileged village children and an organic farm to help finance the school. Thanks to this money from you and a small charitable trust, Satya's school and farm have been able to buy much needed items including a plough, water pump and cows, to build a cow shed and to reforest local areas devastated by a super-cyclone in 2003. Satya's second-hand computer died a few months ago, cutting him off from contact with donors and from others engaged in holistic education and organic farming. Now he's only able to use a cyber café every few weeks when he bikes to town miles away. Satya doesn't know this, but John and I hope to raise about US$500 to buy him a replacement computer.

Another organisation we are supporting is Nanban, a project to house and educate Indian children in Madurai run by a wonderful Indian priest named Bother James. Our South India tour groups regularly visit Nanban and are always deeply moved by the tremendous projects for abandoned, orphaned and desperately poor street children. Nanban has a thriving bakery, an organic farm, a school and other training programs, including India's first (perhaps only) scooter-taxi business for young women owner-drivers!

"Will you help us? We personally know and respect the people heading these projects, and we can testify to how much difference even a small donation can make. To give you an example: A Tibetan or Indian family can be supported adequately for a mere US$60 a month, compared to the hundreds or thousands most of us spend on our own families each month. A little bit of money goes a very long way in India.

"You can designate the project or projects to which you want your money to go or allow us to distribute it. Please know that every penny you send will go directly to these projects. John and I cover all administrative costs, and also tithe 10 to 12 percent of our income each month to these and other worthy projects. We fully understand that many of you support your own charitable causes and may not be able to contribute to these, and we bless you for the work you are already doing.

"In the meantime, we send you our love and gratitude for the extraordinary kindness you have extended to us during these last seven months. A thousand thank yous!"

With her spirits lifted by our return to Te Wairua and feeling in much better health, Jo joked about death. In her journal she wrote, "I have made John promise that if I die, he will try to milk all our friends for more donations for our India projects. We're calling it the Croak Fund, which makes me giggle every time I think of it!"

Throughout her illness, she had been impressed by her experience of the New Zealand health system, and this was reinforced after our return to Te Wairua by a phone call she received from one of the radiation technicians on her Christchurch team checking on her welfare.

"John suggested I write to the Listener, which serves as a national forum on all sorts of issues, so I did. The health service is perpetually under fire – too many demands on too tiny a system – but Kiwis don't have anything to compare it to. I find it vastly more caring and compassionate and personal than anything I had in the US, as well as far less expensive. I have never once received a bill for anything except some of my prescription drugs, and most of those are government subsidised. The government is also paying for our travel and accommodations throughout this. The only thing that isn't covered – and this is substantial – is my alternative complementary care, though with great generosity John Black gives me free acupuncture treatments still."

~ ~ ~

In May 2007, I was interviewed by Dawne Sanson, a Massey University doctoral candidate, who was at work on a dissertation entitled Taking the Spirits Seriously: Neo-Shamanism and Contemporary Shamanic Healing in New Zealand. I began the interview with a statement of what I described as "my general view of reality."

"My view of the universe it that it is at core a great consciousness, a great mind. This doesn't mean that the non-material is more basic, but everything flows out of consciousness. I don't like the dichotomy sometimes made between the non-material and material. Matter is also consciousness; everything is consciousness, everything is mind. Beginnings are not really important. Stuff manifests, but it is all temporary. I like those philosophies that see the world as a great flux, with everything constantly changing its form. Some of that – in human terms – takes vast periods of time, while in other cases it happens all the time, instantaneously. Nothing is really fixed; the appearance of things is only an appearance.

"My search in life is to try to get glimpses of what lies behind the appearances. I believe it's possible for people with the right disciplines – or possible for all of us on occasions – to slip behind the appearances. Hindus call this maya. Sometimes maya is translated as 'illusion.' I don't think it's illusion; it's only illusion if you think it's the totality of reality. In other words, it can be described as illusion if you've made the mistake of thinking that what we see is all there is.

"I believe it is possible to penetrate to other dimensions – other realities – and there are trainings that can bring this about. Hindu and Tibetan Buddhist yogis, drawing on years of training in the practices of their traditions, have the ability to enter other dimensions. Jesus, I believe, was a spiritual master who could see the greater reality, or aspects of it. If you like, the great mind is divinity.

"Powerful shamans are adept at penetrating the appearances and communicating between different aspects of reality. Consciousness is manifest in different forms, some plant, some animal, some human, and some that I would describe as spirit. Shamanism rests on a belief that all of nature is conscious and inspirited and that human health – the health of individuals and whole communities – depends on a harmonious balance with nature. The great shamans are communicators between diverse forms. I accept Mircea Eliade's definition of shamanism as the use of ecstatic access. Shamans use a trance state to access other dimensions. Around the world, entering into a trance state (through mind-altering sound or movement or the ingestion of a drug) is one of the ways our ancestors and our contemporaries in many cultures access healing knowledge by communication with the spirit world in all its diversity."

~ ~ ~

August 28, 2007, gave us a beautiful experience, a total eclipse of the full moon. Accompanied by the two cats, Jo and I wrapped up warmly and took chairs onto the end of the jetty. It was a totally calm, cloudless night and the moon at 8:45 was a large, brilliant silver disc in the north-eastern sky. Over the next hour it was devoured by the earth's shadow, as we ate canapés and drank champagne, serenaded by little blue penguins, weka, and moreporks, our most common owls. By 10 pm, we had Luna Rosa – a brick-red moon that had transformed from a disk to a solid sphere hanging in the sky like some marvellous vision from a fairy tale. At first it was edged with silver, but as time wore on it became darker and darker – as did everything around us. Meanwhile, the stars shone brighter and brighter, reflecting brilliantly in the mirror surface of the Sound. When all was dark, the moreporks (of which we could hear half-a-dozen at least) went a little crazy and gave rapid-fire calls like we've never heard before. It was not until the moon started to brighten again that they resumed their steady calling rhythm. We were out on the jetty for three hours until we could walk back to the house in brilliant, restored light.

For September 2007 to mark the golden anniversary of our New Zealand Universities swimming and water polo team's 1957 Australian tour, I organised a weekend reunion in Nelson. Only two members of the team were absent, the oldest Theo Verhoeven and the youngest Jim Marks, both of whom had died. Two team members came from the US: John Orbell from Eugene, Oregon, where he was a Professor of Political Science at the University of Oregon, and Stan Paris from St. Augustine, Florida, where he lived as a millionaire as a result of founding a number of for-profit physiotherapy universities. Jo declined to participate, as she did in almost all group activities in which I was involved, but all the other New Zealand team members were accompanied by their wives, Ian and Bev Macdonald, Fin and Barb MacKenzie, Graham and Alison Leach, Jim and Heather Sneyd, Keith and Jo Boswell, Otto and Maree Snoep, and Murray and Elizabeth Francis. We had a very convivial weekend of eating, drinking, and reminiscing.

On the tour, I had kept a daily diary, and I read extracts for my fellow team-members' entertainment.

~ ~ ~

In 2008 with her stamina returned, Jo joined me in teaching workshops, including one of five days in March in Queensland organised by Lynne Seddon, with whom we had formed a friendship at the Social Artistry Conference on Fraser Island in 2005.

Early in June 2008, we had a festive evening to celebrate Jo's two-year survival anniversary. Armed with piping hot baked potatoes and piping cold champagne, plus many other good things to nibble, we set up picnic chairs in the shelter of trees near our jetty with a fire to provide the right atmosphere. We were accompanied by the two cats, incredulously delighted by such unusual night-time behaviour by their normally staid human companions. Lots of weka in attendance as well, and a serenade from the beach by little blue penguins coming ashore to feed their nesting mates. To complete the entourage, we had an inquisitive young brush-tailed possum in the tree right overhead. We were well wrapped up, but the night proved unexpectedly warm, and we were contently out there for 2½ hours. It was a delightful evening.

For October-November 2008, Jo and I planned a three-week tour of Rajasthan, which drew on the experience gained on our exhilarating visit to the state in the winter of 1989. We recruited a group of 17 from the US, Canada, the UK, Australia, and NZ. Our promotional literature quoted an Australian journalist resident in Delhi:

"Rajasthan is a dream in sand and saltbrush, a martial desert where a mountain is not just a mountain, but a natural fortress. The Rajputs are a proud but mellow people with a culture of puppetry and balladeering. Their confidence is rooted in their role as warriors, whose ancestors acquitted themselves honourably during centuries of defiance against Muslim, Hindu, and Sikh invaders. They also cut deals, most notably with the Mughal Empire, which they served as governors and military commanders. The men are burnished and swaggering, with flamboyant moustaches and earrings; and the women dress like nomad princesses, even those who labour on the roads. To clothe themselves in this harsh wilderness, the Rajasthanis prefer colours that stand out – shades of scarlet and electric yellow, royal blue and neon green – a vivid wardrobe distinguishing friend from foe amid earth colours."

Dramatic though it is, this description is not an exaggeration. Rajasthan may be India's most vibrant region, and our tour sampled some of its best. The accommodations included a palace and a fortress, luxury tents along the shore of a water-bird sanctuary, a hotel in a city's medieval lanes and converted *haveli*, merchant families' traditional villas. In her journal, Jo described the tour's opening stages:

"Our first stop was a fabulous little village, Kishangar, just the right size and degree of quietude for newcomers to India. We stayed at a wonderful old palace set on a lake apart from the village. From our room, we looked across the lake to an island where there were a few old temples. Each morning I awoke looking out through the picture windows to the exquisite sight, plus the sounds of boat people singing as they went out to pick water chestnuts and devotional chanting coming from the temples.

"We surprised the group with a folk-dance performance one night, and it was superb. Picture gypsy-like women dancers with four men sitting on a rug playing strange stringed instruments and tabla drums. Another day we went for a guided walk through the sleepy village, which is renowned for its many artists.

"From Kishangar we took our air-conditioned bus to another village, even more remote, for two days of true luxury in elegant tents (complete with marble-tiled bathrooms) set on a family-owned reservoir with lots of birds and animals. The family was marvellous, taking our group for walks in the surrounding countryside and giving them cooking lessons. Terrific food, served at a luxurious open-air restaurant overlooking the reservoir. The second of our two nights there was Diwali, the festival of lights, so servants laid out elaborate walkways of tiny oil lamps in front of the tents and all around the lounge and restaurant. It was magical."

Our next stop could not have been a greater contrast: the teeming city of Jodhpur, dominated by the huge fifteenth-century fort of Mehranghar, an awesome edifice built on 400-foot cliffs. Directly below the fort, the old part of the city is an intriguing tangle of houses, temples, cafes, and shops. Our guesthouse was a converted *haveli* on one of the lanes that made up the tangle, lanes too narrow for our bus, so we had to off-load outside the old city gates and send the group in pairs in scooter rickshaws with the hope that everyone would find the hotel. The luggage required an additional three rickshaws. Everybody and everything made it safely.

The hallways and stairs of the *haveli* were almost as tangled as the surrounding lanes, but on the rooftop was a fabulous open-air restaurant. Jo wrote: "I will never forget the first evening, climbing all the steps up the five floors to the restaurant and discovering the whole city setting off fireworks for a second night of Diwali celebrations, against the background of a floodlit fortress."

The US Presidential election took place during our Jodhpur stay, and the Americans, who comprised two thirds of the tour group, greeted Barack Obama's victory with jubilation. Jo again:

"We all crowded into Claudia's and Lisa's room for Obama's victory speech broadcast live by CNN. Most of us were in tears, crying for joy. I'll never forget it. We had servants coming up to us later, also very excited about the election results and saying repeatedly, 'Obama! Obama!'"

~ ~ ~

From Jodhpur it was west into the great Thar Desert and Rajasthan's most magical city, Jaisalmer, a walled outpost on the old Silk Route linking China to the ports of the Arabian Sea. When we had first visited in 1989, Jo had described the city in her journal: "Jaisalmer has been called a city out of the Arabian Nights and that it is – a golden city of stone walls and fortresses with cosy bazaars in narrow lanes tucked within the walls. Ridge after ridge of tawny desert sand stretch to the western horizon."

Again, we were accommodated in a converted *haveli*, and the bedrooms were decorated with beautiful tribal artifacts. In our room, we found in one corner a brass replica of a tortoise – at least we thought it was a replica until it walked slowly into the centre of the room. A pet of our host family, it had free range of the establishment. Included in our hotel fee was an evening folk-dance performance and a half-day camel safari in the desert. This was followed by a barbecue under the stars and overnight tent accommodation.

Udaipur in the far south of the state was our next destination, and Jo and I returned happily with the group to Lake Pichola Hotel. During our 1989 stay there, we had formed a friendship with the owners and had subsequently assisted them in having their teenage son admitted to New Zealand's Whanganui Collegiate School. With the collusion of the hotel staff, we organised a secret banquet to honour recently married Nicky Mendenhall and Wendell Speers served in the open-air rooftop restaurant overlooking the lake. We were all seated at one large table lit with candles. Festivities opened with a puppet show and concluded with a fabulous fireworks display.

Our last stop was Bharatpur in the state's north-eastern corner with its famed Kalaladeo National Park, a UNESCO world heritage nature reserve. It is a refuge and breeding ground for hundreds of species of birds that migrate for the winter from across Eurasia. In addition to wonderful bird sightings, on this visit Jo and I saw cobras, jackals, and a civet cat.

Bharatpur is close to Fatehpur Sikri and Agra, and all but one of the tour group opted for an unaccompanied two-day trip to these old Mughal capitals. Jo and I, meanwhile, went for a quick exploration of places farther east that might anchor a future central India tour. Our last stop was Varanasi where we stayed in a guesthouse right on the banks of the Ganga. What an incredible location! Our room on the third floor had a veranda facing the river on which we could sit to sip tea and watch the cavalcade on the ghats below and out on the river itself. Monkeys rambled on the rooftops around us, and little squirrels climbed down to our balcony to cadge food.

At daybreak on the first morning, we took a rowboat (with boatman) for an hour-and-a-half along all the major ghats to observe the early morning ritual ablutions and the assorted gurus leading devotees in prayers. Tiny oil lamps floated past us on the current and occasional dolphins broke the surface amongst the crowded boats – yes, the Ganga has dolphins a thousand miles from the ocean; strange, sharp-nosed dolphins almost like swordfish. The following night, we took out another boat for two hours, which was even more spectacular. In addition to observing the fiery activity on the burning ghats, we had front row seats for the most powerful choreographed ritual of seven priests honouring Mother Ganga for an hour-and-a-half. This was the most amazing religious spectacle I have ever witnessed.

Our guesthouse was in a network of tiny lanes, with some of the four- and five-story buildings leaning inward to touch overhead. These lanes are inaccessible to motor vehicles other than motor bikes. We just loved exploring, peering into the closet-sized shops with their myriad sale items and into the innumerable wayside temples. Colour, colour, clamour, clamour everywhere. That clamour was less welcome in our guesthouse bathroom, which was right above what must surely be the noisiest lane in all India. It was filled (day and night) with voices, gongs, music, TV programmes of "inspiring" Hindu drama, choirs of less-than-heavenly angels, dog fights, water buffalo bellowing, hawkers' cries, you name it. A visit to the toilet was a plunge into a fascinating version of Dante's Inferno. Ah yes, India!! What a mixed bag it is.

It was the end of the first week in December before we were home at Te Wairua. Late in the month, we were happy to receive a letter of appreciation from two of the tour participants, Ian and Bev MacDonald in Christchurch:

"We got home comfortably enough although both of us lost about 4kg and took about three weeks to stop feeling tired all the time. We are fine now and would not have missed the trip for worlds. We did expect to be moved out of our comfort zone and at times we certainly were that. I enjoyed getting to know our fellow travellers and appreciate their strengths and accept their differences. The extra trip to the Taj Mahal was worth it. What a magnificent edifice. I do not recall any building in two trips to Europe to match it. You must have been very glad to be able to relax at the end of such an epic tour with all the communication problems and logistics of 17 disparate others to contend with. You both certainly earned it. Bev and I would like to thank you for the opportunity of a lifetime that we would not have contemplated without your knowledgeable guidance.

— CHAPTER EIGHTEEN —

The Storm of Loss

"We are ourselves ghosts of other times, not fully present in our own; and we see what is no longer here and feel the future as a wind through the streets, a wind that is for us who look backward always blowing away what we cherish, the storm of loss."
                                        – Rebecca Solnit

We were so pleased with the success of the Rajasthan tour that initially we thought of repeating it in October-November 2009, but we already had an Outback Australia tour organised for early June 2009 and a New Zealand tour for late February and early March 2010 preceded by a "Spirit in Nature" Workshop at Te Wairua. In addition, we had received expressions of interest in a Himalayan tour in October-November 2010, so reluctantly we decided to wait a year or two for a return to Rajasthan.

~ ~ ~

On Christmas Eve 2008, we were given a fabulous gift by Tangaroa, the sea god. I was standing on the jetty at about 8:00 am when six to eight orcas surfaced just five meters away. One swam directly beneath me and then cruised rapidly around our bay close inshore. I rushed up to the house to call Jo, and she came down with binos to watch them fishing around the point at the entrance to the bay. And they returned late afternoon. Again, I was on the jetty, and I heard a loud blow of air. There was a large orca chasing two stingrays in the bay, pursuing them almost onto the beach. It was so far in, more than half its body was above water. It swiftly swam back, and under the jetty it joined another orca I hadn't noticed. Together they checked out our neighbour's beach before swimming off up the channel towards Cook Strait.

~ ~ ~

In 2009, in my mid-seventies, I began writing my autobiography. Rather than starting with my childhood and youth in New Zealand, I decided to devote the first volume to my three decades in America, 1963-1994, interwoven with my experiences in those years in India, the UK and Australia. Idiosyncratically, I would then write about the early years of my life in NZ, my doctoral study in Australia and India, and the decades since my return home to NZ in 1994. Parallel to these memoirs, I also had in mind the publication of a collection of my India papers under the title Many Warm Winters.

In his autobiographical *Peeling the Onion*, Gunter Grass writes that "Memory likes to play hide-and-seek, to crawl away. It tends to hold forth, to dress up, often needlessly .... It is seldom unambiguous and often in mirror-writing or otherwise disguised." Fortunately, to supplement memory, I had more than 60 years of personal documents dragged tenaciously around the world against the reasonable objections of my partners.

My earliest papers were childhood letters to and from pen pals (one in England, the other in South Africa) and a daily account of my 1949 cycling adventure from Christchurch to Owaka and back. From 1960, after I had left NZ, I wrote regular letters to my parents and sister – weekly in the early years, reduced to fortnightly or monthly in the eighties because of my workload as President of CIIS. My mother preserved all my letters and returned them to me before she moved to a nursing home in 1991. I had typed most of my academic correspondence and made carbon copies of many of my letters. I had kept almost every letter of significance I received. I also had newsletters of organizations of which I was a member, and journals and newspapers that carried reports on events in which I was involved.

While at university in Christchurch in the 1950s and for a few scattered periods later, I kept a diary, but the outstanding diarist in my life was Jo, who made daily journal entries (often voluminous entries) from her teens on. For the years we were together from 1983, her journal would prove an invaluable source.

Jo herself was at work on a book in 2009. In the nineties, she had mined her journals to produce an account of our 1989 Himalayan experience in the Kullu and Kangra Valleys, but she gave up the idea of publication when she received critical feedback on the manuscript from a friend. Personally, I thought it was excellent and urged her not to shelve the project, but I could not persuade her. In 2009, her subject was what she called "the CT" (the cancer thing). She took as a framework for her book Joseph Campbell's *The Hero's Journey*, and again her journals were a primary source of her reflections.

Reading Jo's journal for this time period, I came upon the following entries:

October 17, 2009

"One exercise in a book I am reading, required that I come up with the people I most admire, living or dead. So far, my list is Oprah Winfrey and fellow TV guru Iyanla Vanzant; Jamie Oliver; the Dalai Lama; Maya Angelou; and Eleanor Roosevelt. During my journalism career, I also most admired Edward R. Murrow and Ernie Pile. 'Compassion': That's what I love about all these people.

They care about others deeply and want to effect social change."

October 18, 2009

"John's list of heroes: The Dalai Lama; Fritz Schumacher, author of Small is Beautiful; Michael Harner; Joanna Macy; Andre and Magda Trocme, French Protestant Minister and wife who rescued hundreds of Jews during WW2; Willis Harman of the Institute of Noetic Studies; Te Puea, kuia who revitalised Tainui iwi; Martin Luther King Jr.; and Mahatma Gandhi. He says the main trait they embodied was 'courage.' All of them are social activists who broke out of the mainstream to change society and help others."

~ ~ ~

At about this time, Jo and I decided we definitely had kiwi on our land. Every now and then in the decade-and-a-half since we arrived at Te Wairua, we had heard calls soon after dusk and shortly before dawn that sounded like the recorded calls of kiwi that we could listen to on the Internet, both female and male calls. Late in 2009, we also discovered the distinctive holes that kiwi make as they dig for worms. For most of the twentieth century, the Marlborough Sounds were home to Little Spotted Kiwi, but as victims to settlers and their dogs they were thought to have been wiped out except on Cook Strait islands. Despite the protests of residents, DOC had transferred the last kiwi from D'Urville Island to more remote islands in the early 1980s.

Aware that if we publicised the fact that there were kiwis living at Te Wairua, DOC rangers would almost certainly bring tracking dogs to hunt out the birds and remove them to a "safe place." We told no one, not even our closest friends. We did, on one occasion, ask the Leovs if they had ever seen evidence of kiwi on their land, and they told us that a few years earlier the whole family had camped for a night high on Mt. Shewell (the mountain behind Te Wairua), and shortly before daybreak they had heard an unusual bird call that they thought might be kiwi.

~ ~ ~

Our beloved black cat Kia died in August 2009. He and his fluffy grey companion Rai had been with us since they were kittens in 1995. Kia's death was protracted and painful, and as he became weaker and weaker, I felt incompetent in caring for his needs. On the night he died, Jo cuddled him for hours on the bed, and he uttered plaintive wails as though he were calling for spirit companions for his final journey. Rai's reaction to his calls was to stand at the window and peer intently into the darkness.

Rai lived another two years. She became incontinent, and with deep sadness we had her euthanised.

~ ~ ~

From mid-February 2010, I was to lead a week-long "Spirit in Nature" workshop on our land, followed by a two-week NZ tour. Early in the month in the middle of the night, I had jumped energetically out of bed to go to the toilet, blacked out and fell headlong onto an oil-column heater, which fortunately was not turned on. How long I was unconscious I have no idea, but I came to with my right ear and side of my head bloody. There was evidence of a concussion in intermittent dizziness and a persistent headache, which was still with me when the time came for the workshop. It made teaching difficult, but fortunately it had eased before the tour group assembled in Christchurch on February 23.

The workshop had 12 participants and nine of these continued on the tour. It was a diverse group drawn from the US,

Canada, the UK, Belgium, and Australia. Unlike previous NZ tours, this one did not include the North Island, but we travelled almost the length of the South Island and visited Stewart Island.

In Kaikoura on our sixth morning, we awoke to news of a massive earthquake in Chile. A tsunami warning was issued for the whole east coast of NZ, with Kaikoura and Banks Peninsula singled out as especially endangered. Our motel was right on the beach, so we high tailed it out of Kaikoura without eating breakfast, and as Akaroa on Banks Peninsula was our destination for the day, I kept an ear on the news as we travelled south. Warnings were scaled back, so I decided Akaroa would be safe. The tsunami did arrive soon after us in mid-afternoon in the form of a one-meter surge on the high tide. We all survived!

The tour highlight for me was Stewart Island. We flew there from Invercargill on six-seater planes and returned by ferry. The only town, Oban, is a picturesque, quiet little place: A beach and a wharf in a lovely bay, with lodges and houses on forest-clad hills overlooking the harbour, fishing boats moored offshore. Apart from Oban and a few other small areas privately owned, Stewart Island is now a mountainous national park, its 650 square miles covered by regenerating and old growth forest. It is one of the few remaining places where kiwi feel safe enough to forage for food during daylight hours.

The tour ended in Invercargill, and from there I took a rental car to revisit places in Invercargill and the Catlins important to me from my childhood. I saw two of my childhood houses, but discovered that three of my primary schools had been demolished and relocated. A highlight of the trip was one of the Catlins' scenic gems: McLean Falls, a lovely high waterfall deep in a narrow gorge, access to which requires a 30-minute hike through dense, towering old forest. The other highlight was seeing yellow-eyed penguins in the wild at Curio Bay. They stand almost three-feet tall, the world's second largest after Emperor Penguins. Moreover, they are decked out in great colours. Their big feet and stocky legs are bright pink; they have navy blue backs and white bellies; their flippers are attractively striped with blue, gold, and white, as are their heads, with dashes of orange; and they have yellow eyes and yellow crests.

My fall and concussion had raised an old issue between Jo and me. As she did whenever I had a health problem, she felt my concern was exaggerated, and I felt she was being uncaring.

Jo wrote in her journal, February 7, 2010:

"After John fell, I felt so ill-equipped to handle my substantial fears, as well as keep offering solicitous care of him. He kept constantly commenting on how dizzy he was, till I wanted to scream. I wanted so badly to escape from my own terror, to have him reassure me he would be OK, would soon be OK, would always be OK, whereas his mode on the rare occasions he gets sick is to get really scared himself and catastrophise. That in turn made me back off, not ask the next day how he was feeling as immediately he thought I should, and, predictably, we argued once again about this same old issue: I feel he is always over-dramatic when he gets ill, and he thinks I will abandon him and not care for him if he gets sick in his old age.

"It's true that in the past I've not been a good nurse Nancy due to childhood resentments and fears surfacing about the most significant adult in my life getting ill. I know that dates from my mother's many illnesses and my summons as daughter to nurse her through them. I can never seem to do enough. It's like I'm supposed to metamorphose into Mummy Broomfield, and I always fall short."

Jo and I left the issue unresolved.

~ ~ ~

We had a Himalayan tour scheduled for October 21-November 10, 2010, and Jo decided to accompany me, as this was her favourite journey. By contrast to the flamboyance of Rajasthan, this tour was to a gentler slice of India, the Kangra and Kullu Valleys where we had lived for the greater part of 1989. These valleys were carved by the Beas River through the awesome Himalayan ranges that lead to the Tibetan Plateau. Most of our tour accommodations were small, refurbished hotels from the Raj-era set amid beautiful gardens near quiet villages. The pace of the tour was leisurely. In three weeks, we visited just six places, giving us three to four days in each. Jo wrote to a friend:

> "One of the many highlights for me is always our time in two centres of Tibetan Buddhist culture. One is Dharamsala, where the Dalai Lama resides, a lively small bazaar town with great little restaurants and shops, monks debating in courtyards, artisans creating traditional art and lots of amazingly cheery Tibetans to meet. We always take our groups to Tibetan Children's Village, where more than 1,000 children live, most of them orphans: it's a real heart-tug. The second place is Tashi Jong, a small refugee settlement of about 400 craftspeople and monks. We stay nearby at the former summer residence of the Maharaja of Kashmir. John and I have been connected to Tashi Jong for more than 20 years, and we sponsor two families there who lavish the group with hospitality and ensure we can meet with some of the lamas and yogis, see their temple and craft workshop, etc.
>
> "We also spend a couple of days in Naggar, the small village in the Kullu Valley where John and I lived. Our group is always invited to have tea at the homes of two very special families. One is a Brahmin family compound

set amid apple orchards with these amazing snow-capped peaks all around. The other is the home of our former servant, Ramchand, a Dalit ('untouchable') who is now married with three children at last count. His humble family home and the warm welcome we get from his parents, wife and kids, usually brings me to tears each time."

After the tour in 2010, we were able to gather in New Delhi three of the six Tibetan nurses for whose training we had secured financial support from our friends in various parts of the world. The inspiration for the project was our Tashi Jong goddaughter, Pema Dekyi, who wanted to follow in her mother's footsteps and become a nurse. She worked hard in nursing school and was an outstanding student. She was now 29, working in ER at an excellent Delhi hospital.

Pema brought two of the other nurses to meet us at IIC: the second graduate, Sonam Choedon, who had been working at Holy Family Hospital in New Delhi for two years; and Tenzin Zomkyi, at 18 the youngest of the six, who was studying at the nursing school attached to the same hospital.

~ ~ ~

In February 2012, Nikki asked me in an email if I knew what had become of Stephen. When I said I didn't think anyone in the family had had contact with him in years, she revealed that he had been in prison in Georgia for the previous four years. Jenni had hired a private detective to find him, and she had been visiting him fairly regularly, but she had kept the information from me at Stephen's request. He felt ashamed and did not want me to know.

Then in the middle of May, Nikki emailed to say Stephen was possibly about to be released from prison, that his mother was willing for him to come live with her in Florida but that the US Immigration Service (INS) had visited him in prison and might deport him to Australia when he was released by the Georgia Corrections Department. Stephen was born in Canberra, when I was doing my doctorate at the ANU, and he arrived with us in the US in 1963 as a ten-month-old babe-in-arms. He had all the right papers, but then in his twenties on booze and drugs he assumed other aliases and never took US citizenship. When he was arrested, he was using an assumed name and claiming to be an Australian.

Late in May, I received an email from Jenni, accompanied by a message from Stephen to me. It was good to be in touch with him again, but the immediate future was totally uncertain. He was jailed for forgery in 2008 (forged papers to support the false identity, I assume). Jenni said the Georgia State prison system was one of the worst in the US, but fortunately Stephen did his time in better-than-average facilities, mostly with men younger than himself. But Georgia provided no educational opportunities for its prisoners. Moreover, Stephen would leave prison with one set of clothes and $35. She said he might, indeed, be handed over to the INS for deportation to Australia. He had, however, lost all his papers, and, without them, establishing his real identity was a huge problem – in the US and, presumably, in Australia as well, if he were sent there. Jenni and I set about locating documents to support his efforts to re-establish his identity. He was in limbo. Although his release date from Georgia Corrections came and went, the INS made no move to clarify his future, so he stayed in prison for another year. According to his mother, the INS proved virtually impossible to reach, with no live phone operators and no apparent willingness to return calls.

Stephen was still expecting to be shipped off to Australia at some point. Even in this sad situation I got an inappropriate chuckle out of the fact that my eighteenth- and nineteenth-century ancestors managed to avoid being transported from Ireland and England to the Australian penal colonies, but now ironically in the twenty-first century my son would probably be sent involuntary to "The Lucky Country"!

To prepare Stephen for Australia, I sent him guidebooks and letters of advice about the society in general and possible work opportunities in particular. My Sydney friend, Carmel Gold, also got information on the government welfare departments he should contact on arrival. He was finally flown to Sydney in April 2013 and immediately got unemployment payments. Shortly afterwards, government employment advisors pointed him to work opportunities as a security guard. One of the places he was guarding was the iconic Sydney Opera House – the perfect job for a convicted American felon, I thought! In subsequent years, he said he liked Australia greatly and was doing much better than if he had been released in the US

~ ~ ~

Early in 2011, Jo and I led a "Spirit in Nature" workshop at Te Towaka and Te Wairua, and for November I offered a journey to Arnhem Land in Australia's far north. Promising as it did new Aboriginal experiences, I was keenly looking forward to this, but regrettably I did not get enough participants and had to cancel. After another workshop on our land early in 2012, Jo and I decided to take advantage of exceptionally low airfares to treat ourselves to a vacation in India towards the end of the year. We would tell none of our Indian friends we were coming, so we would be free to visit wherever and whomever we chose.

A centrepiece of this journey would be a visit to the state of Uttarakhand in the central Himalaya, which we had postponed from 2006 because of Jo's cancer diagnosis. This would be virgin territory for us, as was Karauli in north-eastern Rajasthan, where we went first. This was a former princely state, with an ancient palace in the heart of the city and a newer one built in the suburbs in the late-1930s which had been converted into a charming hotel run by the younger generation of the princely family. It was surrounded by gardens and a functional farmyard with friendly animals, and it had a beautiful inner courtyard where dinner was served under the stars. Numerous members of the family still lived onsite, including the Raja and Rani, who entertained us to tea once they discovered I was an historian of India. They both were widely read, and she was a sitting member of the Rajasthan State Legislature.

They arranged an escorted tour for us of the old city, a maze of narrow lanes within massive walls, and of the original fortress palace built in stages from the fourteenth century, which was among the grandest we had seen in Rajasthan. During our tour of the old palace, we were told there would be folk music there in the evening, so we went back for this.

Once he had parked his car, our taxi driver became our guide, and he took us through a back entrance into the fortress. In a large central courtyard paved with stone worn smooth by the footsteps of centuries we found a dozen musicians, all men, playing violins and other stringed instruments, flutes, and drums. There were also three male singers. An audience of hundreds packed the courtyard, men standing at the back and women sitting close to the musicians. Our guide secured places for us on a raised platform behind the musicians, but as women started to dance below us, Jo could not restrain herself from climbing down to join them. She was dressed in *salwar-kamis* with her *dupatta* covering her head. The dancing women welcomed her into their midst, and when she took a rest after fifteen minutes or so, the seated women drew her down to sit with them. Our guide told me these were mostly peasants who loved to come into town for the musical evenings. Jo, who was having the time of her life, danced several times over the next hour. As I look back now, I am in awe of the vigour and stamina of my 63-year-old wife, who had survived serious illness not long before.

Returning from Karauli to New Delhi, we found a festival of folk arts and crafts at IIC where we were staying. I have a treasured photo of Jo admiring one of the exhibits. It is my last photo of her.

Since our arrival in India, I had been low in energy and struggled when carrying luggage or climbing stairs. It was proving difficult for me to walk any distance even on the flat. Jo urged me to consult a doctor, but I said it could wait until we were back in NZ.

After a fortnight in Delhi, we travelled by train and taxi to Almora in the Himalayan foothills of Uttarakhand. I was eager to see this "hill station" because it had been a rare centre of criticism of the Raj by British radicals associated with its Christian colleges. It proved to be a pleasant town, but unlike Manali and McLeod Gang in the western Himalaya it lacked views of high ranges. The same could not be said of our next destination, the village of Kausani. Here there was a 300-km-wide panorama of the ice peaks of the Garhwal Himalaya, including 25,600-foot Nanda Devi. Stupendous!

I was having more trouble with my energy in Almora and Kausani, both above 6000 feet, and things did not improve when we moved on to Ranikhet, at the same altitude. Fortunately, our hotel was on a flat site, and we were not encouraged to walk into the neighbouring woods where we were warned panthers roamed. Our room, however, was at the top of two flights of rickety stairs, and after we fell asleep on our first night, we were woken by a fire on one wall sparked by defective electrical wiring. We put it out with jugs of water, but not before it had filled the room with acrid smoke. We were spluttering and coughing as we threw open the windows, and it was almost an hour before the air was sufficiently clear for us to go back to bed. Next morning, we were Brooved to a ground-floor room in another building.

On this second night at the hotel, I woke before dawn and tried to get out of bed. I could not keep my balance. I fell back on the bed with my only consciousness a pinpoint of light in total blackness. I did feel I had had a stroke. When I began vomiting, Jo rushed to the hotel office to get help. From that point onwards, I have only fragmentary memories. I was aware of being carried out and laid on the backseat of a car, and I remember lying on a stretcher on the floor of what Jo told me was the reception area of the local health clinic. She said it was appallingly dirty and disorganised. I do remember a crowd of people, with some bending over me, asking what had happened. Then I was in an ambulance with Jo on my way to a public hospital in Halwani at the foot of the mountains.

Apparently, this was also severely disorganised, and I have painful memories of medical orderlies – three young men – making fun of me. I have forgotten the detail of what they did and said, but I remember shouting at them that they should be ashamed of themselves, and this did stop them. Jo told me I was saved from the mayhem by a doctor who had me moved by another ambulance to his private clinic in the same town, where a procedure was taken to stabilise my heart. Jo and I spent the night there and next morning began a day-long road journey to Delhi. Somehow this required a succession of ambulances (we travelled in a total of six between the Ranikhet hotel and the New Delhi hospital), but all I remember is back pain from the steel surfaces on which my stretcher was laid and the non-stop wail of a siren. The whole experience in these first days after the stroke was surreal. The thing that amazes me now is that I remember no fear of dying.

Throughout the gruelling journey from Halwani, Jo was in cell phone contact with our old New Delhi friend, Pradeep Mehendiratta, who arranged wonderful care for me at the superb Apollo Hospital, with which he had been involved since its inception. It was the fourth largest hospital in the world, I later discovered.

I was diagnosed with arteriosclerosis, requiring triple-by-pass open-heart surgery. I have a clear memory of regaining consciousness after the surgery. I felt unbearable pain in my chest and, convinced I was dreaming, I tried to go back to the comfortable state I had been in. When this did not work, I realised the pain was reality. Five horrible weeks in an over-crowded ICU followed. This was an Indian cultural experience in the extreme. Whereas in a Western hospital there would have been an effort made to keep light and noise levels down, here there was bright artificial light 24 hours a day and no concern about noise. In severe pain, I drifted in and out of consciousness, feeling as though I were in a mad house. When I was sufficiently aware of my surroundings to ask if I could possibly be moved to a private room or at least into an al-cove in the ICU ward, I was met with expressions of concern that I would suffer from loneliness there. In crowded lifts and hallways, as I was being taken on a gurney to the operating theatres for follow-up procedures, hospital visitors lent over me peering and discussing my condition with the orderlies. I felt like screaming at them to leave me alone.

Early on, I had another meeting with Death, who offered to put an end to my pain and suffering, but I told him I must live on to repay Jo's love, which had saved my life. I also had the strange feeling that I was fulfilling an obligation to nurse a seriously ill man who was sharing the bed with me. When I did not adhere strictly to medical instructions, I felt guilty that I was failing this person who had been placed under my protection.

The care given by doctors and nurses was excellent. My surgeons were a middle-aged husband-and-wife team, who had studied in Australian medical schools, and when after a fortnight I gave them a copy of my book, *Other Ways of Knowing*, they read the medical chapter overnight and sat by my bedside the next day to discuss it with me! The nurses were drawn from two groups: Kerala Christians (women and men) and Tibetan Buddhists (all women). The former were delighted that I had visited their home towns or places nearby, and the latter, when the news spread that Jo and I had funded training for six of their compatriots, organised evening visiting parties of Tibetan nurses from hospitals all over the city. They were unfailingly cheerful and constantly encouraged me to smile. Churlishly, I wished often they would just leave me alone.

Meanwhile, Jo was staying on her own at IIC and, suffering from shock, was having a very hard time. On one visit to me in hospital, she collapsed and ended up in a hospital bed for half a day. She was desperately lonely, craving female company in particular. Meanwhile, she was wrestling online daily with New Zealand's Southern Cross Health Travel Insurance to get my medical bills paid.

When after five weeks I was discharged from hospital and joined her at IIC, she made me profoundly sad and perplexed by refusing to share a room with me. The stroke had left me unable to walk or even stand unaided, and fortunately Pradeep arranged round-the-clock nursing care and daily visits by a physiotherapist. He also bought me a wheelchair so I could go to the dining room and be wheeled into the IIC gardens. Even so, Jo would rarely dine with me or take me for walks. Nor would she discuss this with me.

Eventually, Southern Cross Health flew a Kiwi nurse to Delhi to accompany us back to New Zealand on Singapore Airlines. I have only the vaguest memory of the journey. I must have been heavily drugged, but I do recall becoming enraged by something at one stage and having to be forcibly restrained by cabin crew, with the assistance of one of the pilots. The anger I often felt during my recovery is apparently typical of some people following a major operation. For me, it was very out of character.

We landed in Nelson on December 27, and I was taken immediately by yet another ambulance to the rehab ward at Nelson Hospital, where I stayed an additional month and a half. How grateful I was for the quiet calm during the daytime and for the silence and almost complete darkness at night. By contrast to the Indian hospital where I could not see the out-of-doors, each of the Nelson Hospital rooms had windows, and rehab had a lovely small garden in which patients could sit. The most scary thing I had faced when I came out of hospital in India was that my eyes would not focus, which prevented me from reading and writing. Happily, my vision now came right. Convinced I could also regain fully the balance I had lost with the stroke, I worked hard in my scheduled sessions with the hospital physiotherapists, and I found an unused set of parallel bars in a hallway where I could put in an hour or two of additional walking practice each day.

My stay in hospital would have been shorter had the Occupational Therapists been convinced that there was a welcoming and caring environment waiting for me at home. They had doubts about this because Jo came to visit me once only during my six weeks in hospital. Our Enner Glynn neighbours had rallied around her on our return from India, and observing that she was not coming to the hospital, they started dropping in to chat with me. It was rather embarrassing.

To test the water, the Occupational Therapists finally arranged a trial weekend's "home leave" for me. It was another fortnight before they would agree to my being finally discharged. The reluctance Jo had to visit me in rehab I had explained to myself as a consequence of her profound dislike of hospitals. I recalled that in 1993 she had visited her mother only twice as she lay dying in hospital not far from where we lived in Marin, California, and then only when pressured to do so by her brother Gene. When I returned home in February 2013, however, it was obvious that the Occupational Therapists had been justified in their concern. Jo was as emotionally distant as she had been when I came out of hospital in New Delhi. She made it clear she was not going to be my caregiver.

With my balance still impaired, I could stand only with a walking stick or holding on to something. For the outdoors, the hospital had given me elbow crutches. I found it difficult to resume household chores as Jo seemed to expect. She would shop for groceries, but we would have to share the cooking as we had done previously. Inexplicably, she would not take me anywhere in the car. Fortunately, to assist with paperwork while in hospital I had signed on Jan DeCorcy, a young woman whose family were neighbours on our street, and she now drove me wherever I needed to go.

I did recognise that Jo was probably suffering from PTSD, but that did not seem to be sufficient to explain her attitude to me. When I came home, I found she was working with psychotherapist Geoffrey Samuels, and Jo agreed to my joining their bi-weekly sessions. I tried to use these to fathom what was going on with her. I recall asking at the first session why, after 20 years or more of playing cards with me each morning, she now refused to do this. She simply shrugged and said she didn't feel like it anymore. I got no further with other questions.

Had I had access to her journals at the time, I might have been able to comprehend better. At Christmas 1993, she had written:

"My mother ill in hospital triggers the worst, shuddering memories of her and her many illnesses. I fully realise it sounds selfish, self-centred and childish, and it's also the truth. Kicking and screaming, I go once again to a lesson I have not wanted. What do I want? Minimum involvement."

She said she did not like sick people and had no desire to care for them.

After her mother's death ten days later, she expressed relief. "My overwhelming sense was one of gratitude for the universe working out in what I still feel is best for everyone. I felt liberated, so glad that the ordeal I thought was unfolding is over." Best for everyone? Not for her mother, surely.

Jo resented the fact that her mother, because of recurrent illness, had failed to fulfil her "proper" role as caregiver for her when she was a child. Now I was repeating the pattern. After I was concussed by my fall in February 2010, she had written in her journal:

> "It's true that in the past I've not been a good nurse Nancy due to childhood resentments and fears surfacing about the most significant adult in my life getting ill. I know that dates from my mother's many illnesses and my summons as daughter to nurse her through them. I can never seem to do enough. It's like I'm supposed to metamorphose into Mummy Broomfield, and I always fall short."

At that time, she wrote: "John thinks I will abandon him and not care for him if he gets sick in his old age." She was right. That was my fear, and now it had come true. It seemed almost incomprehensible after 30 years of loving companionship. Hard as it was for me to acknowledge, Jo seemed to be acting with narcissistic selfishness, and I felt saddened and angered as she turned her back on me.

~ ~ ~

She and I stayed in town for six weeks after my hospital discharge so I could continue work with a physiotherapist and access other medical care. At the beginning of April, we recruited an Elaine Bay friend, Neil McLennan, to drive us out to Te Wairua. We had decided with huge regret that we had to sell the place, and we felt overwhelmed by the task of packing. This impelled Jo, without any consultation with me, to start burning books in a drum on the back lawn. Even though I insisted she take no books from the shelves in my study, I found she had slipped in when I was otherwise occupied and burnt some of my cherished volumes. My anger with her was ratcheted up a notch.

On our second Sounds stay in late May, Jo started vomiting. When this was repeated off-and-on for almost a week, I got Harry Leov to drive us to the Nelson emergency clinic. Numerous tests, scans, doctors' visits, and a short hospitalization followed in the subsequent week, the result of which was the conclusion that Jo's cancer had returned. The verdict was that this new cancer was terminal.

Jo took this dire prognosis amazingly calmly, saying that death held no fears for her. She wrote to a friend:

"The news was a relief and a source of strange joy, because it suddenly made sense of all the strange phenomena and the depression I have been experiencing since John collapsed in India in November. I have felt as if everything was being pulled away from me, as if I were trapped on a beach as the strongest tide of my life was dragging everything and everyone away from me. I felt a total void looking ahead, which all made for a depressing state of mind, because I have always had so many passionate interests in life!

I had virtually all my lymph nodes affected at the time of my original breast cancer, so my new oncologist says I had an amazingly good run of seven years. It never occurred to me seriously that I would ever have cancer again, but it is an ideal way to die. Who among us knows the approximate time and manner of their death?? I do! About six months, which strikes me as not too short and not too long, just right. The cancer is in the liver and a kidney, as far as anyone knows. I declined more tests and will only do maybe a single pill-popping a day of a hormone that might buy me more time, as long as it doesn't have bad side effects. So mostly NO appointments!!"

I nursed her at home in Nelson for the first six months following the advice of Hospice doctors and nurses and with the assistance of our Australian friend, Carmel Gold, a former nurse who flew over from Sydney. In early December 2013, Jo was taken to Hospice after suffering extreme pain. Once her "meds were tweaked" (as the Hospice nurses say) she was moved to the hospital unit of a retirement village in Stoke. As I was still unable to drive, our friend Jan Cleghorn took me there and back each day, and I spent six to seven hours sitting with Jo. She liked the place, being especially pleased with the food and the frequency with which they offered it. She remarked that if she's given a choice about her rebirth, she would like to come back as a pastry chef! Initially she felt that the nurses' response to her call button was too slow, but we got that sorted out, and often afterward she had periods of total bliss, when she felt that everything in her life was exactly right.

On the weekend of December 13, a group of ten friends from many parts of NZ joined me to pack up Te Wairua. They went to work with a will on the packing and cleaning of the house, sleepout, workshop and sheds, and achieved miracles. Meanwhile, two of them were hauling all the stuff out to the Leovs homestead in their 4WD utes and trailers. To my amazement and huge pleasure, those two plus various members of the packing eight hauled it on from there to Nelson. All my worries about how to get the stuff from the house were evaporated in three days! What a fabulous job and what fabulous friends – many of whom said they had a thoroughly enjoyable weekend.

Jo died on February 9, 2014. As she had chosen a natural burial, she had to be buried within a few days. No coffin, just a shroud. There were eight of us at the graveside to lay her to rest, including her brother Gene and his partner Sandy, who arrived from California the day before. On March 1, we held a Remembrance Service for her, a very beautiful ceremony. Jo had chosen the music, and it reflected her hippy generation: the Beatles, "Let It Be;" Simon and Garfunkle, "Bridge

Over Troubled Water;" Kate Wolf, "Give Yourself to Love;" and Annie Lennox, "Into the West" from the "Lord of the Rings." I was touched that a large group of friends from Nelson and the Sounds was joined by others who had flown in from the North Island.

I recognise now that all I had been through in the preceding 16 months had left me emotionally numb. I went through Jo's death, burial, and farewell ceremony rather like an automaton. I feel so sad that it ended this way for me with Jo.

Perhaps it was a blessing that I was in this numb state as I faced the task of selling Te Wairua. The pain otherwise would have been very deep. On the recommendation of Neil McLennan, I engaged as my real estate agent, Graham Kay, who himself had land in the Sounds. Honouring the Leovs' request, the property was listed as "boat access only." Combined with the fact that the land could never be subdivided or the bush cut because of the QEII Trust Open Space Covenant, this made Graham concerned that the number of prospective purchasers would be seriously reduced, but I felt confident the right buyer would emerge.

We initially listed the property at $450,000, but after several weeks I decided to drop the asking price by $100,000. Almost immediately I received an offer from Richard Patterson and Trudy Burgess, a couple farming in Hawkes Bay. Richard had grown up in the Sounds and had kept a good-sized boat in Havelock. I feel I had spirit guidance in dropping the price as they proved to be perfect buyers, aligned with my vision for the place. For them, it was a positive that the forest was permanently protected, they loved the animals and birds, and they were delighted by Jo's mosaics scattered all about the place. They said they could not possibly have paid more than $350,000. They took possession on July 1, 2014. I sold my ute and boat to Graham Kay's brother-in-law, who lived in nearby Cissy Bay. A few years earlier, he had done some welding for me on the boat trailer, and he now floated this with mussel buoys to tow it home behind the boat.

~ ~ ~

Three weeks earlier, I had received a message on Facebook expressing condolences on Jo's death. This was from Maggie Cambra, whom I had met only once years earlier when she was considering joining one of my workshops. She lived in Nelson, so I responded with an invitation to drop by for a cuppa. The suggestion came as a surprise to her, as she thought I was still living in the Sounds, but she did say yes. She came to visit on June 14, 2014, and a new chapter opened in my life.

— About Atmosphere Press —

Founded in 2015, Atmosphere Press was built on the principles of Honesty, Transparency, Professionalism, Kindness, and Making Your Book Awesome. As an ethical and author-friendly hybrid press, we stay true to that founding mission today.

If you're a reader, enter our giveaway for a free book here:

SCAN TO ENTER
BOOK GIVEAWAY

If you're a writer, submit your manuscript for consideration here:

SCAN TO SUBMIT
MANUSCRIPT

And always feel free to visit Atmosphere Press and our authors online at atmospherepress.com. See you there soon!

— About the Author —

John Broomfield is the author of award-winning books on modern Indian history. Involvement in the radical movements of the 1960s and 1970s led to his development of courses in comparative studies at the University of Michigan that aimed to jolt students into the realization that contemporary organizational and technological developments could lead to ecological catastrophe. This concern was also the inspiration for his book *Other Ways of Knowing.*

In 1983, John was appointed President of the California Institute of Integral Studies, an independent graduate school in San Francisco that combines Asian and western studies to offer new models of holistic education. In the early 1990s, with his partner, Jo Imlay, he coordinated the development of an international network of organizations committed to transformative work in education, health and environmental protection. In 1994, John returned to his homeland, Aotearoa/ New Zealand.

John Broomfield's books include *Elite Conflict in a Plural Society: Twentieth-Century Bengal* (1968 & 2018), *Mostly About Bengal: Essays in Modern South Asian History* (1982 & 2020), *Other Ways of Knowing: Recharting Our Future with Ageless Wisdom* (1997), and *Carried on Great Winds* (2022).

John Broomfield died in 2022 at the age of 87.